DEVELOPING FACULTY LEARNING
COMMUNITIES AT TWO-YEAR COLLEGES

DEVELOPING FACULTY LEARNING COMMUNITIES AT TWO-YEAR COLLEGES

Collaborative Models to Improve Teaching and Learning

EDITED BY

Susan Sipple and Robin Lightner

Foreword by Milton D. Cox

STERLING, VIRGINIA

COPYRIGHT © 2013 BY
STYLUS PUBLISHING, LLC.

Published by Stylus Publishing, LLC
22883 Quicksilver Drive
Sterling, Virginia 20166-2102

Library of Congress Cataloging-in-Publication Data
Developing faculty learning communities at two-year
colleges : collaborative models to improve teaching and
learning / edited by Susan Sipple and Robin Lightner ;
foreword by Milton D. Cox.
   pages   cm
Includes bibliographical references and index.
ISBN 978-1-57922-844-6 (cloth : alk. paper)
ISBN 978-1-57922-845-3 (pbk. : alk. paper)
ISBN 978-1-57922-846-0 (library networkable e-edition)
ISBN 978-1-57922-847-7 (consumer e-edition)
1. Community college teachers—In-service
training—United States.   2. Professional learning
communities—United States.   3. Group work in
education—United States.   I. Sipple, Susan (Susan M.),
editor of compilation.   II. Lightner, Robin, editor of
compilation.
LB1738.D47   2013
378.1'250973—dc23   2012039480

13-digit ISBN: 978-1-57922-844-6 (cloth)
13-digit ISBN: 978-1-57922-845-3 (paper)
13-digit ISBN: 978-1-57922-846-0 (library networkable
e-edition)
13-digit ISBN: 978-1-57922-847-7 (consumer e-edition)

Printed in the United States of America

All first editions printed on acid-free paper
that meets the American National Standards Institute
Z39-48 Standard.

Bulk Purchases

Quantity discounts are available for use in workshops
and for staff development.
Call 1-800-232-0223

First Edition, 2013

10   9   8   7   6   5   4   3   2   1

To the faculty of
University of Cincinnati Blue Ash College
for their dedication to teaching and learning

CONTENTS

FOREWORD

The two-year college has played an important role in the development of faculty learning communities (FLCs), and this book provides examples of a variety of adaptations of these FLCs. I am pleased to elaborate on some key themes that emerge from these chapters as well as in the literature about FLCs at two-year colleges.

The development of FLCs in higher education has occurred in three phases: (a) 1978–88, the initial Miami University years of local, one-dimensional cohort development in FLCs for early-career faculty; (b) 1989–98, local multidimensionality—the broadening of the FLC model to other cohorts and to a few topic-based FLCs at Miami University; and (c) 1999 to the present, dissemination of the model through state, national, and international efforts across different types of institutions along with the resulting emergence of a wide variety of topic-based FLCs.

The dissemination began with a 1999 grant from the Ohio Board of Regents, the statewide organization overseeing education. This grant enabled the creation of the Ohio Teaching Enhancement Program (OTEP), an informal group of faculty developers who accepted an invitation to join implementation efforts to establish FLCs for early-career faculty at institutions in Ohio. In the first year of the dissemination, 1999–2000, one of the eight institutions that participated in the program was Sinclair Community College. As Cox and Jeep (2000) explain, "Sinclair teamed the concept of the Ohio Teaching Enhancement Program for Junior Faculty with the need to develop a Freshman Experience Course in Liberal Arts and Sciences. Junior faculty recruited for the program will work to craft the interdisciplinary course, which is hoped to form the foundation for the development of learning communities in the LAS Division" (p. 17). Although the model for FLCs recommended that the number of FLC members range from 8 to 10, circumstances required Sinclair to adapt its FLC approach owing to its limited number of new faculty. Five junior faculty participated and developed the course, which they then team taught in 2001–2.

For the second year of OTEP, 2000–1, four additional institutions joined, including another two-year college. This institution adapted the FLC model by expanding beyond the junior faculty cohort. The Raymond Walters College of the University of Cincinnati was "started in 2001–02 with 7 faculty from 6 disciplines. Because the college is small, the community included some mid- and late-career faculty. It is the first major program offered by the new Teaching Center" (Cox, 2002, p. 20). The effectiveness of FLCs at Raymond Walters College (now named University of Cincinnati Blue Ash College) prompted faculty and administrators to strive to make the college the showcase for FLCs at two-year colleges.

There is an important theme to note in this early development of FLCs as well as for those FLCs described in this book: the adaptability of the FLC structure to meet a variety of different needs and approaches required by two-year colleges. In their introduction to this book, editors Sipple and Lightner call these "nontraditional FLCs."

Another theme that emerges from this book is the potential for FLCs to provide opportunities for two-year college faculty to develop scholarly teaching and the scholarship of teaching and learning (SoTL). *Learning Communities Journal*, established in 2009, offers a venue for publishing scholarship about and generated by learning communities. Two articles in *Learning Communities Journal* by authors at two-year colleges provide examples of excellent contributions to scholarly teaching and SoTL. The first describes an assessment project conducted at Everett Community College. The study focused on participants in teaching labs, the term used for the college's version of FLCs. The purpose of this assessment was to determine the extent to which participants gained knowledge from the teaching labs and applied it in professional settings. The authors, Goto, Marshall, and Gaule (2010), surveyed all 61 current and former FLC members at their community college. From an analysis of open-ended questions on the anonymous survey, the authors inductively derived four categories based on the FLC members' primary expectations about what they wanted from their FLC experience: networkers, learners, implementers, and wait-and-seers. *Networkers* wanted to interact with their FLC members; they viewed their peers as sources of expertise. *Learners* wanted to explore general concepts, were nonspecific and flexible, and were willing to engage in learning for the sake of learning. *Implementers* wanted to acquire specific approaches and strategies that they already had in mind, could learn about, and then apply in their courses. *Wait-and-seers* were open to the experience but not sure what to expect; they trusted that a productive encounter and worthwhile outcomes would occur. In this survey, the most common primary expectation described by participants was networker. Learners, wait-and-seers, and implementers were ranked second, third, and fourth, respectively.

In the second article about FLCs at two-year colleges, Kincaid (2009) contends that to become more learner centered, two-year colleges must connect and engage faculty and professional staff in scholarly, evidenced-based teaching. With these goals in mind, Mesa Community College implemented a faculty and professional learning community (FPLC) program that enrolled 61 active members in six different FPLCs. The program was evaluated with a pre- and postparticipation survey including both quantitative and qualitative items. Results indicated that the FPLC program successfully connected and engaged members and achieved significant community and professional development outcomes.

Although these are encouraging results, I must now extend a word of caution and a call to vigilance with respect to Mesa Community College's FPLC program. In spite of its excellent outcomes, during the 2008–9 academic year, the program was severely cut and eventually terminated. This event underscores the concern that the editors of this book raise: Community colleges are facing a great funding challenge. Kincaid (2009) stated the following about the demise of Mesa's FPLCs:

> This diminishes neither the achievements of our program nor the potential of FPLCs. Our institution endured multiple traumas over the past two years: college enrollment continued to decline, all top administrators were replaced, the national economic downturn precipitated painful budget cuts, and all employees were immersed in averting an impending crisis. FPLCs might have helped the institution weather this storm, but the program was neither stable enough nor politically strong enough to survive. (p. 92)

Palmer (1998) has noted a related paradox of institutional transformation: To change an institution, a movement must overcome organizational resistance, but once achieved, reforms require organizational support to sustain them. In two-year colleges, faculty, administrators, and teaching and learning center colleagues must design and advocate for an effective assessment plan that provides strong evidence about the effectiveness of their FLCs. When challenged, we must seek continued support from college senates, unions, and boards of trustees. As Kincaid (2009) notes, FLCs can be formed to offer important solutions to problems that confront an institution—these could be the very problems that place its FLC programs in jeopardy. I encourage this book's readers to gather evidence in order to ensure that their FLC programs and advocates have a voice in investigating, proposing, and implementing solutions should a time of crisis arise.

Because a key factor in documenting an FLC's success is assessment, the editors of this book raise a concern about the difficulty of finding authentic (not just self-reported) evidence about student learning as a result of FLC programs. My response is that this evidence must be generated individually by each member of the FLC as he or she designs an individual teaching and learning project connected to the topic of the FLC. This project should enhance student learning in the member's FLC focus course. The design of the project includes an assessment of student learning that occurs as a result of the project. FLC meetings can then move beyond the conversation stage to one in which members consult throughout the year to enlighten and support each other in their project's design, implementation, assessment, and interpretation of outcomes. Among the 30 components of an FLC (Cox, 2009), components 18 through 24 guide this project development, which can result in a course portfolio and presentation from each member that includes resultant student work and learning outcomes. For example, this year my six-member early-career cohort FLC produced project student learning outcomes such as engaging the hunger banquet, using intellectual autobiography essays, engaging peer-to-peer teaching, comparing conventional and digital approaches to promoting spatial literacy, teaching via graphic organizers and disorganizers, and comparing learning involving student portfolios versus research papers. The FLC members presented papers about their projects at a symposium on campus and then at the Lilly Conference on College Teaching in Los Angeles.

Another emergent theme of this book is not unfamiliar to those who work with FLCs: making connections. One chapter describes the interaction of university and two-year regional campus faculty members. These links expand horizons at both institutions. For example, one of my FLC members this year is from a Miami University regional campus. Of the 33 consecutive years that this early-career cohort FLC has existed (it was the original flagship FLC), membership has included faculty from one or more of our regional two-year campuses in 26 of those years. This interaction builds community across campuses and provides an opportunity for the regional campus members to share their experiences about adult and commuting learners, an opportunity we rarely have on the Oxford campus.

Continuing with the theme of making connections, another of the book's chapters describes FLC efforts to connect full-time and part-time/adjunct faculty in one department. Narrowing this gap is a major challenge in higher education. I have been involved in FLC efforts to accomplish this goal on my campus using a multidepartmental campuswide effort. It was a difficult task with surprise twists, taking several years to implement and to find part-time colleagues with the time to participate. The first planner was a faculty member whose dissertation had been about part-time faculty, and later the first facilitator was himself a part-timer. The topic that finally attracted part-time colleagues to membership in this FLC was not directly connected to teaching and learning. Instead, it was about policy: to undertake a proactive role on issues related to the position of part-time faculty in the university community (Lambert & Cox, 2007).

I now look ahead and share with readers the efforts that a statewide community college (CC) system is making toward initiating and implementing FLCs at some of its 23 two-year colleges (Cox, 2011). On November 15 and 16, 2011, the Virginia Community College System (VCCS), under the auspices of its professional development office, provided a noon-to-noon workshop to initiate the training of future FLC facilitators for some of the system's two-year colleges. For next steps, the five VCCS Regional Centers for Teaching Excellence will establish FLCs for facilitators who will initiate and implement FLCs on their campuses for 2012–13. The November FLC training workshop produced the following variety of plans for FLC topics:

- Teaching Creativity (Virginia Western CC)
- Cooperative and Active Learning: How the various learning styles are connected (Tidewater CC)
- Building Bridges: Read. Write. Connect. (Thomas Nelson CC)
- Global Education (Northern Virginia CC)
- Active Learning in the First-Year Core Course Curriculum: A rubric to be applied for all departments (John Tyler CC)
- Cohort FLC for New Faculty (John Tyler CC)
- Early-Career Faculty: Teaching via Distance Learning (Southside Virginia CC)
- Geospatial Information Systems (GIS) Across the Curriculum (Rappahannock CC)
- Creating Student Learning Communities: Incorporating developmental reading, writing, math, and other gateway courses as a first-year experience (Woodbridge Center, Northern Virginia CC)
- Improving Student Research (Lord Fairfax CC)
- Student Development (Northern Virginia CC)
- New Faculty Cohort FLC (Southwest Center for Teaching Excellence)
- The Science, Physiology, and Business of Art-Making (Northern Virginia CC–Annandale)

- A Series of Developmental Education Information Festivals: Sharing experiences, sharing ideas that work, and discussing sample scholarly articles (Piedmont Virginia CC)
- Student Research in Stem Courses (Central Virginia CC)

This rich array of topics illustrates the wealth of intellectual curiosity that two-year college faculty are eager to explore with their colleagues. The themes about FLCs at two-year colleges that I have discussed in this foreword include the adaptability of the FLC model, the FLC's opportunities to initiate and engage in scholarly teaching and SoTL, the FLC's establishment of connections across challenging gaps, and student learning assessment as a path for the establishment of FLC program sustainability. I close with an acknowledgment of and thanks to those faculty who first pioneered FLCs at two-year colleges at the beginning of this century: Dona Fletcher at Sinclair Community College, and Ruth Benander and Beverly Knauper at Raymond Walters College. They provided a beginning for FLC models that are now offering deep learning, community, and a scholarly approach to teaching at two-year colleges. To all of the faculty and administrators at two-year colleges I extend encouragement and best wishes as you consider and engage the opportunities that are brought forth by FLCs.

Milton D. Cox

References

Cox, M. D. (2002, January). *Heeding new voices? Additional recommendations provided for community and engagement.* Paper presented at the 10th annual Conference on Faculty Roles and Rewards, Phoenix, AZ.

Cox, M. D. (2009). *The FLC program director's and FLC facilitator's handbook* (6th ed.). Oxford, OH: Miami University.

Cox, M. D. (2011, November). *Forming–storming–norming–performing–adjourning: Facilitating effective faculty learning communities.* Workshop presented at the Virginia Community College System Training Session for FLC Facilitators, Richmond, VA.

Cox, M. D., & Jeep, J. M. (2000, November). *Taking your best faculty development program statewide in the 21st century: Mentoring other campuses regarding junior faculty.* Paper presented at the 25th Annual POD Conference, Vancouver, British Columbia.

Goto, S. T., Marshall, P., & Gaule, S. (2010). Assessment of faculty learning-communities: Considering social dimensions of participant choice. *Learning Communities Journal, 2*(1), 5–26. Retrieved from http://celt.muohio.edu/lcj/

Kincaid, W. B. (2009). Connecting and engaging faculty and staff to promote scholarly teaching in community colleges. *Learning Communities Journal, 1*(2), 75–95.
Retrieved from http://celt.muohio.edu/lcj/

Lambert, H. E., & Cox, M. D. (2007). The two-year effort to build a program
that provides part-time faculty pedagogical support, community, and a sense of
mission. In R. E. Lyons (Ed.), *Best practices for supporting adjunct faculty*
(pp. 217–240). Bolton: Anker.

Palmer, P. J. (1998). *The courage to teach: Exploring the inner landscape of a teacher's
life.* San Francisco: Jossey-Bass.

INTRODUCTION

Susan Sipple and Robin Lightner

Teaching excellence and engaged learning are the foundation of the two-year college mission. Without an exceptional faculty, diverse and sometimes unprepared students will not meet their educational goals. From vocational schools to community colleges to branch campuses of major universities, two-year colleges expect faculty to spend the majority of their professional lives in the classroom or in preparation for time spent there. In fact, the 2004 National Study of Postsecondary Faculty (Cataldi, Bradburn, & Fahimi, 2005) shows that instructors at public two-year colleges spend a significantly greater amount of time teaching than faculty at four-year or public doctoral institutions. In light of these data, significant faculty development and some measure of sustained scholarly activity related to teaching and learning at two-year colleges are crucial, or even the most dedicated educators may find themselves languishing. With so many hours spent in the classroom, two-year college faculty may have little time to develop new strategies to address problems with teaching and learning—and even less time to devote to reading or conducting scholarship related to it. Lackluster methods, outdated ideas, and waning enthusiasm for classroom practices have a significant impact on education.

Reinvigoration is possible, though. By providing sustained, in-depth faculty development opportunities, two-year colleges can recharge faculty, improve teaching and learning, and remain true to their central missions. This book provides faculty, administrators, and faculty developers with the information they need to form several faculty learning communities (FLCs) that link work in the classroom with scholarship and reflection. These FLCs provide renewed engagement and allow educational excellence to emerge.

An FLC is "a cross-disciplinary faculty and staff group of six to fifteen members . . . who engage in an active, collaborative, yearlong program with a curriculum about enhancing teaching and learning and with frequent seminars and activities that provide learning, development, the scholarship of teaching, and community building" (Cox, 2004, p. 8). While Cox describes what might be the best FLC configuration, variations do exist. In this book, three nontraditional FLCs are represented: two that can be run as "sprint" FLCs, and one that is intradisciplinary rather than interdisciplinary. No matter how they are configured, FLCs have enjoyed a solid decade of success in four-year colleges and universities, and many two-year colleges now employ them as well. But too many two-year colleges still rely solely on the one-day workshop model—a model that although useful, does not do enough to facilitate interdisciplinary collaboration, contribute to the scholarship of teaching and learning (SoTL), or foster student-centered changes in curriculum (Fletcher & Patrick, 1998). By contrast, FLCs when well run are especially effective for producing all of these changes (Cox, 2004). Successful FLCs have far-reaching effects that may influence teaching and learning and help to transform the culture of an institution.

Any two-year college that seeks to enhance faculty development and support teaching excellence can benefit from a single FLC or even a full slate of these communities. Differences exist between community colleges and university branch campuses, but these institutions possess similarities that make the FLCs in this volume ones from which either might benefit, especially because their faculty share similar teaching and service workloads. While the emphasis on scholarship might be greater at the university branch campus where promotion and tenure decisions often hinge on some level of scholarship, most two-year college faculty define their roles as more teaching oriented than research oriented. Faculty at public community colleges report spending 79.8% of their time teaching but only 3.5% on research, whereas public doctoral university faculty report spending 50.8% of their time teaching and 28.2% on research (Cataldi et al., 2006, p. 29). Although research and scholarship play a smaller role on the two-year college campus, FLCs that promote scholarly teaching and SoTL advance pedagogical excellence. Therefore, these FLCs are especially relevant to their faculty and their institutions' missions.

Overview of FLCs

Most of the FLCs in this volume follow the Miami University model set forth by Milton Cox. Some of these groups focus on a particular topic or problem, and others are cohort based, focusing on the needs of faculty at different career stages. FLCs are more than a workshop series. As Cox (2004) states, they

> meet for a period of at least six months; have voluntary membership; meet at a designated time and in an environment conducive to learning; treat individual projects in the same way with the group contributing suggestions and a timely schedule to completion; employ the Kolb (1984) experiential learning cycle; develop empathy among members; operate by consensus, not majority; develop their own culture, openness, and trust; engage complex problems; energize and empower participants; have the potential of transforming institutions into learning organizations; and are holistic in approach. (p. 9)

Miami University began the FLC movement when Cox established a community for junior faculty in 1979 as a part of a Lilly Endowment program. He expanded it, and between 1979 and 2004, there were 80 FLCs at the university. Cox's scholarship and promotion of faculty development across the nation has led to FLCs becoming a widely used best practice for faculty development. An institution new to FLCs may wish to follow the developmental steps suggested by Richlin and Cox (2004, pp. 130–131) that encourage SoTL:

1. Create an application for membership.
2. Plan early for the FLC, such as by choosing books and reference material.
3. Plan an opening retreat before the start of the year.
4. Ask participants to choose one of their own classes to study.
5. Hold seminars and retreats led by facilitators, consultants, and participants.
6. Work on projects.
7. Present to the group and larger college audience for peer review.
8. Hold a closing retreat.
9. Continue the project over the summer or following year.
10. Publish the project.

Once facilitators run one successful FLC using this model, they may find that they can suit the needs of their college better by being more flexible in the structure of future FLCs.

No matter what structure the FLC takes, research shows some specific strengths of this type of faculty development. MacGregor and Smith (2005) report on the status of learning communities in participating colleges and universities since 1996. The report covers student learning communities, but the findings are relevant to the FLC literature, because when a student learning community is formed, the participating faculty simultaneously form a kind of topic-based FLC in order to work through course and curriculum design. The authors explain how learning communities have "become important seedbeds for pedagogical innovation" (p. 4) as a result of cross-disciplinary sharing of techniques, and they have become the context for new pedagogies such as problem-based learning or service-learning. Student learning communities have contributed to professional development in that, like FLCs, they make teaching public: "Participating in another instructor's class, preferably in an area outside one's own discipline, is one of the most powerful and sustained faculty development opportunities available to instructors" (p. 4). The authors describe another important finding in the student learning community literature that is also relevant to FLCs: Focusing on larger problems, such as student engagement or programwide success, builds partnerships across the institution. Faculty work with the institutional research office or student affairs and analyze problems as a gestalt, beyond typical isolated concerns with their own classrooms.

The literature about FLCs is largely descriptive, but a handful of studies measure their effectiveness. A survey of 50 FLC participants showed that 92–96% agreed that there was an increase in their students' ability to perform higher level critical-thinking tasks, work with others, and think for themselves (Cox, 2004, pp. 7–8). Faculty also reported positive results of the active learning exercises that grew out of the FLC. Furthermore, they reported having a more positive attitude toward teaching and receiving more positive responses from their students.

In our own survey of our college's FLCs, 44 faculty rated the impact of their FLC participation on a scale of 1 (negative) to 5 (positive). They reported that the impact of FLCs on teaching ($M = 4.6$), collegial relationships ($M = 4.6$), and scholarly projects ($M = 4.25$) was highly positive. Furthermore, using a rating scale of 1 (strongly disagree) to 5 (strongly agree), they reported that they would recommend FLCs to colleagues ($M = 4.40$) and that they would participate in them again ($M = 4.27$). In another study, scholars at Howard University recorded the results from collaborative, interdisciplinary science, technology, engineering, and mathematics (STEM) FLCs (Smith et al., 2008). They reported that as a result of the work done in their FLCs, student success rates in their newly designed, linked courses (61%) were higher than in other sections of the courses (45%) (p. 211). Faculty rated the FLC and its resulting student experience as high in promoting collegiality, helping them to use teaching methods other than lecture, and teaching higher order thinking concepts. Likewise, in this book, several of our authors report anecdotal results of the impact of FLC participation and results from specific FLC-inspired SoTL projects; however, widespread evaluation of the effects of FLCs on student learning remain elusive. Most of the studies rely solely on instructor perceptions of learning or report changes in teaching. However, one study in the K–12 literature reports data about the effects that learning communities can have on student learning.

Vescio, Ross, and Adams (2007) review 11 studies about the impact of professional learning communities (PLCs) on the behaviors of teachers in elementary and secondary education and the learning of their students. These K–12 PLCs are analogous to FLCs in higher education. PLCs have the following characteristics: shared values about children and the school; a focus on learning, not teaching; reflection; making teaching practices public; and collaboration. In the studies reviewed, teachers' perceptions and classroom observations showed that "participants became more student centered over time. . . . Participants increased the use of techniques such as added flexibility of classroom arrangements and changes in the pace of instruction to accommodate for varying levels of student content mastery" (p. 83). The authors also reviewed disparate types of data about student learning gains in schools with PLCs and concluded that "although few in number, the collective results of these studies offer an unequivocal answer to the question about whether the literature supports the assumption that student learning increases when teachers participate in PLCs. The answer is an unequivocal and resounding yes" (p. 87).

The Need for Faculty Development in Two-Year Colleges

The findings of the 2010 Center for Community College Student Engagement (CCCSE) survey provide a wealth of information related to teaching and learning in two-year colleges. The report summary focuses on "bringing effective strategies to scale to promote learning, persistence, and college completion" for larger numbers of students in these colleges (p. 16). The report also asserts that development for both full- and part-time faculty is central to this movement: "Any effective strategy for dramatically increasing college completion must include a substantial commitment to professional development for individual faculty members and for college teams" (pp. 16–17).

On the two-year college campus, faculty development is needed to address a variety of teaching and learning-related issues. Perhaps one of the most challenging issues faced by two-year college instructors involves the wide array of learners in their classrooms who require a variety of instructional strategies and techniques. Grubb and Associates (1999) argue that "community colleges do surprisingly little to support the pedagogical practices needed by instructors who are serving vast and diverse learners, typically melded within a single classroom" (p. 576). Because the typical two-year college classroom includes a spectrum of learners from developmental through high achievers, faculty must attempt to meet *all* of their needs. In addition, two-year colleges frequently attract both traditional and nontraditional students, students who work toward an associate's degree and those who will transfer to a baccalaureate program. Even excellent teachers can find this diversity challenging, and without faculty development to support their efforts to teach diverse groups well, they may find this difficult. Short-term, tips-based workshops may not fix such problems, which may require a shift in the teaching paradigm. Because they do not provide the time and support, workshops may not accomplish these larger transformations, for example, a shift to inquiry- or team-based learning including self-regulated learning (SRL) exercises. Workshops rarely promote significant reflection, research, or redesign by participants, and they rarely include follow-up by faculty developers.

This emphasis on quality development comes during a time of deep budget cuts in higher education, leaving some administrators and faculty developers struggling to expand faculty development on a shoestring budget. According to the American Association of Community Colleges (AACC, 2012a),

> Community colleges are facing a great funding challenge in that state funding is not keeping pace with increasing costs due to inflation, an expected increase in high school graduation rates, and consequent college enrollment increases. In addition, the majority of states have a structural deficit in funding current services. Because of these factors, community colleges are faced with the tough decisions of cutting services or increasing tuition.

When budgets are tight, faculty development can suffer.

As public funding has diminished, many two-year colleges have hired more adjunct faculty members to cover classes and reduce salary costs (Modern Language Association, 2009). Although many part-time instructors are excellent teachers, the conditions of their employment may work against excellence. Schuetz (2002) describes the 2000 Center for the Study of Community Colleges survey of more than 1,500 full- and part-time faculty in more than 100 community colleges in the United States. The survey examined whether the increased use of adjunct faculty affects teaching. Her analysis shows that although part-time and full-time community college faculty spent about the same amount of time on various classroom activities (e.g., lectures, class discussions, examinations), other differences between the two faculty groups' teaching practices exist: "This analysis confirmed that part-timers tend to have less total teaching experience, teach fewer hours per week at the responding institution, use less innovative or collaborative teaching methods, and interact less with their students, peers, and institutions" (p. 43). Likewise, Grubb and Associates (1999) say that "a less obvious effect of having so many part time instructors is that it undermines collegiality" (p. 334). They assert that in many two-year colleges adjuncts are rarely reviewed by other faculty, they do not always participate in faculty development programs, they have no permanent office space, and they rarely attend faculty or committee meetings. In other words, adjunct faculty suffer from a particular kind of isolation that could impact teaching effectiveness. Even if faculty development opportunities are open to part-time faculty in two-year colleges, the fact remains that an adjunct may have to string together classes at one or more institutions in order to create something approaching a living wage. This kind of overloaded schedule and subsequent low pay leaves little time for faculty development—especially if that development is uncompensated.

These are not the only impediments to real faculty development in two-year colleges. A case can be made that quality development includes helping faculty conduct research and engage in scholarly reflection; these activities are sometimes avoided by two-year college faculty and even discouraged by administrators. This is a serious loss for the faculty member and the institution. When college faculty fail to remain current in their fields or engage in continuing development of teaching skills, teaching and learning suffer. Furthermore, significant reflection on existing research and scholarship is necessary for engagement and collaboration. Tinberg, Killian Duffy, and Mino (2007) argue, "Inquiry, reflection, and critical exchange ought not to be 'add-ons' to that work; rather, these need to be at its center (with all the recognition for such work that institutions can provide). I'd even add that without such introspection and collaboration, teaching becomes more labor intensive" (p. 28). In the absence of significant reflection and scholarship, faculty have to learn from trial and error, rather than from their colleagues or from consulting SoTL literature.

Too often on two-year college campuses, though, administrators stifle scholarship and reflection, claiming that it is at odds with the real work of the institution: teaching.

> Where the fight at research-centered universities and colleges is to valorize teaching as a legitimate subject of scholarship and research, the struggle at two-year colleges is to convince faculty and administrators that intellectual inquiry and scholarly exchange are activities appropriate to the mission of the institutions. (Tinberg et al., 2007, p. 28)

Frequently, two-year colleges consider teaching narrowly, defining it only as time spent in (or in preparation for) the classroom. When even activities that ultimately support teaching (e.g., faculty development or research on classroom learning) are seen as conflicting with the college's mission, faculty and students suffer (Murray, 2001; Tinberg et al., 2007).

But it is not simply the institutional culture or the college mission that explains the difficulty that some two-year colleges have in creating significant ongoing faculty development initiatives. One major problem is incentive. In a study of 300 publicly supported two-year colleges, Grant and Keim (2002) found that 99% of responding colleges offered some kind of faculty development opportunities, but the researchers concluded that for these programs to be truly effective there needed to be some incentive for faculty involvement. When an institution shows it values professional development by providing financial support, offering travel money, or considering professional development activities in promotion and tenure decisions, faculty respond (Goto & Davis, 2008; Shulman, Cox, & Richlin, 2004; Smith, 2007). When these things are lacking, faculty may not choose to be involved in professional development.

Of course, even with a variety of incentives in place to encourage faculty development, other deterrents exist in two-year colleges. Heavy teaching loads mean that committed two-year college faculty spend an enormous amount of time planning classes, grading, teaching, and mentoring students. Free time for development in this environment may be hard to come by. In addition, ever-expanding advances in technology—and two-year colleges' expectation that faculty be technologically proficient—mean that much existing time for professional development is often spent in technology workshops. These workshops might teach skills, but they might not affect what the teacher does in the classroom. Still, mastering these skills is essential at two-year colleges—and doing this takes time away from other kinds of development in which faculty might engage.

Technology aside, other problems and possibilities exist. According to the AACC (2012b), one of the biggest challenges facing community colleges today is the loss of full-time faculty to retirement. During the peak of community college growth and expansion in the 1960s and 1970s, two-year colleges hired large numbers of faculty. Although the loss of these seasoned professionals could be a problem in the future, there is another way to look at this challenge. The AACC (2012b) states, "The departure of so many people during the next few years offers community colleges an excellent opportunity to update outdated practices, create new workplace policies, and introduce organizational structures and models that promote greater efficiency." The time is right, then, to expand offerings for faculty development for both full- and part-time instructors. FLCs emphasize ongoing development, collaboration, and activities designed to change for the better all aspects of teaching and learning. In this time of shrinking budgets, FLCs do all of this at a low cost. Furthermore, well-run FLCs have the potential to help change institutional culture in places where change is needed.

Benefits of FLCs for the Two-Year College

FLCs provide multiple benefits for faculty, professional developers, the institution, and ultimately, students. When run well, FLCs offer a forum for effective change at a variety of institutional levels. The results of an FLC can be concrete products—research studies, classroom interventions, documents for a promotion dossier—or they can be intangible changes, such as a shift in a faculty member's perspective on active learning.

Benefits for the Teacher

FLCs provide a variety of benefits for two-year college faculty. First, many FLCs offer participants opportunities to improve their teaching and to create and test classroom strategies that might impact student learning. Second, FLCs improve the professional lives of faculty by chipping away at the stultifying effects of burnout and isolation that can accompany the heavy teaching and service loads they carry. Third, FLCs create opportunities for mentoring relationships that can enrich the professional lives of the faculty who participate in them. Finally, FLCs that support classroom research or that give members the time and space to reflect on the scholarly aspects of their teaching can begin to create a more professional and well-respected faculty. This, in turn, could positively influence FLC participants' progression toward tenure, promotion, awards, or other kinds of institutional recognition.

Improving Teaching and Learning

Perhaps the most important benefit FLC participation can provide is to help members become more effective, enthusiastic teachers. Sometimes, FLCs, like many of those represented in this book, help faculty develop, test, and peer-review new classroom strategies or technologies. Other FLCs push faculty toward scholarly teaching, asking them to consult the teaching and learning literature, choose and apply relevant information from that literature, observe and assess outcomes, and invite peers to evaluate changes (Richlin, 2001). In this way, teaching is subject to the same rigorous design and review as a scholarly article would be. The benefits are clear: Teaching is professionalized and faculty who engage in this activity develop additional expertise in teaching and learning that supplements their own discipline-based expertise.

Professionalizing Teachers

Although two-year colleges play a vital role in the education of college students in the United States, the faculty employed in them are frequently regarded by those outside of these institutions as second-rate educators (Outcalt, 2002; Twombly & Townsend, 2008). In academic circles, two-year college faculty may be taken less seriously than their counterparts in four-year colleges, in part because they are not as seriously engaged in scholarly activities (Kelly-Kleese, 2004; Spigelman & Kami, 2006). Encouraging research and scholarship about their area of expertise—teaching—changes these attitudes by professionalizing two-year college faculty (Twombly & Townsend, 2008) and recognizing their classroom practices as worthy of serious scholarship.

Recognizing Professional Accomplishment

Another way participation in an FLC can benefit two-year college faculty is by helping them to build a solid argument that they have accomplished what it takes to achieve promotion and tenure at their institutions, or to help them garner well-deserved professional respect and recognition. Faculty participants in FLCs have reported that participation has been a strong contributing factor in promotion and tenure decisions (Lightner & Sipple, 2013).

FLCs provide a path toward growth that two-year college faculty need to advance in their careers. Sometimes career advancement means moving from a two-year to a four-year institution, and without any evidence of scholarly activity, a two-year college faculty member is unlikely to be able to make that move. Active SoTL research may be the only avenue for scholarship for many faculty at two-year colleges, and without experience in this field of research, they need the support of an FLC to introduce them to the field and its methods. Research circles, groups of two or three new faculty who work together to support each other's research goals, have had a powerful impact on productivity and sense of belonging (Gillespie et al., 2005). Finally, presentations and publications that grow out of FLC work improve the faculty member's credentials.

Eradicating Isolation and Burnout

Because two-year college faculty spend so much time in class and in the office with students, they have little time for socializing and collaboration on campus, which can lead to burnout. Maslach and Leiter (1997) identified workload, lack of control, and isolation as factors that cause burnout in organizations. Lackritz (2004) surveyed faculty at traditional four-year universities on their work environments and subsequent burnout. Although he found that the level of burnout was approximately half that in other industries, 20% of participants were in fact experiencing burnout. Furthermore, he found that heavy teaching and grading loads, more time spent in office hours with students, and more college service obligations were positively correlated with facets of burnout such as emotional exhaustion and the depersonalization of others. Given that these particular job characteristics are indicative of two-year college teaching jobs, Lackritz's findings are applicable.

FLCs alleviate burnout, in part, by alleviating isolation. Tinberg and colleagues (2007) describe the "pedagogical solitude" at two-year colleges that results from packed teaching schedules and insufficient travel money to attend conferences that might allow for more professional interaction among peers (p. 28). Sustained involvement in an FLC connects faculty and overturns isolation (Goto & Davis 2008; Spigelman & Kami, 2006). Furthermore, faculty who participate in FLCs report that the work they do there actually alleviates burnout (Sipple & Lightner, 2009). Our faculty reported that participation in FLCs does not contribute to the burden of a heavy teaching load, but rather presents an opportunity to solve problems and to engage in collaborative work that informs their classroom activities.

In addition to addressing isolation, FLCs address the need for intellectual stimulation and growth, which prevents burnout. In his review of faculty development efforts at two-year colleges, Murray (2001) asserts that "the difference between revitalization and burnout may depend on the presence or absence of effective faculty development programs" (p. 488). FLCs can provide an avenue for professional growth, giving burned-out or soon-to-be-burned-out faculty opportunities for investigating new topics, while simultaneously serving the interests of students and their college missions. In fact, Blaisdell and Cox (2004) found that midcareer faculty burnout and marginalization were effectively reduced by FLCs that helped encourage new learning, rich collegial discussions, and new classroom applications.

Benefits for Faculty Developers

Developers want their faculty to have all of these benefits: rich, productive collaborations; opportunities for scholarship; classroom reinvigoration; and decreased burnout. In addition to these direct benefits for participants, FLCs help faculty developers meet their goals and address specific challenges. Our missions are varied, but at most institutions, we aim to improve teaching and learning; support faculty toward promotion, and where relevant, tenure; address faculty's technological competence; and move specific mission-driven initiatives forward.

Working Within Small Budgets

Despite the need for this faculty support and institutional service, budgets for faculty development in two-year colleges are floundering. Many institutions just do not have the option of expanding the staff of a faculty development office or of paying for participation in faculty development. In 2002 Grant and Keim surveyed 272 two-year institutions. Only 47% of the colleges awarded compensation for attending faculty development events. When administrators rated the important factors for participation, the top-rated factors were release time, personal and professional growth, salary advancement, monetary compensation, professional activity credits, and certificates. However, to recruit faculty when the ability to give release time or compensation is absent, institutions have to rely on the growth motives of the participants, the cultural currency that participation carries, and the practical benefits to faculty.

Recruiting—Intangible Benefits Matter

Recruiting is one place where the intangible benefits of the FLC really matter. The social nature of an FLC makes the faculty developer's job of recruiting new members easier. In the absence of compensation, faculty have to want to participate, and many faculty sign up for FLCs because of the social benefits. Having friends at work is one of the top predictors of engagement on the job (Crabtree, 2004). Faculty developers appreciate this social benefit as an excellent recruiting tool for FLCs, and the same cannot be said about webinars or workshops. Another intangible benefit to the faculty developer is that FLCs inspire intellectual curiosity, turning mundane problems into fascinating research questions worthy of time and energy. The creative intellectual energy of an FLC sells itself, allowing the faculty developer to focus on programming rather than advertising and recruiting. When FLCs have a reputation for intellectually interesting work, faculty will sign up even if they are uncompensated.

Building Leaders

At many institutions, an academic dean with a myriad of other responsibilities, a faculty member with release time, or one or two staff are responsible for an institution's faculty development programming. Given their breadth of responsibilities—improving the teaching of hundreds of faculty, serving on committees, giving workshops, and dealing with new technologies—developers frequently feel understaffed. Building a cadre of FLC leaders shifts faculty development from something that is delivered by the developer's office to a force at work within the faculty. When faculty lead programs, the developer certainly benefits directly. This shift allows the developer to offer more programming without doubling the workload. In addition to these practical benefits for the developer, having faculty lead FLCs is a good idea for other reasons. First, this facilitation experience builds leadership skills among faculty. Faculty can earn credibility among their peers and develop the skills of setting a vision, planning, and working through disagreements. Second, when faculty lead FLCs, they claim responsibility for and ownership of these groups, thereby growing commitment to the programs. Third, faculty facilitation (along with faculty-led FLC design and recruitment) allows the FLC to attract participants different from those in the faculty developer's "fan club" who regularly attend events. For example, a leader from biology might attract more science faculty who could otherwise view teaching and learning topics as fluffy social science. Fourth, having a faculty member lead the FLC injects new expertise into a rich multidisciplinary conversation about teaching and learning. These benefits help faculty developers achieve their mission and strengthen the entire faculty.

Implementing Changes

Faculty developers are interested in the effects of the material they present and want faculty to use and apply what they learn in their classes. Workshops are ideal for tips-based solutions, such as how to use Prezi or how to write an effective rubric. In these examples, it is easy for an expert to show a faculty member how to apply the technique on his or her own. However, workshops have limitations—they are rated most useful when they teach one specific skill or technique. Many faculty members will attest that they may learn a good idea in a workshop, but by the time they get back to their offices, deal with stacks of papers to grade, and teach a few classes, the idea is forgotten. Unless workshops have a focus on implementation, many of the ideas get filed away under the category "when time permits." Faculty developers appreciate that participants working in an FLC have the time and space to apply what they are learning and discussing in order to make lasting changes in their classrooms and in their approaches to teaching.

Benefits for the Institution

The changes FLCs produce affect not only faculty and faculty developers, but also the institution. Over time FLCs can produce change in the college culture and can inspire faculty to find new ways to meet the mandates of the institutional mission.

Tackling Bigger Problems

For exploring large, complicated issues that require study, collaboration, problem solving, and long-term support, an FLC can provide the needed momentum and structure. For example, one of the FLCs described in this book started when faculty were frustrated with students' apparent inability to transfer what they were learning from one course to another, such as learning American Psychological Association (APA) style in an English class but not applying it in a psychology class. Though a workshop could have informed those faculty on issues related to transfer of learning, it would not have led down the winding, interesting path that the group took—from cognitive research on near and far transfer to the study of metacognition to SRL. Ultimately, the group conducted a research project and designed a book of study skills activities to help first-year students. This process took two years and 15 faculty members who benefited along the way by trying and tweaking new classroom techniques. They also presented at conferences and published articles on the topic. The institution directly benefited in that there is now increased collaboration on transfer issues and expectations. The FLCs' materials are used by faculty beyond the immediate learning community. An FLC tackling amorphous problems such as this has benefits for its attendees and produces transformations that ripple across the institution.

Changing the Culture

As FLCs are supported by our leaders and administrators, faculty learn that collaboration and peer review are valued and even expected as part of being a teaching professional. When employees are committed to solving problems collaboratively, an institution meets some of the criteria inherent in the description of a learning organization as defined by Peter Senge in *The Fifth Discipline* (1990). The idea of learning organizations is popular in corporate management, and many companies strive to embody its hallmark characteristics: being mission focused, innovative, cooperative, and proactive in ways that benefit employees and customers. Shulman et al. (2004) explain how FLCs enable institutions to function as learning organizations. FLCs promote thinking about larger systems rather than just individual problems and encourage connections across the campus. They help individuals become expert teachers, communicate the values of the culture, and articulate goals and shared methods to achieve these goals. Since the early 1990s, learning organizations have become a powerful concept because organizations identified as such are seen as nimble, creative, focused, and ultimately, successful.

Kuh, Kinzie, Schuh, and Whitt (2005) describe these very characteristics in their article about 20 four-year colleges and universities that had higher than predicted graduation rates and scores on the National Survey of Student Engagement. Their interviews and site visits to these schools showed that institutions took a variety of pathways toward success. "Supporting this orientation toward improvement is a 'can-do' ethic that permeates the campuses—a tapestry of values and beliefs that reflect the institutions' willingness to take on matters of substance consistent with their priorities" (p. 46). Another finding from these institutions is that "senior and junior faculty members are encouraged to find ways to weave their ideas for improving teaching and learning into every practice" (p. 49). Finally, the authors identified the importance of faculty collaboration and introducing new faculty to the culture of valuing teaching. All of these descriptors can be achieved through successful FLCs. In fact, Miami University was highlighted as one of these exemplary institutions because of its successful reliance on FLCs to solve problems, focus on teaching, and create a culture of "positive restlessness" (p. 46).

Serving the Mission

Improving student learning, meeting the needs of the community, engaging in service—the missions of community colleges can all be served by FLCs in ways that workshops and other types of faculty development cannot. Murray (2001) concludes the following from his survey of faculty development activities at two-year colleges:

> Unfortunately, the study reported here uncovered no evidence that faculty development at most community colleges is anything more than a randomly grouped collection of activities lacking intentional coordination with the mission of the college or the needs of faculty members. There appears to be little or no attempt on the part of leaders at most of these community colleges to use faculty development resources to further institutional goals. (p. 497)

This is a missed opportunity. The chapters that follow provide rich examples of FLCs that have moved college missions forward in important ways. The flexibility of topic and delivery in an FLC allows an institution to tweak the examples in this book into models that fit perfectly with the aims of the school, the current culture, and the passions of its faculty. Without the connection between professional development and a college's mission, these activities can be perceived as time-consuming add-ons to the regular work of the college, attracting few participants and leading to little institutional change. FLCs can communicate and advance college priorities in ways that benefit the individual and the entire institution.

Summary of the Chapters

Faculty or developers interested in creating a slate of FLCs need examples of successful ones that might work at their home institutions, tips on how to best implement them, and programming recommendations. The following 11 chapters provide an argument for several different, highly successful two-year college FLCs, along with crucial implementation strategies. Our authors come from four two-year institutions with strong or emerging faculty development programs. University of Cincinnati Blue Ash College is a two-year branch college of a large urban research university; the other three schools, Miami Dade, Tacoma, and Columbus State, are large to medium community colleges. The chapters describe these institutions' successful FLCs, which range from innovative to tried-and-true.

In chapter 1, Lightner describes an SoTL FLC designed to mentor participants through a classroom research project that is conducted over the course of one academic year. The chapter details biweekly meetings that include study design options, institutional review board approval, decisions about measures, data collection, analysis, and presentation outlets. The chapter also provides examples of classroom research projects from several disciplines.

In chapter 2, Denton, Sipple, and Cooper-Freytag present an FLC model that helps participants become scholarly teachers. In the peer review of scholarly teaching FLC, members write about their teaching practices, research relevant SoTL literature, and provide feedback to each other to improve teaching.

In chapter 3, Benander describes a course redesign FLC. Working collaboratively and using principles of backward design, participants draft student learning outcomes, design activities and assessments, and learn new teaching techniques.

Elizaga and Haynes describe a successful intradepartmental adjunct connectivity FLC in chapter 4. This FLC was designed to improve the communication between full- and part-time faculty, as well as to help faculty share best practices in teaching and collaborate on projects.

Skinner describes an FLC that focuses on SRL in chapter 5. SRL is characterized by monitoring, managing, and thinking strategically about one's own learning process. This chapter describes faculty projects that promote students' metacognition through the use of goal setting, reflective exercises, error detection, and revision.

Cummins-Sebree and Wray take up the implementation of a critical thinking FLC in chapter 6. This FLC involves the development, review, and implementation of critical-thinking activities and assessments in two-year college classes.

In chapter 7, Munroe describes an innovative studio learning FLC that encourages participants to use design thinking to expand their creativity and apply it to pedagogical redesign. This FLC brings together eLearning and information systems staff with faculty from all disciplines to help participants try new tools, concepts, and techniques. Munroe offers insight into the ways studio critique helps FLC members practice and review new skills before they take them live in the classroom.

In chapter 8, Benander, Lightner, and Kramer review the key issues in transfer of learning and describe an FLC that applied those issues to first-year students. The authors present the outcomes of the FLC's research, along with a series of exercises designed to help students become more successful in applying skills from one discipline to another.

In chapter 9, Berger and Nellis look at a short-term technology FLC that allows participants to design a customized approach to learning to use instructional technology in their classrooms. Faculty at their college design their own training and development schedule and work with staff and a community of colleagues to create projects that allow them to master a specific technology.

In chapter 10, Lynch and Cheatham discuss the formation and growth of a "teaching commons," a multicampus, multidisciplinary community dedicated to providing members with a supportive environment in which to discuss selected readings and related teaching topics. The chapter offers practical advice for the development and ongoing "care and feeding" of such a community.

Finally, in chapter 11, Refaei, Sipple, and Skutar make an argument for the benefits of a writers group and offer insights on how their institution created and managed such a group. They offer tips for implementing a writing community that can support the need for time, space, and feedback to help faculty write anything from teaching materials to manuscripts for publication.

References

American Association of Community Colleges. (2012a). *Characteristics of community colleges.* Retrieved from http://www.aacc.nche.edu/AboutCC/Trends/Pages/characteristicsofcommunitycolleges.aspx

American Association of Community Colleges. (2012b). *Faculty and staff at community colleges.* Retrieved from http://www.aacc.nche.edu/AboutCC/Trends/Pages/facultyandstaffatcommunitycolleges.aspx

Blaisdell, M. L., & Cox, M. (2004). Midcareer and senior faculty learning communities: Learning throughout faculty careers. In M. D. Cox & L. Richlin (Eds.), *Building faculty communities: New directions for teaching and learning, 97* (pp. 137–148). San Francisco: Jossey-Bass, doi:10.1002/tl.140

Cataldi, E. F., Bradburn, E. M., & Fahimi, M. (2005, December). *2004 National Study of Postsecondary Faculty: Background characteristics, work activities, and compensation of instructional faculty and staff (NSOPF: 04): Fall 2003.* U.S. Department of Education National Center for Education Statistics. Retrieved from http://nces.ed.gov/pubs2006/2006176.pdf

Center for Community College Student Engagement. (2010). *The heart of student success: Teaching, learning, and college completion (2010 CCCSE Findings).* Austin: University of Texas at Austin, Community College Leadership Program.

Retrieved from http://www.cccompletioncorps.org/ccccorps/sites/default/files/pdfs/CCCSE_2010_national_report.pdf

Cox, M. (2004). Introduction to faculty learning communities. In M. D. Cox & L. Richlin (Eds.), *Building faculty communities: New directions for teaching and learning* (pp. 5–23), *97*. San Francisco: Jossey-Bass. doi:10.1002/tl.129

Crabtree, S. (2004, June 10). Getting personal in the workplace. *Gallup Management Journal.* Retrieved from http://gmj.gallup.com/home.aspx

Fletcher, J. J., & Patrick, S. K. (1998). Not just workshops any more: The role of faculty development in reframing academic priorities. *International Journal for Academic Development, 3*(1), 39–47. doi: http://dx.doi.org/10.1080/1360144980030106

Gillespie, D., Dolsak, N., Kochis, B., Krabill, R., Lerum, K., Peterson, A., & Thomas, E. (2005). Research circles: Supporting the scholarship of junior faculty. *Innovative Higher Education, 30*(3), 139–162. doi:10.1007/10755-005-6300-9

Goto, S. T., & Davis, A. C. (2008). Promoting the scholarship of teaching and learning colleges. *To Improve the Academy, 27*, 249–266. Retrieved from http://www.podnetwork.org/publications/academy.htm

Grant, M. R., & Keim, M. C. (2002). Faculty development in publicly supported two-year colleges. *Community College Journal of Research and Practice, 26*, 793–807. doi:10.1080/10668920290104886

Grubb, W. N., & Associates. (1999). *Honored but invisible: An inside look at teaching in community colleges.* New York: Routledge.

Kelly-Kleese, C. (2004). UCLA community college review: Community college scholarship and discourse. *Community College Review, 32*(1), 52–68. doi:10.1177/009155210403200104

Kuh, G. D., Kinzie, J., Schuh, J. H., & Whitt, E. J. (2005, July–August). Never let it rest: Lessons about student success from high-performing colleges and universities. *Change, 37*(4), 44–51. doi:10.3200/CHNG.37.4.44-51

Lackritz, J. (2004). Exploring burnout among university faculty: Incidence, performance and demographic issues. *Teaching and Teacher Education, 20*, 713–729. doi:10.1016/j.tate.2004.07.002

Lightner, R., & Sipple, S. (in press). Scheduling scholarship: Promoting faculty engagement in two-year colleges. *Community College Journal of Research and Practice.* doi:1080/10668921003609293

MacGregor, J., & Smith, B. L. (2005, May–June). Where are learning communities now? National leaders take stock. *About Campus, 10*(2), 2–8. doi:10.1002/abc.123

Maslach, C., & Leiter, M. P. (1997). *The truth about burnout: How organizations cause personal stress and what to do about it.* San Francisco: Jossey-Bass.

Modern Language Association. (2009). *A community college teaching career: MLA Committee on Community Colleges 2006.* Retrieved from https://www.mla.org/commcollege_teachcar

Murray, J. P. (2001). Faculty development in publicly supported 2-year colleges. *Community College Journal of Research and Practice, 25*(7), 487–502.

Outcalt, C. (2002). *A profile of the community college professorate, 1975–2000.* New York: RoutledgeFalmer.

Richlin, L. (2001). Scholarly teaching and the scholarship of teaching. In *Scholarship Revisited: Perspectives on the scholarship of teaching.* C. Kreber (Ed.) *New Directions for Teaching and Learning, 86,* San Francisco: Jossey-Bass, 57–67. http://dx.doi.org/10.1002/tl.16

Richlin, L., & Cox, M. D. (2004). Developing scholarly teaching and the scholarship of teaching and learning through faculty learning communities. In M. D. Cox & L. Richlin (Eds.), *Building faculty communities: New directions for teaching and learning, 97* (pp. 127–136). San Francisco: Jossey-Bass. doi:10.1002/tl.139

Schuetz, P. (2002). Instructional practices of part-time and full-time faculty. In C. L. Outcalt (Ed.), *Community college faculty: Characteristics, practices, and challenges: New directions for community colleges, 118,* 39–46. San Francisco: Jossey-Bass. doi:10.1002/cc.62

Senge, P. M. (1990). *The fifth discipline: The art and practice of the learning organization.* New York: Currency Doubleday.

Shulman, G. M., Cox, M. D., & Richlin, L. (2004). Institutional considerations in developing a faculty learning community program. In M. D. Cox & L. Richlin (Eds.), *Building faculty communities: New directions for teaching and learning, 97,* 41–49. San Francisco: Jossey-Bass. doi: 10.1002/tl.131

Sipple, S., & Lightner, R. (2009). Two-year college faculty: Energy and entropy at mid-career. *Ohio Association of Two Year Colleges Journal, 33,* 17–24. Retrieved from http://www.oatyc.org/journal.htm

Smith, A. (2007, Fall). Professional development issues for community colleges. *Peer Review, 9*(4), 23–25. Retrieved from http://www.aacu.org/peerreview/about.cfm

Smith, T. R., McGowan, J., Allen, A. R., Johnson, W. D., II, Dickson, L. A., Najeeullah, M. A., & Peters, M. (2008, Summer). Evaluating the impact of a faculty learning community on STEM teaching and learning. *The Journal of Negro Education, 77*(3), 203–226. Retrieved from http://www.jstor.org/stable/25608688

Spigelman, C., & Kami, D. (2006). Valuing research at small and community colleges. *Teaching English in the Two-Year College, 34*(2), 135–150. Retrieved from http://www.ncte.org/journals/tetyc

Tinberg, H., Killian Duffy, D., & Mino, J. (2007, July/August). The scholarship of teaching and learning at the two-year college: Promise and peril. *Change,* 26–33. doi:10.3200/CHNG.39.4.26-35

Twombly, S., & Townsend, B. K. (2008). Community college faculty: What we need to know. *Community College Review, 36*(1), 5–24. doi:10.1177/0091552108319538

Vescio, V., Ross, D., & Adams, A. (2007). A review of the research on the impact of professional learning communities on teaching practice and student learning. *Teaching and Teacher Education, 24,* 80–91. doi:10.106/j.tate.2007.01.004

I

COLLECTING EVIDENCE ABOUT WHAT WORKS

Scholarship of Teaching and Learning FLC

Robin Lightner

Historically, faculty learning communities (FLCs) started with the purpose of exposing faculty to the scholarship of teaching and learning (SoTL). "SoTL goes beyond scholarly teaching and involves systematic study of teaching and/or learning and the public sharing and review of such work through presentations, publications, or performances" (McKinney, 2007, p. 10). Creating an FLC focused on SoTL is the ideal first FLC to start at a college if FLCs are new to the institution. Many faculty are surprised to learn that there is an entire field devoted to teaching, and they benefit from being acquainted with it by participating in a semi-structured group such as an FLC. Graduate training often does not prepare faculty to be professional teachers, with an emphasis instead on disciplinary content. In two-year colleges in particular, with a strong reliance on adjunct instructors who work in fields entirely separate from education, faculty may not know the most basic concepts related to course design, classroom management, or assessment. Furthermore, they may have no idea how to engage in scholarly teaching—drawing from the literature and making teaching public. Shifting to a teaching focus requires a change in attitude, and the SoTL FLC conveys a culture of supportive, results-driven teaching. This FLC transforms faculty into scholarly teachers and supports them as they contribute to the growing base of knowledge about how students learn (e.g., Cox, 2003a).

Solving Problems for Faculty

The SoTL FLC offers participants all of the benefits of FLCs in general that are described in the introduction to this book: reduced isolation; idea exchange; collegiality and connectedness; improved job satisfaction; and, thus, reduced burnout. Its primary goal is, ultimately, to improve teaching by training faculty to conduct research on their classroom practices. However, the FLC also addresses other immediate concerns for the participants. For instance, our college, as well as a number of two-year colleges, requires scholarship; even at colleges where scholarship is not a requirement, faculty may need to engage in scholarship to maintain their marketability. Many of our faculty rely on this FLC to help them start a research program that fits with their heavy teaching load and is manageable given the research resources at the institution. Faculty at two-year colleges frequently struggle to be seen as professionals in their discipline. They do not have time or lab space to conduct disciplinary research. They do not have graduate assistants or grant funding. With the majority of their time spent teaching, research becomes an additional task added onto an already full schedule.

Furthermore, faculty are required to demonstrate their effectiveness in the classroom beyond end-of-quarter course evaluations. Data on student learning are key, persuasive components of teaching portfolios and can illustrate that a faculty member's approach is working. Over time, data on student learning can reveal that an instructor is learning from the results and making changes to improve student success. For example, our faculty participants frequently include a summary of the results from their SoTL FLC project in their reappointment, promotion, and/or tenure dossiers. This summary, along with a reflective essay about the scholarly process involved in making changes in their classes, conveys that the teacher is an expert professional who is committed to continual improvement and in touch with the best practices in the field.

Introducing SoTL

Tinberg, Duffy, and Mino (2007) make a compelling argument for promoting SoTL at two-year institutions. SoTL raises the intellectual profile of the two-year college and provides recognition to the faculty member. Additionally, SoTL contributes to job satisfaction, reducing "pedagogical solitude" and increasing fulfillment: "Without such introspection and collaboration, teaching becomes more labor intensive, not to mention less rewarding, because it is less informed" (p. 28). The authors also describe how two-year colleges are uniquely suited to make important contributions to the base of knowledge about student learning. Faculty are more likely to embrace interdisciplinary investigations than their four-year counterparts, and two-year college faculty have more expertise with underprepared students and face a wider range of student performance, so projects unique to the two-year audience can be invaluable to the field. A number of authors assert that SoTL is an important pursuit for community college faculty (Boggs, 2001; Boyer, 1990; Kelly-Kleese, 2004; Spigelman & Day, 2006) and worthy of a busy faculty member's time. Some even make a compelling case that SoTL is a necessary condition of responsible teaching (Pecorino & Kincaid, 2007).

Rather than being persuaded by intellectual arguments, faculty are often more convinced about the value of SoTL by seeing good projects and envisioning how SoTL is applicable to their own teaching. Kathleen McKinney's (2007) book *Enhancing Learning Through the Scholarship of Teaching and Learning* has been a primer for our SoTL FLC participants since its publication. She explores the nature of the confusing definition of SoTL and its subtle differences from the term *scholarly teaching*, which is linked to reflective and informed practice as opposed to classroom research. The book moves quickly into more practical concerns of faculty with suggestions for generating a problem, considering methodology, and presenting work. It is a must-read for faculty new to SoTL and required summer reading for faculty beginning the FLC at our college.

Models for SoTL FLCs

There are different approaches that facilitators can take with SoTL FLCs. Some schools treat the groups as a training program for quantitative social science research. The facilitator teaches participants about topics such as sample size, study design, hypothesis testing, and statistics. Others treat SoTL FLCs more as discussion-based support groups for research. In this type of model, faculty conduct studies within the research paradigms of their disciplines fairly independently from the group, sharing progress with colleagues at different stages. At our college, we aim for a middle ground—we offer some instruction on study options, present different models of research in the field of SoTL, and encourage faculty to choose a methodology that will have some legitimacy within their disciplines. The FLC leader should survey the needs and preferences of the group to adjust the level of structure and schedule flexibility that the group prefers.

Faculty are encouraged to stretch their research skills by including some methods that they otherwise would not; for example, a biology instructor collects some data from interviews when he or she otherwise would be inclined to rely solely on numerical performance data. This kind of stretching not only improves the research study, but also helps the faculty member acknowledge the difficult task of navigating between disciplines and evaluating different kinds of evidence. When faculty appreciate how difficult it is to understand disciplinary differences, they are more empathetic toward students, and more apt to explain the implicit assumptions that they hold about their discipline.

The scholarly literature describes some models for SoTL FLCs. For example, Goto and Davis (2009) report on different models of SoTL FLCs that have met success at two, two-year colleges, Mesa Community College and North Seattle Community College. At Mesa, the FLC uses a "centralized model" in which faculty create research projects about a common topic, such as student retention or writing strategies. There is funding for all facilitators. Participation counts toward professional growth credits that can be applied toward a salary scale adjustment as well as fulfills service requirements. One of the benefits of the structure and institutional support of this kind of model is that participation is broad—with about 70 faculty members participating each year.

Goto and Davis also describe a slightly different model that is implemented at North Seattle Community College, a "decentralized model" in which faculty are encouraged to collaborate as they work together on linked classes that form a student learning community. There are workshops and forums available to the faculty teams about developing SoTL, but the program does not lead them through in a step-by-step fashion. This allows the projects to develop organically out of the faculty members' interests and receive more student input and involvement than the more centralized model.

Both of these groups have given SoTL institutional legitimacy and made it a recognized part of a faculty member's contributions to the college. Authors Goto and Davis recommend the following for creating SoTL FLCs: the FLC should remain in faculty control; the use of projects in reappointment, promotion, and tenure portfolios should be optional; faculty should always see the relevance of the project and larger program; and faculty should maintain control over the scholarly agenda.

Implementation

SoTL FLCs are not a new idea, but at our college, we have found a way to create a yearlong experience that is transformative, enjoyable, and practical.

In operation for 11 years, this is the longest-running FLC at our college. We started the FLC as part of Milt Cox's Ohio Teaching Enhancement Program (Cox, 2001), and the FLC's success has encouraged faculty to sign up for other FLCs and even start new ones to address other college topics. For example, the Biology and Chemistry Departments worked together to design a new first-year experience class. Rather than create a "committee" for the task, the department chairs invited interested department members to form an FLC on the topic. The culture of FLCs at the college changed the tasks from being committee work to instead being an area of scholarly inquiry. Faculty approach the task as a research problem and bring their skills as researchers and their creativity as practicing teachers to create the new course.

In our SoTL FLC, faculty apply to be part of the group in the fall. A call for participation is sent to all full-time faculty. On the application, we ask for participants' background information and an idea of the type of project they would like to pursue. Idea formation is part of the FLC activities, but it is helpful for participants to begin identifying areas of interest. We have taken groups as large as 12 and as small as 3. However, ideally a group of 6–10 provides ample opportunity for peer review as well as for individuals to have sufficient airtime during discussions.

The resources needed for this FLC are fairly small. The facilitator should have some compensation or release time because the FLC requires coordinating, providing resources, and giving feedback, much like leading a graduate seminar would. At our college, participants are awarded only with funds for registration at a teaching conference. Other schools provide larger incentives, such as a stipend when the SoTL project is finally published, or course releases for completion of the project. Funds for books or external speakers can be helpful.

The facilitator of this FLC needs to have a few specific characteristics. First, she must have the skills for organization, team building, and facilitation that are central to leading any type of group. Second, she must have credibility as a respected classroom teacher. Third, she must have expertise in a variety of methods of study used in SoTL. Fourth, she must be aware of different disciplinary approaches to research and be flexible about encouraging faculty to adopt models that fit with their disciplinary expectations. Fifth, she must be able to provide consultation on the simple statistics used for these studies or have referrals for services that faculty need. In addition to statistical help, our faculty have relied on outside support for help with research-related tasks such as qualitative data transcription and professional conference poster design. Sixth, ideally, the facilitator must also be able to offer suggestions and help with the manuscript preparation phase of SoTL. For example, in our FLC, participants spend a session late in the year on exploring publication options, and we keep a list of journals in which our faculty have published SoTL work and notes about turnaround time and the helpfulness of the editors.

Our group follows a schedule that allows for completion of a project over one academic year. In the summer, participants read McKinney's book and complete certification of the university's institutional review board (IRB) to be ready to conduct this classroom research. In the fall, participants meet biweekly. We discuss models of SoTL, including classroom action research (e.g., Mettetal, 2001), quasiexperimental designs (e.g., Carmichael, 2009), qualitative studies (e.g., Khandelwal, 2009), mixed-methods designs (e.g., Jones, Ruff, Snyder, Petrich, & Koone, 2012), and more anecdotal reports. A useful, systematic explanation of the different methodologies in SoTL is provided by Huball and Clarke (2010), who organize the diverse approaches by type of research question, research context, data collection methods, and outcomes. This discussion with sample articles is critical for SoTL FLC participants so that they understand the variety of approaches that can be used for SoTL. The facilitator can guide them to choose the method that both matches their research question and has credibility with their home disciplines.

Next we work through identifying the research questions that will begin each participant's research project. Middendorf and Pace's model of decoding the disciplines is an excellent framework for organizing thoughts about classroom problems (Middendorf & Pace, 2004). In the model faculty identify where students encounter obstacles by asking, "What is a bottleneck in learning in this class?" (p. 3). To identify obstacles, "faculty have to dissect their own innate thinking" (p. 5) by exploring the steps that an expert in the field would go through to accomplish the task identified as a bottleneck. Participants then assemble an annotated bibliography of scholarship on the topic. We draw from literature on educational psychology, cognitive science, their own disciplinary teaching publications, and SoTL. Then, we brainstorm with each other about the interventions that might address the classroom problem. Faculty are encouraged to consult with students about their interventions, such as by informally asking students what they think about a new approach. In some instances, faculty hold focus groups to gather input on each other's ideas. We build measures and complete the required IRB submission materials. Appendix A is a useful handout developed to help participants find or create measures of student learning. Participants are encouraged to triangulate the results by finding multiple measures for learning, ideally including performance and attitudinal data. At every step participants are peer-reviewed by colleagues and the facilitator.

During the fall quarter, participants attend a teaching conference, most frequently the Lilly Conference on College Teaching. Before the conference, participants work together to create a rubric for evaluating a good SoTL presentation. This activity serves two purposes: It builds participants' assessment expertise, and it prepares them for the effective communication of their work in the future. A sample rubric that our group created is given in Appendix B.

In the winter quarter, if the participants received IRB approval for the study, they begin data collection. During this time, the group's focus shifts from the design of the research project to the more general topic of scholarly teaching. We use a variety of activities to engage faculty in the practice of becoming reflective teachers. We expose them to the literature on SoTL and build the habit of discussing what works with their peers. During this term, we complete questionnaires to identify our teaching style, reflecting on our strengths and weaknesses. We do a lecture critique exercise in which we watch a lecture of a Technology, Entertainment, and Design (TED) talk online and critique the speaker. The goal of this activity is to start a discussion about what parts hold attention. Frequently, the participants note features of effective communication, including eye contact, gestures, and vocal variety. We talk about the importance of summarizing key points and creating an overarching structure for a lecture. Another activity in the winter quarter is for the participants to design a midterm survey for their classes as an informal, formative course evaluation. We peer-review these, offering suggestions for improvement.

In the spring, some faculty are still collecting data in their classes. We check in on progress, some participants seek help with statistics or resources for data analysis of quantitative studies, and we plan for dissemination of our results. Ideally, faculty emerge from this FLC with a conference presentation at an SoTL venue, a conference presentation at the teaching arm of a disciplinary conference, a tips-type article, and an SoTL research article. We talk about manuscript creation techniques and direct participants to lists of conferences and journals. Many of the participants want ongoing support of teaching and decide to join the SoTL alumni FLC, which is a more informal SoTL support group for sharing and brainstorming, or they join the writers group FLC, described later in this book, in order to gain momentum on publication.

A culminating event for this group is the presentation of work at a large all-college event during convocation the following fall. Each participant has between 8 and 15 minutes to present his or her study. Importantly, the dean and department chairs attend, in addition to the participants' departmental colleagues. This shows that they value these activities and support the professional development of their faculty. This presentation is one way that the entire culture of the college is informed by SoTL. Brand new faculty are particularly impacted by the presentation. They quickly get the message that we take teaching seriously here and that we are professional teachers who systematically evaluate and improve student learning. It also shows them that we are an institution that offers structure and support to help faculty become successful researchers.

Effects of the SoTL FLC

The following section describes how SoTL FLCs support teachers and ultimately improve student learning. In addition, they serve a larger purpose of growing the field of knowledge about college teaching and informing issues at the institution. Kreber (2006) argues that reflecting on teaching practices with colleagues serves broader goals, for example, clarifying the goals and purposes of higher education, adding to the knowledge base about student learning, and informing curricular and cocurricular issues affecting students. Using a broad definition of scholarship professionalizes the practice of teaching and respects the expertise and care that practitioners put into their daily work.

On Teachers

Faculty participating in the SoTL FLC report that they have a better understanding of the field of SoTL and that they are more likely to turn to the literature when they have a teaching question. In this way, participation in this FLC encourages both scholarship and scholarly teaching. In addition, they report that they have better, more supportive relationships with their colleagues and that their teaching is improved. For example, one participant remarked in a follow-up survey, "After almost every meeting, I came away with new things to try in my class." Another wrote, "I don't feel so alone in my teaching. I have people to go to for advice. I can attend conferences, and I can look up new ideas in articles" (Lightner & Sipple, 2013). At our college, scholarship is an expected part of the reappointment, promotion, and tenure process and often a stressful one for faculty with full-time teaching loads, heavy service commitments, and no research support. This FLC provides a mechanism for accomplishing scholarship in a semistructured, supported way.

A number of faculty produce presentations and publications, and this benefits the whole field—offering research results than can help other community colleges. However, occasionally, the participant does not make his or her work public beyond the college presentation. Regardless, this group experience can be valuable. It builds the habit of assessing what works in the classroom, examining data, and adjusting for improvement. For example, one participant noted, "I am collecting my rubric results now to see how students perform quarter after quarter. It encourages me to try something new to move the needle on some problem areas" (Lightner & Sipple, in press).

On Our Students: Sample Projects

In the last 11 years at our college, the SoTL FLC has enrolled between 3 and 14 participants yearly and, in doing so, has affected hundreds of students. The projects that follow represent the kind of research that faculty in an SoTL FLC can produce in a year. These projects show how the classroom interventions that participants designed and tested improved student learning.

Service Learning in French

French instructor Jody Ballah designed an SoTL project about a new service-learning class for students of French (Ballah, 2011). Students met once per week to design materials and activities for teaching kindergarteners through fourth graders in a French club at a local elementary school. Additional course components included pre- and post-language testing, written reflection papers, weekly group debriefing meetings after each teaching period, and regular discussion board postings. Ballah measured French language proficiency in her college students as well as confidence in speaking French outside of the college classroom. On a grammar test, students improved from the pretest (69.54%) to the posttest (75.46%). On oral interviews scored by a rubric, students improved from 79.5% on the pretest to 83.7% on the posttest. Student confidence increased as rated on a scale of 1 (not at all confident) to 5 (extremely confident) from the pretest ($M = 2.92$) to the posttest ($M = 3.48$). All of these changes were statistically significant. Student quotes illustrated the impact of this new course: "I have decided to change my major to education and become a teacher." "Even though my ability in French hasn't changed a lot, I am now a better student because I look at the language differently." "I am thinking of changing my major to French after doing this class." "This experience has made me a better person. I never thought I could ever teach!" The instructor concluded that the course was meeting its intended goals and expanded it to serve more students. The service-learning course is now in its third year.

Current Events for Microbiology

Professor Amy Miller used popular newspaper articles about current events related to microbiology to make connections between the course material and students' lives (Miller, 2011). She gave students pretests about the topics of pathogens, virulence, and antibiotic misuse, and then administered current events assignments. She measured improvement in her students' factual knowledge and their ability to apply what they know. Students significantly improved from pretest to posttest on both measures, but there was a significant interaction effect. Students improved more on applied items from pretest (14%) to posttest (63%) than on factual items (41–77%). Students rated the current events activities very favorably, a 4.7 on a scale of 1–5, and commented on how engaging they found the articles, for example, "I like tying course material to events outside of class" (p. 60). These results supported the instructor's rationale for using current events and encouraged her to incorporate them for even more topics in her courses.

Active Learning in Physics

Physics professor Krista Wood adapted some of Eric Mazur's peer instruction techniques (e.g., Crouch & Mazur, 2001) for use in her teaching about circuits. The instructor led a discussion and gave concept test multiple-choice questions. Students then paired up to share ideas about the items on the test. Next, volunteers offered their answers and explained why they chose them. After the concept tests, students worked with application problems. In recitation sections of the course, the instructor circulated among peer groups working on application problems. Pre- and posttest scores on a quiz about electrical circuit knowledge indicated a modest but significant improvement after instruction in this unit. Attitudinal surveys indicated that students were not particularly fond of learning about circuits, but that they found the group methods and their classmates' explanations helpful. The instructor kept a journal to note students' explanations about the circuit questions. Qualitative analysis of the responses indicated that "students come to the topic of electric circuits with preconceived ideas about the topic. Initially students used conceptual reasoning to explain their thinking, but not necessarily correct terminology. As they developed a greater understanding, they tended to explain using both algebraic and conceptual reasoning, as well as the appropriate terminology" (Wood, 2010, p. 5). Knowing these misconceptions, the instructor can target these problem areas in her explanations and in the setup of the problems, for example, introducing the algebraic explanations earlier. The instructor continues to use a variety of active learning strategies and has conducted several workshops around our university to introduce STEM faculty to these methods.

Dental Hygiene Curriculum

An instructor in dental hygiene completed a survey to collect information about current practices in the field that affect her graduates (Stegeman, 2005). The objectives of this research were (a) to ascertain the percentage of dental health professionals who feel that blood glucose monitoring is a necessary component in a dental procedure, and (b) to identify the groups of dental health professionals who require additional education about the importance of blood glucose monitoring. To gather this information, she sent an attitudinal survey to dental health professionals who indicated that it is unnecessary to provide blood glucose monitoring in a dental setting. Surveys were distributed to second-year students in the college's dental hygiene program, members of the local dental society, and dental hygiene educators in Ohio.

The results indicated that students (32%) and dental hygiene educators (60%) agreed or strongly agreed that it was important to provide blood glucose monitoring to patients with diabetes, while only 20% of the dentists agreed or strongly agreed that it was important. Therefore, the attitude of the students and educators conflicts with that of future employers. This information is valuable to educators because it indicates the need to incorporate pedagogies into their classes that empower students to be advocates of monitoring. In addition, they can present strategies for discussing the topic and educating the dentist in a diplomatic and tactful way. The department made changes to the curriculum as a result of the study, and the results were presented at a number of regional and national organizations.

Genetics Instruction and Course Type

Another colleague addressed his concern about the effectiveness of his online courses in genetics, compared to that of traditional face-to-face courses (Wray, 2010). Over two academic terms, he compared the performance of online and face-to-face sections of his genetics course in terms of students' knowledge of genetics (pre- and posttest), attitudes about the field, and attitudes about the course. His online courses included recorded lectures, worksheets, challenge questions for deep critical thinking, instructor feedback, and reflection activities. His face-to-face courses included problem-based learning, mini lectures, and homework. He assessed learning with a 20-item multiple-choice genetics quiz. Despite scoring lower on the pretest, by the end of the course, the face-to-face students ($M = 15.29$) significantly outscored those taking the class online ($M = 13.12$). Attitudinal items revealed little difference. However, the online students reported a significantly higher workload in the course than the face-to-face students. The instructor used these findings to inform decisions about which classes should be offered online. He is currently engaged in a separate study surveying instructor empathy and immediacy behaviors in both online and face-to-face courses.

Simulation in Nursing

A nursing faculty member designed a study to test the effects of using a human patient simulation versus traditional case studies on nurses' approaches to hypoglycemia (Trotta, Overbeck, Gibbs, & Barton, 2011). Students in a nursing aging course were randomly assigned to either a human patient simulation scenario or the case study describing the symptoms with text on paper. Both groups received the same scenario about caring for a patient who experiences hypoglycemia. Students took a pretest and posttest, and faculty evaluated the clinical decision-making and critical-thinking skills using a rubric. After their intervention, students completed a survey about their attitudes toward their learning. The pretest scores for both groups were 55%, and the posttest averages increased significantly—to 69% for the simulation group and 80% for the case study group. The clinical evaluation revealed a different pattern of improvement, with the simulation students scoring almost twice as high as the case study students on the rubric. Students saw the value in the simulation. For example, one student said, "[It] allowed me to see things I should be looking for and I wouldn't have if I was only looking at a piece of paper." However, students frequently said that neither simulations nor case studies could be a substitute for actual clinical experience. The results of this study convinced the instructor that the simulation and the case study play different roles in student education, although both are equally important.

SoTL in All FLCs

While our FLC promoted the general topic of SoTL as its main goal, other models focus the FLC on a single specific topic (e.g., problem-based learning, concept mapping, or first-year experience). These topic-specific FLCs, like several included in this book, use SoTL to investigate their research question, and then, after collecting data about their topic, participants contribute to SoTL with their findings. Milt Cox (2003b) described SoTL as a component and logical outcome of the topic-based FLCs. He applied the various theories of cognitive development to faculty learning about SoTL and identified several stages of SoTL involvement. In the first stage, silence, the faculty member feels locked out of SoTL in his or her discipline. The participant feels voiceless, at a loss for how to contribute, and relies on outside experts or the knowledgeable facilitator rather than conducting his own research. In the next stage, subjective knowing, the FLC member believes that there are many different ways to get a positive teaching outcome, including intuition, informal suggestions, or student experiences. Next, procedural knowing involves articulating learning objectives, constructing an SoTL project to test them, and collecting data. Finally, constructed knowing includes having a contextualized understanding of SoTL and a commitment to it. In his investigation at Miami University, Cox found that 55% of all of its FLC participants had participated in SoTL at the national level with refereed conference presentations or peer-reviewed articles in journals. With participation in multiple FLCs, the likelihood of SoTL contributions increased. In all of the FLCs included in this volume, SoTL is a logical outcome of the FLC, assessing its effects in the classroom and making those results public.

Conclusion

An SoTL FLC is an ideal first FLC for a college new to this type of faculty development. It introduces scholarly teaching and the field of research about student learning. Ideally, the practices of an SoTL FLC, such as those described in this chapter, would lead to growth in the body of knowledge about our two-year college students, who often need extra support and innovative teaching practices to meet their unique needs. Even if the participants' first studies do not reach the level of quality needed for peer-reviewed publication, being a part of this community introduces the practices of consulting

SoTL and collecting and examining assessment data. Trigwell, Martin, Benjamin, and Prosser (2000) describe the dimensions of the SoTL: Knowing the literature, improving teaching, improving learning in the discipline, and producing generalizable knowledge about learning. At all levels—from reflecting to publishing—engaging in SoTL is a critical part of being a reflective teacher and helps participants take steps toward systematic improvements in teaching.

References

Ballah, J. (2011, Spring). Students as teachers—design and implementation of a service learning course in French. *Journal of Selected Proceedings of the 2011 American Association of Teachers of French (AATF) National Convention, 2*, 1–7.

Boggs, G. R. (2001). The meaning of scholarship in community colleges. *Community College Journal, 72*(1), 23–26. Retrieved from http://www.aacc.nche.edu/Publications/CCJ/Pages/default.aspx

Boyer, E. L. (1990). *Scholarship reconsidered: Priorities of the professoriate.* Stanford, CA: Carnegie Foundation for the Advancement of Teaching.

Carmichael, J. (2009). Team-based learning enhances performance in introductory biology. *Journal of College Science Teaching, 38*(4), 54–61. Retrieved from http://www.nsta.org/college/

Cox, M. (2001). *Ohio Teaching Enhancement Program.* Miami University. Retrieved from http://www.units.muohio.edu/otep/background.shtml

Cox, M. D. (2003a). Fostering the scholarship of teaching and learning through faculty learning communities. *Journal on Excellence in College Teaching, 14*(2/3), 161–198. Retrieved from http://celt.muohio.edu/ject/

Cox, M. D. (2003b). Proven faculty development tools that foster the scholarship of teaching in faculty learning communities. *To Improve the Academy, 21*, 109–142.

Crouch, C. H., & Mazur, E. (2001). Peer instruction: Ten years of experience and results. *American Journal of Physics, 69*, 970–977. doi:10.1119/1.1374249

Goto, S. T., & Davis, A. C. (2009). Promoting the scholarship of teaching and learning at community colleges. *To Improve the Academy, 27*, 249–266. Retrieved from http://www.podnetwork.org/publications/academy.htm

Huball, H., & Clarke, A. (2010). Diverse methodological approaches and considerations for SoTL in higher education. *The Canadian Journal for the Scholarship of Teaching and Learning, 1*(1). Retrieved from http://ir.lib.uwo.ca/cjsotl_rcacea/vol1/iss1/2

Jones, B. D., Ruff, C., Snyder, J. D., Petrich, B., & Koone, C. (2012). The effects of mind mapping activities on students' motivation. *International Journal for the Scholarship of Teaching and Learning, 6*(1), 1–21. Retrieved from http://academics.georgiasouthern.edu/ijsotl/index.htm

Kelly-Kleese, C. (2004). Community college scholarship. *Journal on Excellence in College Teaching, 14*(2/3), 69–84.

Khandelwal, K. A. (2009). Effective teaching behaviors in the college classroom: A critical incident technique from students' perspective. *International Journal of Teaching and Learning in Higher Education, 21*(3), 299–309. Retrieved from http://www.isetl.org/ijtlhe/

Kreber, C. (2006). Developing the scholarship of teaching through transformative learning. *Journal of Scholarship of Teaching and Learning, 6*(1), 88–109.

Lightner, R., & Sipple, S. (2013). Scheduling scholarship: FLCs in two-year colleges. *Community College Journal of Research and Practice.* doi:10.1080/106689 21003609293

McKinney, K. (2007). *Enhancing learning through the scholarship of teaching and learning: The challenges and joys of juggling.* San Francisco: Anker.

Mettetal, G. (2001). The what, why, and how of classroom action research. *Journal of the Scholarship of Teaching and Learning, 2*(1), 6–13. Retrieved from https://www.iupui.edu/~josotl/

Middendorf, J., & Pace, D. (2004). Decoding the disciplines: A model for helping students learn disciplinary ways of thinking. *New Directions for Teaching and Learning, 98,* 1–12. doi:10.1002/tl.152

Miller, A. (2011). The use of current events as assessment tools. *Journal of Microbiology and Biology Education, 12*(1). doi:10.1128/jmbe.v12i1.263

Pecorino, P., & Kincaid, S. (2007). Why should I care about SoTL? The professional responsibility of post-secondary educators. *International Journal for the Scholarship of Teaching and Learning, 1*(1), 1–6. Retrieved from http://academics.georgiasouthern.edu/ijsotl/index.htm

Spigelman, C., & Day, K. (2006, December). Valuing research at small and community colleges. *Teaching English in the Two-Year College, 32*(2), 135–150. Retrieved from http://www.ncte.org/journals/tetyc

Stegeman, C. (2005, May). *Blood glucose monitoring: A paradigm shift.* Paper presented at the Centers for Disease Control and Prevention, Diabetes Translation Conference, Miami.

Tinberg, H., Duffy, D. K., & Mino, J. (2007, July/August). The scholarship of teaching and learning at the two-year college: Promise and peril. *Change,* 26–29.

Trigwell, K., Martin, E., Benjamin, J., & Prosser, M. (2000). Scholarship of teaching: A model. *Higher Education Research & Development, 19*(2), 155–168.

Trotta, D., Overbeck, A., Gibbs, J., & Barton, R. (2011, November). *Human patient simulation vs. case study: Which teaching strategy is more effective in teaching nursing care for the hypoglycemic patient?* Paper presented at the National Organization for Associate Degree Nursing Annual Conference, Chicago.

Wood, K. (2010, March). Collaborative practice: Improved pedagogy. In H. Meyer (Chair), *Science teaching: Middle and high school—characteristics and strategies.* Symposium conducted at the Annual International Conference of National Association of Research in Science Teaching, Philadelphia.

Wray, F. P. (2010). A comparison of student understanding of inheritance patterns and perceptions of science in traditional versus online non-majors biology courses. *International Journal of University Teaching and Faculty Development*, *1*(2), 1–16. Retrieved from https://www.novapublishers.com/catalog/product_info.php?products_id = 10541

APPENDIX A

Choosing Measures and Writing Good Survey Questions

When you choose measures to assess a classroom intervention, you will want to triangulate your assessment. In other words, get several sources of data to examine the findings from several angles. One suggestion is to find and/or create sources from the affective, cognitive, and behavioral domains. Following are some examples:

Affective: What Do Students Feel?

- Consider measures of self-efficacy/confidence.
- Consider measures of subjective preparedness.
- Consider measures of anxiety. (Remember that anxiety is not always bad. Some concern serves as a motivator for studying/preparation.)
- Include measures of liking/enjoyment of the activity/intervention.
- Keep in mind that measures could be quantitative (ratings) or qualitative (reflective narratives).
- Find a published scale if you can. These have already established validity (getting at what you are really trying to measure) and reliability (producing consistent results). Examples are the GRIT scale (measures persistence) and the STAI (state/trait anxiety inventory).

Cognitive: What (or How) Do Students Think or Know?

- Try to go beyond the course grade by using a Primary Trait Analysis or rubric to measure student performance on written items or tests. Having one additional rater blind to your hypothesis can provide interrater reliability.
- Score different aspects of an assignment and record them separately so that you might realize that a method affects organization of the information, but not factual knowledge.
- Objectively score performance on videotaped presentations or other projects by using outside raters.
- Use rating criteria that are tied to a theory, such as Perry's intellectual development or Bloom's taxonomy (e.g., describe, explain, predict).
- Include measures of metacognition:
  - Determine whether there are changes in how the students are learning the material and whether they use different study methods, mnemonics, organizing strategies, and so on. This could be

measured by scales (published or just a few questions) or by having students write about their processes.

○ Measure monitoring or accuracy of predicting the grade.

Behavioral: What Do Students Do?

- Record how many students are able to complete a series of tasks correctly.
- Take notes about characteristics that could be rated by an observer (nervousness, warmth, confidence).
- Keep a tally of student behaviors, such as the number of questions asked, visits to office hours, times students referred to a study aid, and class attendance.
- Ask students to self-report behaviors, such as time studying with class-mates, number of times erasing a test answer, and duration for taking a test or solving a problem.
- Include observations of your *own* experience in the classroom as well. Take notes on time spent on topics, discussion trends in the class, student interest, questions, and so on. You could also write a reflection after a lecture/course about the impact.

Other Considerations

- Carefully consider whether you want your measures to be more global versus specific. It is more difficult to effect change on global measures than on measures specifically about your classroom intervention.
- Do not measure everything. Pick three to five strategic dependent variables.
- Plan for how you will report the data. Whether you want to show a graph, report averages, or conduct tests of significance affects how you will need to ask the questions and what kind of rating scales you will want to use.
- Consider the practicality of data collection given your workload.
- Consider the different types of rating scales. They might be ratings, rankings, or checklists.

Writing Good Survey Questions

- Use a published measure or items from a published measure instead of creating your own if possible.
- Give your questionnaire a title, and label/title subsections.

- Start the questionnaire with interesting, gentle questions. Put sensitive questions at the end of the instrument.
- Keep wording of items simple (e.g., assist = help, sufficient = enough, acquaint = tell).
- Ask one thing per question (avoid double-barrel items; look for compound sentences).
- Use the same rating scale within a block of items. To do this, many people prefer to use statements over questions with ratings from 1 (strongly disagree) to 3 (neutral) to 5 (strongly agree).
- Make a decision about whether it makes sense to force a preference (i.e., a scale of 1–6) or to allow participants a neutral choice.
- Decide on the types of statistics you will want to use or report before/while you are writing the items. If you are not doing statistics yourself, consult with your statistician before finalizing the survey.
- Avoid negatively worded questions.
- Block questions into similar chunks.
- Be cautious about how response options may compromise anonymity, for example, asking students about age group when there are only a few nontraditional students.
- Do a think-aloud procedure with a few people who pilot the measure. Have them tell you what is going through their mind as they complete the items. What do they wonder about? Are they confused about what a question means?
- Time one or two people as they pilot the measure.

APPENDIX B
Rubric for Evaluating SoTL Conference Presentations

	Needs Improvement	Satisfactory	Excellent
Title/Session Outcomes	The title does not match the presentation, and learning outcomes do not match or are unclear.	There is some mismatch between expectations and the presentation. The title matches the session contents.	The outcomes are clearly stated and match expectations.
Visual Aids/ Handouts	The visual aids or handouts are unclear or distracting. Or, no visual aids or handouts are provided when they would have been helpful.	The visual aids or handouts do not detract from the presentation, nor do they enhance understanding.	The visual aids or handouts improve understanding. They are easy to read and contain references for further study.
Problem or Need	The need or purpose of the study is unclear.	There may be some questions about the purpose or need for the study.	The audience understands the need for the study.
Background Research	No relevant research is described.	Some research is mentioned but may not be adequately described or the description may lack a theoretical perspective.	Relevant research or theoretical perspectives are described and appropriately referenced.
Methods	The methods are unclear in the presentation, or they may be inappropriate for the problem.	There may be unanswered questions about some of the methods used in the study.	The methods are described in sufficient detail for replication. The audience understands why a particular method was adopted over others.

Data/Results	There are no data beyond disorganized anecdotal reports of effectiveness.	Some of the results may be unclear or may not completely address the research questions.	The data are presented clearly. The data are persuasive about the effectiveness of classroom practices. They are presented clearly and address the hypothesis of the SoTL project.
Conclusions	The conclusions are unwarranted from the results.	There may be questions about the conclusions and how they match with data.	The conclusions are careful to avoid problems with statistical conclusion validity, particularly inferring causality from nonexperimental designs.
Implications for Other Teachers	There are no apparent applications to other classrooms.	The audience may still have doubts about the ability to apply lessons from this presentation.	The presenter suggests applications for teachers in different disciplines.
Audience Involvement	There is no audience involvement, nor are there opportunities for questions.	The presenter allows for questions but does not structure further audience participation.	The presenter involves the audience, for example, by asking questions, having them complete samples of materials, or doing a think-pair-share about the results.
Presenter	The speaking/presenting style distracted the audience from the content.	The speaker could have improved a few key elements of his or her style.	The speaking style enhanced the audience's interest in and understanding of the content. This includes pacing, vocal variety, gestures, loudness, and expressiveness.

2

PEER REVIEW OF SCHOLARLY TEACHING

Formative Feedback for Change

Janice Denton, Susan Sipple, and Lesta Cooper-Freytag

Two- and four-year colleges use a variety of summative procedures to evaluate teaching effectiveness, but many institutions still fail to facilitate truly *meaningful*, formative teaching conversations—ones soundly situated in current notions regarding scholarly teaching. Furthermore, although many two-year colleges provide faculty development opportunities aimed at improving teaching, they do not always define clearly what constitutes teaching excellence, nor do they always contextualize development opportunities in the larger framework of promoting scholarly teaching. At its best, scholarly teaching is "teaching that is well grounded in the sources and resources appropriate to the field. It reflects a thoughtful selection and integration of ideas and examples, and well-designed strategies of course design, development, transmission, interaction and assessment" (Shulman, 2000, p. 50). Scholarly teaching must include thoughtful and reflective assessment in order to reveal excellence or evoke pedagogical change.

Too often, institutions rely on scant evidence when evaluating teaching: primarily student evaluations (Cashin, 1999) and sometimes poorly executed classroom observations (Centra, 1993; DeZure, 1999). Although student ratings and faculty observations can provide some evidence of teaching strengths and weaknesses—information that could be used as an impetus toward improvement—they are often used instead as the basis for summative assessments. One way to begin to change an institutional culture that seems stuck in less than effective evaluation practices is to implement a faculty learning community (FLC) that encourages scholarly teaching, detailed written reflection on teaching, and in-depth peer critique to provide productive feedback. Through a peer review of scholarly teaching FLC, two-year college faculty can collaborate in order to rethink practices, institute new teaching strategies, and craft and vet teaching philosophies. More important, they can do this through the practice of reciprocal mentoring. This kind of rigorous, formative peer evaluation acknowledges that our own colleagues are the most appropriate and effective reviewers of our teaching, because they understand the student population; the institution's mission; and, perhaps, the scholarship that informs our practices. Furthermore, the two-year college mission itself creates the need for an FLC that encourages these activities; the emphasis on teaching excellence and student learning at two-year colleges makes pedagogical excellence a priority and formative evaluation of teaching crucial.

Literature Review

The notion that teaching should be subject to rigorous scholarly inquiry and peer review—just as scholarly research would be—is at the heart of effective teaching evaluation. The shift in the ways that colleges and universities regard teaching began more than two decades ago when Boyer (1990) reframed scholarship to include teaching. "The work of the professor becomes consequential," he said, "only as it is understood by others" (p. 23). He further postulated that scholarly teaching requires a highly qualified and engaged professional, with teaching strategies deliberately selected to produce hoped-for learning outcomes. Boyer's work fueled in the academy the reexamination of the work that professors do when they teach and challenged the academy to see teaching as a discipline in its own right.

Shulman (2004) built on Boyer's ideas and coined the terms *scholarly teaching* and *scholarship of teaching and learning* (SoTL). Shulman sees these as two different but related concepts:

> Scholarly teaching is what every one of us should be engaged in every day we are with students in a classroom or in our office—tutoring, lecturing, conducting discussions, all the roles we play pedagogically. Our work as teachers should meet the highest scholarly standards of groundedness, of openness, of clarity and of complexity. But the scholarship of teaching requires that we step back and reflect systematically on the teaching we

have done, recounting what we've done in a form that can be publicly reviewed and built upon by our peers. (p. 166)

While many academics have struggled with the distinction between the two concepts, there is no disagreement that reflection and review are necessary parts of both practices. Hutchings (2005) seems to concur and explains how peer review can positively influence an entire institution:

> A scholarship of teaching will entail a public account of some or all of the full act of teaching—vision, design, enactment, outcomes and analysis—in a manner susceptible to critical review by the teacher's professional peers and amenable to productive employment and in future work by members of the same community. (p. 6)

If scholarly teaching is going to be made public and evaluated so that formative feedback can be offered, the professionals conducting the evaluation must share some common sense of what constitutes teaching excellence; however, professors do not necessarily share consistent criteria for excellence. In addition, while many academics might agree that teaching should be peer-reviewed, we might not know how to conduct rigorous, meaningful reviews. For instance, although many faculty and administrators know that student evaluations offer only one piece of the story of what happens in a professor's classroom (Cashin, 1999), they have not always been sure how to get beyond them as the mainstay of the evaluation of teaching. Furthermore, although peer classroom observations add to the evaluation process when done well (Arreola, 2007; Brinko & Menges, 1997; Chism, 1999; Keig & Waggoner, 1994; Lewis & Lunde, 2001; Millis, 1992), they do not present the full range of a professor's teaching effectiveness. In other words, what happens in a particular class session is not the whole picture. These observations generally focus on effective lecturing or stage skills. By contrast, self-reflection on teaching and course design, and peer review of that reflection, as well as evaluation of syllabi, assignments, classroom artifacts, and teaching philosophies are especially valuable (Berk, 2006; Cranton, 2001) and provide a larger picture of the entire learning experience.

In 1994, in an effort to make the teaching review process more rigorous, the American Association for Higher Education (AAHE) launched a two-year project, "From Idea to Prototype: Peer Review of Teaching." This AAHE initiative designed strategies to encourage collegial exchange about teaching. The project mission statement states,

What's needed, then, are strategies for peer review that capture the scholarly substance of teaching, and which might therefore focus not only on what happens in the classroom (where the evaluation of teaching is now almost exclusively focused) but also on matters of *course design, and assessment of results in terms of student learning.* (Hutchings, 1994, p. 4)

In this model, evaluation of teaching becomes something faculty members being evaluated are actively involved in, "putting together appropriate artifacts of their teaching, along with reflective commentary that reveals the pedagogical reasoning behind them" (p. 4). The AAHE project involved 12 universities that came together to develop ways for faculty to do these things most effectively. Pilot teams from each university worked with teams in their own disciplines from other universities and then attended the 1994 Institute on the Peer Review of Teaching at Stanford University led by Lee Shulman and Pat Hutchings.

The AAHE initiative produced three distinct lessons. First, "with the right 'prompts,' faculty *want* to talk with colleagues about teaching" (Hutchings, 1994, p. 5). Second, "classroom observation is only one strategy for peer review, and not necessarily the best one; having additional options to choose from makes progress more likely" (p. 5). Third, "making the peer review of teaching part of the departmental culture is a challenge that needs strategic attention" (p. 6). One way to achieve the kind of "strategic attention" that Hutchings calls for is to create a peer review of scholarly teaching FLC modeled after the AAHE initiative.

Peer Review of Scholarly Teaching FLC: Implementing Change

Changing the culture of teaching evaluation involves a shift in the way teaching is regarded—as a scholarly activity, not merely an intuitive, hard-to-evaluate task—and a rigorous, formative review process with heavy emphasis on self-evaluation, peer review, and reciprocal peer mentoring. Scholarly work on evaluating teaching, particularly the AAHE initiative, can form the foundation for this FLC. At our college, two senior faculty members created a peer review of scholarly teaching FLC, loosely modeled after the AAHE project, in which faculty members examined their teaching, provided reviews of each other's practices and reflections, and then used the feedback in tandem with the teaching and learning literature to make thoughtful changes. Any like-minded two-year college faculty member or faculty developer can create a similar FLC to address the need for substantive, formative teaching evaluation.

Two-year college faculty will frequently identify with the goals of this FLC. The group's focus on teaching excellence and its desire to make teaching a scholarly activity is at the heart of most two-year college mission statements. When well executed, the FLC establishes a cohort of faculty interested in exploring new ways to serve as professional colleagues in the arena of teaching. Furthermore, it offers a model that faculty can use to examine their teaching, present this examination as scholarly work, and have that work peer-reviewed in a nonthreatening manner.

The FLC at our college went beyond what Hutchings and Shulman initially envisioned. Our community—a relatively short-term, intensive FLC—works well on two-year college campuses where faculty spend a great deal of time teaching and, in doing so, encounter the isolation from peers that the FLC can rectify. The group has been highly successful. Since the initial launch of the project in 2004, seven cohorts have participated.

First Steps Toward Implementation

The first step in implementing a peer review of scholarly teaching FLC is to select participants. Unlike some FLCs, the work of this community demands careful consideration about who will participate. Rather than making an open call for members, facilitators should invite a group of full- and part-time faculty who represent a wide variety of disciplines and ranks. By combining junior, midcareer, and senior faculty, the widest range of teaching experience and institutional expertise is represented. Furthermore, this broad representation could help to ensure campuswide acceptance of the project: If it is not targeted solely at junior faculty, who could be perceived as needing more help with teaching, future cohorts of professors at all ranks will be easier to recruit. Additionally, it is important to consider inviting only one participant from each department. In our FLC, junior faculty participants repeatedly reported on FLC evaluations that they felt free to share their successes and failures because no one in their department was there to "judge." Eliminating this fear of judgment by departmental peers allows for an atmosphere of honest self-evaluation and collegial peer mentoring. This leads to another important consideration. To get the richest interactions in this FLC, a maximum of 12 people per community group is best. Having more than a dozen participants makes discussion too difficult to control.

The second step toward implementation involves choosing a meeting format. The peer review of scholarly teaching FLC works well as a community whose work is divided into three meetings spread out over the course of an academic year, or as an intensive, multiday event in which participants meet three times over the course of one week. At our college, we have experimented with both formats, though the work of each cohort has been the same. No matter which format a college chooses, it is likely that the faculty involved will continue to support and even mentor each other after the conclusion of the FLC, thereby providing feedback on teaching and learning throughout the academic year and beyond. At our college, final FLC evaluations of both the three-day intensive format and the format that spread sessions out over the year were equally positive. Initially, facilitators anticipated that spreading the work out over the academic year might dilute the experience and lead to a less cohesive cohort, but evaluations did not bear this out.

At some colleges, a third step in the implementation process might involve writing grant proposals for funding or soliciting administrators to purchase books for participants. However, a peer review of scholarly teaching FLC can function well with a small budget—or with no budget at all. At our college, the initial cohort operated successfully without a budget, though all subsequent groups have received funding from the college to purchase books and provide lunch. As the value of this particular learning community became widely acknowledged within the college, however, faculty recognized that participation in the FLC was often an important step in becoming a scholarly teacher. For that reason, it has been unnecessary to offer participants faculty development money as a way to entice or reward them to join the FLC.

Community Work

Colleges implementing a peer review of scholarly teaching FLC should begin by considering the 1994 AAHE model. This model defined scholarly teaching as having three basic components: course planning as mirrored in a course syllabus, classroom practice as seen through the classroom delivery of a particular topic or concept, and the assessment of student learning. Because the primary work of the group is peer review, one early step must be to help faculty get their work ready for review. To do this, AAHE recommends that participants write a series of three memos: sustained reflective writings about the three components of scholarly teaching written in response to specific prompts (Hutchings, 1995). At our college, the original AAHE prompts for each memo were modified and sent out at least four weeks before the meeting date. After the memos were written, they were each sent out to another member of the group (the peer reviewer) along with a set of review questions. Each participant wrote three memos and each memo was reviewed by a different colleague. Prompts were offered as a guide; however, all participants used them extensively and reported in FLC evaluations that without them they would have found the reflective writing challenging. For that reason, we recommend that prompts of some sort be offered to help participants begin to write.

The first memo exercise (see Appendix A for all FLC memo prompts) asks participants to think about one of their course syllabi as a scholarly activity, and then to write a two- to three-page reflective memo that reveals the choices and rationale underlying the syllabus. This work is done in prep-aration for the first meeting. Faculty are prompted to consider questions such as, "What topic does the course begin with?" and "In your field, or even in your own department, are there distinctly different ways to organize your course—ways that reflect quite different perspectives on your discipline or field?" This exercise encourages participants to frame their work within their larger discipline and within the pedagogical theories and methods that inform best practices in their field or in higher education in general. At our college, participants reported that the first memo was the most difficult to write for two reasons. First, many faculty had never embarked on a formal reflection of their teaching before, and second, many had never viewed the syllabus as an instrument that revealed their teaching philosophy or scholarly teaching. The first exercise encourages participants to think in new ways about course planning and how they communicate their intentions to stu-dents, and this analysis and the revelations it presents can lead to lasting change.

After participants write their first memo, they e-mail them, along with the corresponding course syllabus, to a predetermined peer reviewer—another member of the same cohort. The reviewer reads both documents carefully and considers answers to a series of questions provided by the facili-tators (see Appendix B for a complete list of memo review questions). At our college, we use three common questions for all reflective memos, as well as questions specific to each topic. These are the common questions:

- What do you like about the memo?
- What questions do you have about the memo?
- What specific suggestions do you have for improvement?

In our FLC, reviewers deliver feedback verbally to their peer during an in-person discussion at the first meeting.

When the participants come together for the three daylong meetings, the itinerary allows for informal peer review and discussion of memos, as well as more structured activities surrounding scholarly teaching and student learning. The applied work conducted in these afternoon activities is what differentiates our FLC from the initial AAHE project. Over the years, all the participants have found the structure of the community to be one of the FLC's strengths. First, writing the reflective memos and being charged with reading a colleague's work before meeting means that they arrived prepared to have thoughtful discussions that lead to improvement in their work. Second, their afternoon work meant they left with something concrete that they could immediately apply to facilitate student learning, and because these activities are based on best practices found in the teaching and learning literature, this reinforced the scholarly nature of their work.

On day one of the community, in which the focus was on the syllabus, the afternoon session involved two activities. In the first, participants were asked to take the *Teaching Perspectives Inventory* (Pratt, Collins, & Jarvis Selinger, 2001). The inventory takes 10–15 minutes to complete, and the results generate discussion of whether the instructor's beliefs, intentions, and actions are in alignment for the course. Participants receive a score in each of the five teaching perspectives assessed by the inventory: transmission, apprenticeship, developmental, nurturing, and social reform. The results suggest the philosophical underpinnings of their teaching style. Pratt and his colleagues' (2001) research "shows that when teachers examine their own profiles, they recognize themselves; and in subsequent debriefings, colleagues recognize each other in terms of their orientations to teaching as represented in their profiles" (p. 2). Instructors learn something meaningful about their own teaching that might have escaped them previously.

The second activity on day one should be one related to that meeting's memo topic. At our college, participants wrote student learning outcomes for the course represented in the syllabi that they had discussed in their memos. In the early days of our FLC, most faculty members did not include learning outcomes on the syllabus. However, because inclusion of learning outcomes has emerged as a best practice, the focus of the activity has moved from writing them to refining them and making the language clearer for students.

Before the second FLC meeting, participants write a memo reflecting on a classroom episode or an exercise that reveals something important about their teaching effectiveness. They explain why they chose to document it and how it reveals a characteristic style or approach to material, as well as how others in their field would teach this topic differently. Participants send the memo to a new predesignated peer reviewer who uses the same set of generic review questions, along with exercise-specific ones.

During the second meeting, participants work in pairs to discuss memos and the teaching and learning insights gleaned from them. Later, the focus stays fixed on teaching practices, and the large group discusses ideas that emerged in the morning's review. Specifically, this session focuses on the question, "Where did the idea come from to use this particular teaching strategy?" In our experience, faculty talk effusively about what they do in the classroom to help students learn, but they rarely acknowledge their work as scholarly. Because the central premise of the FLC is that teaching should be scholarly, participants move to the library to search the teaching and learning literature for best teaching practices related to the practice they described in their memos. By the end of the session, everyone has found citations that support the use of the strategy they discussed in their memos. Through this session, faculty come to view their teaching as scholarly. They have heard from colleagues in other disciplines about new strategies to promote learning—strategies that they can adapt for their classes.

The third reflective memo prompt asks participants to think about measuring student learning. Participants choose an assignment that they have some historical perspective on—one that they have used before. The assignment should promote an important aspect of the learning. In other words, it must measure one or more student learning outcomes articulated in the first FLC meeting. The prompts for the third memo ask participants to analyze the assignment, any rubric that they used to assess the completed work, and what they did with the resulting student performance data. As always, participants send memos, corresponding assignments, and, if available, rubrics to their designated peer reviewer before meeting three. Peer reviewers use the same generic review questions, as well as specific ones, as they consider the feedback they will offer.

The third FLC meeting focuses on measuring student learning. Participants pair up with their partners to discuss memos and give feedback. Later, participants discuss and draft rubrics to grade the assignment that they wrote about or a different assignment if an effective rubric exists for the one used in the memo. This is not a trivial exercise; participants work alone and in collaboration, refining their expectations for students' performance across a variety of outcomes. Although much can be accomplished in an FLC session, this work must continue outside the community, especially when faculty learn that effective scholarly teaching involves assessment, data analysis, and change that begins with a tool like a well-written rubric, and these things take time to develop. When participants see how assessment grows directly out of the outcomes that they create, they see it as a crucial part of scholarly teaching. To facilitate this ongoing work, participants in our FLC received a copy of *Effective Grading: A Tool for Learning and Assessment* by Walvoord and Anderson (1998). This book presents a stepwise approach to writing rubrics and offers excellent examples. The afternoon FLC discussion could center on using student learning data to make changes to teaching practices and documenting the changes. In this way, participants see how the work they do in the FLC can lead to classroom action research projects in the future.

By the end of the FLC, faculty have developed a portfolio of materials and mastered tools that demonstrate scholarly teaching. Formative, constructive, nonthreatening peer review of their work provides more feedback for change than usual single class observation by a colleague. In addition, the FLC provides one substantial way for two-year colleges—or any college or university—to make evident the centrality of undergraduate teaching and learning in their mission statements.

Benefits of Participation

At our college, participation across cohorts in the peer review of scholarly teaching FLC led to substantial reflection about teaching and learning by the participants as well as substantial changes in the classroom. Participants returned to their work with new perspectives on teaching. In surveys completed after each cohort's final meeting, many participants stated that what they learned from their peers and in the other parts of the sessions would lead to significant changes in their own classes. In addition, participants reported that they had elevated their work to the realm of scholarly teaching; for instance, one member reported that she would now use "pertinent literature citations to support teaching decisions" in her classes. For many, the FLC's merger of theory and practice combined what one participant called "learning and doing" in a way that led to immediate change. Writing learning outcomes for a specific course, creating syllabus-ready teaching philosophy statements, drafting high-quality rubrics for assessing students' performance—these changes could be put into practice quickly. Furthermore, several participants went on to conduct SoTL projects as a result of their participation in the FLC. For instance, many of them measured student learning in their classes using a rubric, analyzed the results, made significant changes to the class, and then repeated the process to see if learning had improved.

Moreover, by encouraging FLC members to pair up with colleagues outside of their disciplines, the FLC allowed participants to conceive of new ideas that might not have occurred to them. Even short-term collaborations among colleagues from different disciplines can yield new strategies for class-room use. Busy two-year college faculty who spend so much of their profes-sional lives in classrooms might rarely have the opportunity for the substantive conversations about teaching that this FLC can provide. Many participants have reported that this aspect of the FLC was a highlight for them.

Through reflection, review, and discussion, participants come to a *shared* understanding of what constitutes excellent teaching in their institution. Evaluation of teaching at two-year colleges is central to matters such as reap-pointment, promotion, and tenure (RP&T) decisions, as well as award desig-nations, so this is a particularly important outcome. Because the FLC encourages members to review classroom artifacts from unfamiliar disci-plines, the very nature of the work encourages them to talk with peers about the general philosophical underpinnings of their practices and the ways that those practices might lead to specific learning outcomes. These conversations help participants see the general qualities of teaching excellence, and they discover how different disciplines can come to consensus regarding excel-lence. Over time, this emerging, shared, and articulated definition of excel-lence can have a profound effect on the culture of teaching evaluation in a college.

In a similar way, the work of the FLC at our college had a positive impact on the way candidates for RP&T attempted to prove the exceptional nature of their teaching. Many participants have included the reflective memos they wrote in the community as documentation submitted to RP&T committees of the kind of thought and consideration they gave to their classes. These documents have become highly regarded evidence in support of teaching effectiveness.

Above all, the work of the peer review of scholarly teaching FLC can contribute to the process of further professionalizing the two-year college professoriate. Despite the fact that community colleges educate an enormous proportion of this nation's college students, the community college faculty workforce is often undervalued by the academy as "mere" teachers (Outcalt, 2002). When teaching becomes scholarly, and when two-year college faculty participate in rigorous, peer-reviewed, scholarly teaching, then students, professors, and institutions become the beneficiaries.

References

Arreola, R. A. (2007). *Developing a comprehensive faculty evaluation system: A guide to designing, building, and operating large-scale faculty evaluation systems* (3rd ed). Boston: Anker.

Berk, R. A. (2006). *Thirteen strategies to measure college teaching: A consumer's guide to rating scale construction, assessment, and decision making for faculty, administrators, and clinicians.* Sterling, VA: Stylus.

Boyer, E. L. (1990). *Scholarship reconsidered: Priorities of the professoriate.* Princeton, NJ: Carnegie Foundation for the Advancement of Teaching.

Brinko, K. T., & Menges, R. J. (Eds.). (1997). *Practically speaking: A sourcebook for instructional consultants in higher education.* Stillwater, OK: New Forums Press.

Cashin, W. E. (1999). Student ratings of teaching: Uses and misuses. In P. Seldin & Associates (Eds.), *Changing practices in evaluation teaching: A practical guide to improved faculty performance and promotion/tenure decisions* (pp. 25–44). Bolton, MA: Anker.

Centra, J. A. (1993). *Reflective faculty evaluation: Enhancing teaching and determining faculty effectiveness.* San Francisco: Jossey-Bass.

Chism, N. V. N. (1999). *Peer review of teaching: A sourcebook.* Bolton, MA: Anker.

Cranton, P. (2001). Interpretive and critical evaluation. *New Directions for Teaching and Learning, 88,* 11–18. doi:10.1002/tl.33

DeZure, D. (1999). Evaluating teaching through peer classroom observation. In P. Seldin & Associates (Eds.), *Changing practices in evaluation teaching: A practical guide to improved faculty performance and promotion/tenure decisions* (pp. 70–96). Bolton, MA: Anker.

Hutchings, P. (1994, November). Peer review of teaching: "From idea to prototype": Lessons from a current AAHE teaching initiative project. *AAHE Bulletin, 47,* 3–7.

Hutchings, P. (Ed.). (1995). *From idea to prototype: The peer review of teaching (a project workbook).* Washington, DC: American Association for Higher Education.

Hutchings, P. (Ed.). (2005). *The course portfolio: How faculty can examine their teaching to advance practice and improve student learning.* Sterling, VA: Stylus.

Keig, L., & Waggoner, M. D. (1994). *Collaborative peer review: The role of faculty in improving college teaching* (ASHE-ERIC Higher Education Report No. 2). Washington, DC: School of Education and Human Development, The George Washington University.

Lewis, K. G., & Lunde, J. T. P. (Eds.). (2001). *Face to face: A sourcebook of individual consultation techniques for faculty/instructional developers.* Stillwater, OK: New Forums Press.

Millis, B. J. (1992). Conducting effective peer classroom observations. In D. H. Wulff & J. D. Nyquist (Eds.), *To improve the academy* (Vol. 11, pp. 189–201). Stillwater, OK: New Forums Press.

Outcalt, C. (2002). *A profile of the community college professorate, 1975–2000.* New York, NY: RoutledgeFalmer.

Pratt, D. D., Collins, J. B., & Jarvis Selinger, S. J. (2001, April). *Development and use of the teaching perspectives inventory (TPI).* Communication presented at the annual congress of the American Educational Research Association, Seattle, WA.

Shulman, L. (2000). From minsk to pinsk: Why a scholarship of teaching and learning? *Journal of Scholarship of Teaching and Learning, 1*(1), 48–53.

Shulman, L. (2004). Teaching as community property: Essays on higher education. San Francisco: Jossey-Bass.

Walvoord, B. E., & Anderson, V. J. (1998). *Effective grading: A tool for learning and assessment.* San Francisco: Jossey-Bass.

APPENDIX A
Reflective Memo Writing Prompts

EXERCISE I

Scholarly Teaching: Course Conception and Planning

Select a syllabus from one of your courses as the subject of a reflective memo (2–3 pages). The memo should provide a peer in your field with a window on the choices and rationale that underlie your syllabus. Use the following prompts to guide you:

- What topic does the course begin with?
- Why does it begin where it does?
- What are the major topics covered in the course?
- How do you measure student performance?
- What topic does it end with?
- Why does it end as it does?
- In your field, or even in your own department, are there distinctly different ways to organize your course—ways that reflect quite different perspectives on your discipline or field?
- Do you focus on particular topics while other colleagues might make other choices? Why?
- In what ways does your course teach students how professionals/ scholars work in your field and the methods, procedures, and values that shape how knowledge claims are made and adjudicated within your field?
- How does your course connect with other courses in your own or other fields?
- To what extent does your course lay a foundation for others that follow it? Or build on what students have already (one hopes) learned in other courses? Or challenge and contradict what students are learning in your own or other disciplines?
- How in general does your course fit within a larger conception of curriculum, program, or undergraduate experience?
- What do you expect students to find particularly fascinating about your course?

Some of these prompts were modified from those originally published in *From Idea to Prototype: The Peer Review of Teaching (A Project Workbook)* by the AAHE (Hutchings, 1995).

- Where will they encounter their greatest difficulties of either under-standing or motivation?
- How does the content of your course connect to matters your students already understand or have experienced?
- Where will it seem most alien, and how do you address these student responses in your course?
- Lastly, you might try playing with some metaphors for characterizing your course and its place in the larger curriculum or in the broader intellectual and moral lives of your students. Is your course like a journey, a parable, a football game, a museum, a romance, a concerto, an Aristotelian tragedy, an obstacle course, one or all or some of the above? How does your metaphor(s) illuminate key aspects of your course?

EXERCISE II
Scholarly Teaching: Reflections on Classroom Practice

Write a two- to three-page reflective memo about a classroom episode/exercise/session that reveals something important about your effectiveness as a teacher. Use the following prompts to guide you in this task:

- Why did you choose to document this particular classroom session? What is it meant to be evidence of? Is it, for example, a particularly compelling, insightful, or artful rendition of a key concept? Or, in contrast to all of these, is it simply a "typical" day in your class, and if so, why did you choose that basis for your sample?
- What context is needed to understand this class session? Where are we in the unfolding of the quarter? What other topics is this session's topic situated within? How does it relate to what was discussed the day or week before and what is planned to follow?
- What were your goals for this day? Did the class session go as planned or deviate from your expectations? How so? Why? Did you change direction to take advantage of some new opportunity, get around an obstacle, or deal with a new circumstance?
- What does this class sample say about your teaching? Does it show a characteristic style? A distinctive approach to material? Would others in your field be likely to teach this topic/concept/whatever differently? Are you trying something new? Something you will continue to work at and improve? Do you like what you see?

EXERCISE III

Scholarly Teaching: Putting the Focus on Student Learning

Choose an assignment—that is, instructions for a student project, paper, problem set, classroom assessment, computer simulation, and so on—that you have some historical perspective on. This assignment should be one that you have designed to promote and/or elicit an important aspect of the learning you intend for students in one of your courses.

Write a reflective memo (two to three pages) in which you comment on what the assignment reveals about students' learning in your course. As you write your reflective memo, please respond to the following prompts:

- Why did you choose this particular assignment to reflect on? How is it important to your overall intentions, course design, conception of your field, and the way you want students to understand it? Are there distinctly different formats or foci you could have chosen for this assignment that would have highlighted different dimensions of the idea or the field?
- Why did you structure the assignment in the way that you did? How does its particular question, problem, or application reveal differences in student understandings or interpretations of a critical concept you are teaching?
- What, in particular, do you hope your students will demonstrate in their work on this assignment? What are your expectations?
- What does your assignment tell you about how students are constructing the ideas that are central to the course and to your teaching goals? What misconceptions do they have about these ideas? How do you identify and address student errors and misinterpretations?
- On what standards do you judge student work on this assignment? Do you use a rubric? Do you change your assignment based on student performance? What thoughts do you have about improving your assignment as a consequence of completing this reflective exercise?

APPENDIX B
Peer-Review Questions

THE COMMON QUESTIONS

a. What do you like about the memo?
b. What questions do you have about my memo?
c. What specific suggestions do you have for improvement?

SPECIFIC QUESTIONS
EXERCISE 1

a. Does the memo provide you, as a peer, with a window on the choices and rationale that underlie the syllabus?
b. How important is it to document this aspect of classroom teaching?
c. Does the memo help you understand the author's teaching philosophy?

EXERCISE 2

a. Where did the idea to use this particular teaching strategy come from?
b. How important is it to document this aspect of classroom teaching?
c. What are the appropriate and best criteria on which to judge classroom practice?
    • accuracy of the teacher's construct of the material
    • creativity and originality
    • thoughtfulness of the teacher's reflection or rationale
    • significance of that particular topic to the field
d. On what other dimensions might one judge classroom practice?
e. Might the standards/criteria differ if the teacher were teaching the course for the first time versus having several years of experience with it?

EXERCISE 3

a. What did the data (the students' performance) on this assignment tell you about student learning?

Some of these prompts were modified from those originally published in *From Idea to Prototype: The Peer Review of Teaching (A Project Workbook)* by the AAHE (Hutchings, 1995).

b. Did you make any changes to your teaching strategies, the assignment, or the rubric (if you used one) as a result of analyzing the data?

c. How important is it to include evidence of measuring student learning when making a case about teaching effectiveness?

3

REDESIGNING COURSES FROM THE GROUND UP

From Outcomes to Assessment to Activities

Ruth Benander

Redesigning courses has taken on a new urgency as technology and delivery methods change. A given course may be delivered as face-to-face, as a blended class, or as an online class. To complicate matters further, courses are offered with increasing flexibility of time from three-week intensive courses to semester courses. A strong course design foundation makes creating and adapting courses easier and makes the courses themselves better. Morris (2006) notes in her introduction to a series of articles on design and assessment in *Innovative Higher Education*, "The ongoing march of new knowledge across our disciplines and fields, combined with diversity of learner interest, background, and experience, combined with a growing array of assessment tools and techniques only means one thing: it is time to redesign my . . . courses" (p. 82).

However, for many faculty, redesigning a course is a daunting task. Graduate programs rarely include courses on pedagogical design because the focus is, naturally, on the content area. Thus, faculty may be unprepared for this task and need support as they acquire the foundation of design. A course redesign FLC will help faculty meet the demands for more flexibly delivered courses. A yearlong FLC that meets this need for support is ideal, because a onetime workshop cannot cover course redesign in sufficient depth. In addition, the continual support helps greatly in maintaining the momentum required to complete the redesign of an entire course. This is particularly important for two-year colleges, where faculty teaching loads and service obligations are high.

The National Center for Education Statistics (2008) reveals some of the challenges that necessitate a course redesign FLC for faculty of two-year colleges. Teaching is central to the reappointment/promotion/tenure process, and teaching loads are heavy. Therefore, faculty must demonstrate teaching excellence. These busy faculty need support to find the extra time to do thoughtful course redesign. In addition, in two-year colleges, faculty are less likely to have PhDs than they are in four-year colleges (National Center for Education Statistics 2008, p. 9). Thus, they are less likely to have had training and experience with teaching during graduate school. Furthermore, adjunct faculty, who make up a large percentage of the two-year college workforce, are often working professionals who were not trained in education. The formal study in pedagogy and design is new to many faculty, especially those in two-year colleges.

Student demographics of two-year colleges also highlight the importance of supporting faculty in course redesign. The variety of experience and academic preparation of students is wide; therefore, instructors must use the most supportive strategies and design their courses with the learner in mind. According to the most recent data on two-year colleges from the National Center for Education Statistics (2008) and the American Association for Community Colleges (2011), the student body is older, less prepared for college-level work than peers enrolling in four-year institutions, from lower socioeconomic levels, and more likely to be first-generation college students. As a result, students at two-year colleges require more support and more variety of pedagogical strategies to help them succeed. Any help that faculty can receive in innovating design to accommodate students improves learning and, thus, the success of the institution as a whole.

At our college, redesign was motivated by an increase in student diversity, an increase in online learning offerings, and a move from a quarter calendar to a semester calendar. The college required instructors to create consistent student learning outcomes for all courses, so instructors had the opportunity to reconceptualize their courses. This focus on student learning outcomes was also spurred by increased attention on quality assessment and accreditation. Furthermore, as a two-year college, our institution has a strong teaching focus. Teaching excellence is our institutional mission and a personal mission for many faculty. Some of our faculty were interested in course redesign for personal reasons: to improve a course already being taught, or to demonstrate teaching effectiveness in the reappointment, promotion, and tenure process by means of a course portfolio.

Literature Review

Course design has attracted more attention recently in response to higher education's growing emphasis on teaching innovation (Taylor, 2010). Experts recommend that designers follow two related principles: alignment and backward design. The principle of alignment involves making student learning outcomes the focus of the assessment while the course activities directly practice the skills of the learning outcomes. Aligning the course outcomes with the assessment and activities of the course creates consistency and makes assessment more effective. Walvoord and Anderson (2009) advocate this alignment and observe that, for skillful teachers, "grading . . . includes tailoring the test or assignment to the learning goals of the course, establishing criteria and standards, helping students acquire the skills and knowledge they need, assessing student learning over time" (p. 1). Similarly, the Quality Matters Consortium (Quality Matters Program, 2010), an online design assessment group from the University of Maryland, promotes alignment as one of the key elements in assessing a course for quality design. With the course learning outcomes as the guiding center of the course, they direct what is assessed and what is practiced for mastery and provide a focus that promotes student learning.

With the principle of backward design, the learning outcomes become the starting point for designing assessments and activities. Without training in design principles, an instructor might use an informal, less effective design style as a default. For instance, he or she might follow the chapters of the textbook for the course, one each week, and provide a midterm and final taken from a test bank. More effective course design begins with the skills students will have when the course is over. Wiggins and McTighe (1998) popularized this approach to design in their handbook titled *Understanding by Design*. They state, "The logic of backward design suggests a planning sequence for curriculum: 1) identify the desired results, 2) determine the acceptable evidence, and 3) plan learning experiences and instruction" (p. 9).

Learning outcomes must be concrete and measurable if they are to be communicated and assessed. For example, an outcome such as "Being familiar with the big five personality traits identified by psychologists" is not concrete or measurable for an introductory psychology course because it is not clear what "being familiar" looks like when a student is doing it. A clearer learning outcome might be, "Define the characteristics of the big five personality traits and analyze the advantage a trait would provide in given scenarios." This outcome makes it clear to students and instructors what is being taught in the course and how it will be measured.

This backward design model is broadly applicable. Daughtery (2006) recommends the Wiggins and McTighe model for health science course design. She observes that traditional course design is often content-coverage oriented rather than learning oriented. Daughtery notes, "By focusing on the end results first, we can help students see the importance of what they are learning and make our activities more meaningful and based less on what we have seen others do or how we were taught" (2006, p. 135). Often natural and health science courses have a great deal of content that students must master for their professions. By designing courses with a focus on what these students need to do with this knowledge, faculty can make more informed choices about how to deal with the required mass of content.

The concept of backward design is also key in the transition of face-to-face courses to blended and online courses. Online courses must maintain the rigor and quality of face-to-face courses, especially when many two-year colleges seek to increase their online offerings. In fact, the demand for the redesign of face-to-face courses into hybrid or online has been high at two-year colleges recently, with an average 6% increase per year in online degree offerings (Moltz, 2011).

This transformation can be difficult. Vai and Sosulski (2011) provide a useful handbook on online course design in which they offer the same advice for course design as Wiggins and McTighe did a decade earlier but adapted for the online environment. Vai and Sosulski note that starting with the learning outcomes as the centerpiece of the course undergoing the redesign helps maintain the quality of an online course and its consistency with campus-based versions of the course. They also note that good course design, starting with learning outcomes as the guide for assessment and activities, is efficient. They state, "One of the most important factors in saving time comes up during the course building stage. While the course design and implementation of standards may require some upfront time, it can save time in the end" (p. 23). In fact, supporting faculty in this type of course design promotes student learning, creates more streamlined assessment, and designs better targeted activities.

Tewksbury and Macdonald (2005) have created an extensive website with tutorials that facilitate redesign. They lead a person through the same design process of identifying learning goals and then designing an experience that will meet those goals. Tewksbury and Macdonald recommend that faculty practice these principles of course design to make assessment more targeted to what the students are doing, but they also urge instructors to look beyond the end of the course when they design the learning outcomes. They recommend that faculty think not only about what they want students to do by the end of the course, but also how that knowledge will be applied in their professional lives: "A truly valuable course should focus beyond the final exam to add to students' future lives, abilities and skill sets and prepare students to think for themselves in the discipline after the course is over" (para. 3). Thus, faculty learning the principles of good course design can have far-reaching effects not just on students' education but also on their lifelong learning. Because the majority of two-year degrees are technical degrees preparing students to move directly into their fields, these students' classroom experiences are practice for their professional performance. The more course practice is tied to professional practice, the more successful these students will be.

Implementation

Finding the right format for course redesign instruction is tricky. At our college, we tried a number of workshop models and settled on a yearlong FLC. When we moved to the FLC format, the instruction and products improved greatly. By meeting with a consistent group of people over a long period of time, there was more time to discuss the topics and more incentive to complete the work in the intervening time between sessions. As of 2011, we are going into our fourth year of hosting a course redesign FLC.

We recommend the following effective FLC model. Each year, 8–10 faculty members sign up to attend nine meetings over the course of the academic year. Each meeting lasts about two hours and includes these elements:

- *Conversation about what the scholarly research says about the topic of the meeting.* The facilitator distributes articles, book chapters, or other resources.
- *Discussion of how to implement changes in a given course.* It can be helpful to compare and contrast strong and weak models of the materials.
- *Peer review of homework.* Participants bring in the course materials they are preparing for their new course to share and get feedback.

In preparation for the monthly meetings, faculty are expected to complete specific tasks in between meetings to be ready for the peer reviews. For example, participants bring in a sample rubric, they write sections of a syllabus, or they give peer review on a colleague's work on a discussion board. In addition, once every three months, members are asked to reflect in personal journal entries on their progress and discuss any new realizations about teaching. These journal entries contribute to a final, end-of-the-year reflective writing assignment.

Course redesign is as much about delivery as it is about design because the two are related in the teaching of a course (see Appendix A for overlapping delivery and design topics). Therefore, the group also discusses delivery-oriented topics that affect the classroom experience such as classroom management, forms and uses of feedback, syllabus design and communication, and how to structure assignments.

The first session addresses the topic of getting ready to start. Participants learn about some of the principles of transfer of learning. We discuss how students learn versus how instructors, as experts, learn. Each participant creates a set of expectations that he or she has concerning what students should already know on entering the course. We share our expectations and discuss how we might assess students' skills and help them transfer what they have learned. By beginning with the idea of transfer, participants reflect on what their students have brought to the class and how we can assess it. This clarifies instructors' assumptions and provides a way to validate them. At the end of this session, the group creates ground rules for peer review and for attendance in the seminar.

In the next session, we draft student learning outcomes. We look at a number of examples of useful versus less-measurable outcomes. Using Bloom's taxonomy as a reference, we provide feedback through peer review on the wording of our outcomes. To see the alignment among the outcomes, activities, and assessments, participants draw a course graphic, a diagram, or a concept map that helps them visualize how the elements in the class fit together. This graphic representation helps participants identify gaps in the present course design. For example, there may be a learning outcome that has no assessments, or activities that are not linked to an assessment or a learning outcome. This exercise provides an overview of the redesign process.

In the meeting that focuses on assessment, participants learn about good practices in test design, for both multiple-choice and essay exams. We discuss the helpfulness of rubrics or primary trait analysis and how these assessment tools can be used to improve student involvement in the assessment process. Participants draft these scales for peer-review feedback. The peer review of assessment tools is a valuable part of the seminar because what makes sense to the expert instructor might need further clarification to a novice. The facilitator must cultivate an atmosphere of trust in order for collegial critiques to take place. Peer-review feedback can feel personal and must be delivered and received in a supportive way.

In the session on classroom management, the facilitator can lead a discussion on the current literature on college cheating, ask participants to share their experiences about it, and then facilitate a peer review of participants' academic honesty policies. The group can also discuss other topics including the usage of technology, inappropriate sharing, or attendance issues.

In the session about providing student feedback, the facilitator can begin the conversation by discussing research on the effectiveness of timely, personalized, and extensive feedback. Then, the facilitator can describe options for student feedback such as online quizzes, audio commentary on written work, and self-regulated learning activities. Participants can discuss their current feedback practices, rate the adequacy of these practices, and then consult with each other concerning a particular assignment that is giving them trouble in terms of effective feedback.

A particularly emotional topic for participants is often syllabus design, covered in our session called "Representing a Course." Participants feel strongly that the syllabus should speak for itself; however, frequently policies remain unclear, or students do not read or consult the syllabus. In the FLC, participants discuss the literature about best practices for syllabi in terms of design and content. Then, they peer-review each other's syllabi using a syllabus assessment rubric to give feedback that might help update the materials. Having someone from another discipline read one's syllabus is often an enlightening experience for both the peer reviewer and the instructor.

This benefit of peer review is important in the next session: how to structure activities and assignments. The group tries a variety of activity options including concept maps, WebQuests, problem-based learning, and discussion groups. As the group members practice the activities that they are considering for their classes, they think about the skills that students will have to have to complete them successfully. In addition, the facilitator reminds participants to align the activities with learning outcomes. This process can feel overwhelming given the variety of options, but the support and input of peers can help with decision making.

Because these groups are interdisciplinary, members see how approaches vary across disciplines. However, because all the members are working with the same population of students, they also notice where their practices intersect. The discussions in the sessions help faculty to understand the cultural makeup of the institution and recognize the implicit cultural expectations of their own disciplines. Whereas a history professor may prefer to write several paragraphs of text to communicate an assignment, a health sciences professor may prefer bulleted lists. It is important for faculty to have these conversations so that they can gain a broader vision of the student experience. This broader vision allows instructors to make reference to expectations in other courses and make explicit connections to other courses that will increase the transfer of learning across the disciplines. Instructors also gain empathy for the difficulty students face in navigating disciplinary differences, and they learn to be more explicit with their instructions and rationales for assignments. Additionally, instructors learn how other disciplines solve similar problems, and, as a result, they formulate ideas that might work in their own classes. The fresh perspective of multidisciplinary peer review can lead to real excitement in the redesign.

The next task of this FLC is to make the work of the group public by making the portfolios available online. For some faculty, this is the first time they have created a website, whereas others may already be experienced with this skill. Faculty already familiar with website creation used whatever Web platform they liked best. For those unfamiliar with website construction, we chose Web-based authoring systems such as Wikispaces, Google Sites, or Weebly. Even inexperienced users were able to create sites with these platforms to showcase their new course materials. Sharing the work of the seminar has several benefits. First, a participant might include the website in his or her reappointment or promotion materials as evidence of professional development and/or excellence in teaching. Second, a funding or budgeting committee that allocates money for faculty development might be interested in this resource as evidence of work accomplished by the group. Third, colleagues who do not have the opportunity to attend the seminar might glean ideas for their own courses or be inspired to join the next FLC for redesign.

The final task of the FLC is peer review of the courses by the participants. Appendix B shows one of the rubrics created by facilitators that we have used to evaluate the final product. In this final meeting, group members assemble all the parts of their website that document the process of their course redesign. They use rubrics to evaluate each of the final documents, including the final reflective piece of writing, to assess the quality of the participants' final products and offer suggestions for improvement. One reason that the peer review works so well, particularly at this end stage of the process, is that the group has developed social cohesion and trust in the extended time period of the meetings. The level of trust that a group develops can affect how comfortable and useful peer review can be.

Because this kind of FLC requires a significant amount of work on the part of the participants and the facilitator, offering incentives to promote engagement is important. The facilitator is essentially teaching a course as he or she prepares materials, facilitates the meetings, and supports the participants in completing the redesign products. A facilitator can be offered a course release or a stipend of $1,000 to $2,500, depending on the funds available. It would be challenging to convince a facilitator to take on this level of extra work without this kind of compensation. Ideally, participants should be funded depending on the college policies that fund other forms of course development, ranging from $500 to $2,000, in order to reward their time and effort, and to show that the institution values high-quality teaching. With consistent administrative support, and a designated budget for this FLC, the FLC becomes an enduring part of the college's culture, faculty can plan their teaching schedules to accommodate the time commitment, and reappointment/promotion/tenure committees can come to expect the products of the FLC as demonstrations of excellent teaching effectiveness.

To create a course redesign FLC, the following steps may be helpful to the facilitators of the FLC:

1. Gauge faculty interest via a survey. Send out a survey using an electronic survey application that asks faculty if they are interested in course redesign or other topics.
2. Find a facilitator who is willing to assemble materials for meetings, coach the technology skills for creating the Web-based portfolio, and provide the social support needed to keep the group focused on the task over a long period of time. This person could be the college's faculty developer, instructional designer, or a participant in previous FLCs. This leader should have expertise in the topics of course redesign and be seen by his or her peers as an expert teacher with credibility. It is to the college's advantage if a stipend is offered for this position.
3. Create a presence in the college's learning management system like Blackboard or WebCT for discussions and presentation of work in progress that is private to just the FLC.
4. Schedule dates, rooms, and appropriate technologies for all the FLC meetings so that participants can block out those times.

5. Create an application process whereby interested faculty apply to the facilitator with their reason for wanting to join the FLC and the course they intend to redesign.

6. Have a letter of support from the chair of each participant's department that acknowledges the faculty member's participation and that commits to not schedule that person's courses during the meeting time over the course of the academic year.

7. When the FLC meetings begin, reiterate the commitment to attend all meetings and assign a person to bring refreshments to each meeting so that this task is spread among the whole community.

8. As the FLC is meeting, have the facilitator provide encouragement via e-mail to help members complete work in between meetings, assemble timely and pertinent research articles, facilitate the peer reviews, present framing information for the concepts (but not involved lectures), and post relevant information on the community's website.

9. At the end of the academic year, make sure the course portfolios are uploaded to a website. If there is funding, ensure that the funding sources disburse the appropriate funds to the participants (for a sample course redesign website, see https://sites.google.com/site/courseredesignportfolios/).

10. Schedule a final celebration of the hard work the group has done.

Effects on Teaching

Many faculty cite the peer-review function of the FLC meetings as one of the most valuable parts of the experience. In this very personal feedback, tangible changes are made, and it seems that it is in peer review that the real work of course redesign takes place. For example, in one session on activities, members of the group bring a copy of an assignment that they give in their classes. A peer reviewer from another discipline gives feedback on clarity of direction, layout, and task. A common source of resistance to change is the assertion, "My students know me, so they understand what I'm asking." A colleague might be able to help an instructor see how students might misunderstand an assignment. A student's complaint about an assignment might be dismissed as disrespectful or insubordinate. However, when a respected colleague gives feedback on an assignment, it can be more clearly heard and accepted by the instructor as valid. In a peer review of a group exercise that did not seem to be working, one faculty member noted, "My second 'Aha' moment was related to student feedback and rubrics. It came from the idea that students do not have a full understanding of what it means to 'participate.' This makes sense to me now." As in other areas, students need to be guided through the participation process. In the discussion of the assignment, it became clear that an element of the assessment in this activity was not clearly outlined for the students. This faculty member then redesigned the activity to better address the assessment.

An additional outcome of this FLC is the experiential learning opportunity: participants reflect on what it's like to be students. They complete homework, attend classes, and participate. The insight on what it is like to be a student again often translates into new ideas for the classroom. For example, one faculty member posted the following on the group's discussion board:

> However, I find I am really enjoying reading the posts of other people in all of our discussion boards, and I'm learning from it too. Aha!! If I can both enjoy and learn from a discussion board, might my students have the same experience?! I have not used discussion boards before in my classes and assumed they would not really be useful. I'm not quite sure yet how to integrate this into my chemistry class, but I am definitely going to be thinking about what my students could "discuss" on our class blackboard site. Perhaps I will ask them for some ideas.

The value of experiential learning and reflection cannot be overemphasized. This learning is emotionally engaging, and the reflection on the experience helps it become an intellectual exercise. One faculty member came to a better understanding of the importance of group work:

> My final fall Aha came when I sat down to write this reflection (much later than I intended). When we had to change the date of our December meeting, I was not able to attend because of a teaching conflict. Of course, [the facilitator] met with me one-on-one. Wow! It seemed like an individual session would be better than meeting with the group! She was patient and went over all of the material in detail. Still, I felt "lost and behind" when we met as a group in January! I realized I had missed some assignments. What happened? It turns out I am telling the truth when I say to students, "There are benefits to working in groups—you remember more, you learn different perspectives, you get more feedback, the group experience cannot be replaced!"

This faculty member discussed how having this personal realization would affect how she dealt with group assignments in her courses. She planned to keep explicit her assessment of group participation and provide clear guidelines for what good group participation would look like. The opportunity to reflect on the very personal experience of participating in a course while one is redesigning a course is a strength of this type of faculty development.

The faculty participants at our two-year institution have found the course redesign FLC to be useful not only in redesigning the course they entered the community with, but also in continuing development of other courses. The skills acquired in this FLC generalize beyond the FLC to the rest of the participants' courses. Through the experiential learning, new skills, interdisciplinary points of view, and peer reviews, these faculty create more effective courses. Even if only 8–10 faculty members participate each year, at least 2,000 students benefit from these redesigned courses and the expertise these faculty have acquired. Our faculty have overwhelmingly found this to be a beneficial and useful experience. By participating in a course redesign FLC, two-year college faculty can transform their teaching, improve student learning, and profoundly influence the culture of instruction at their institutions.

References

American Association for Community Colleges. (2011). *Students at community colleges*. Retrieved from http://www.aacc.nche.edu/AboutCC/Trends/Pages/studentsatcommunitycolleges.aspx

Angelo, T. A., & Cross, P. K. (1993). *Classroom assessment techniques* (2nd ed.). San Francisco: Jossey-Bass.

Benander, R. (2009). Course-based student learning outcome modules. Retrieved from http://www.uc.edu/content/dam/uc/cetl/docs/CourseBased_SLOmodules.pdf

Brookfield, S. D. (2006). *The skillful teacher: On technique, trust, and responsiveness in the classroom* (2nd ed.). San Francisco: Jossey-Bass.

Daughtery, K. (2006). Backward course design: Making the end the beginning. *American Journal of Pharmacy Education, 70*(6), 135. Retrieved from http://www.ncbi.nlm.nih.gov/pmc/articles/PMC1803709/

Lang, J. (2006). The promising syllabus. *The Chronicle of Higher Education*. Retrieved from http://chronicle.com/article/The-Promising-Syllabus/46748

Moltz, D. (2011). Online ed trends at community colleges. *Inside Higher Ed*. Retrieved from http://www.insidehighered.com/news/2011/05/18/community_college_distance_education_enrollments_continues_to_grow

Morris, L. (2006). Integrating new ideas in course design, implementation, and evaluation. *Innovative Higher Education, 31*(2), 81–82. doi:10.1007/s10755-006-9014-8

National Center for Education Statistics. (2008). *Community colleges special supplement to the condition of education 2008.* Retrieved from http://nces.ed.gov/pubs2008/2008033.pdf

Quality Matters Program. (2010). *What is the QM program?* Retrieved from http://www.qmprogram.org/

Taylor, M. (2010). Teaching generation NeXt: A pedagogy for today's learners. *A Collection of Papers on Self-Study and Institutional Improvement.* The Higher Learning Commission. Retrieved from http://www.taylorprograms.com/images/Teaching_Gen_NeXt.pdf

Tewksbury, B. J., & Macdonald, R. H. (2005). Designing effective and innovative courses. *On the Cutting Edge: Professional development program for geoscience faculty.* Retrieved from http://serc.carleton.edu/NAGTWorkshops/coursedesign/tutorial/

Vai, M., & Sosulski, K. (2011). *Essentials of online course design.* New York: Routledge.

Walvoord, B., & Anderson, V. (2009). *Effective grading: A tool for learning and assessment.* San Francisco: Jossey-Bass.

Weimer, M. (2002). *Learner-centered teaching.* San Francisco: Jossey-Bass.

Wiggins, G., & McTighe, J. (1998). *Understanding by design.* Alexandria, VA: Association for Supervision and Curriculum Development.

APPENDIX A

Sample Topics for a Course Redesign FLC

Getting Ready to Start

- How we learn: participants offer a story about what they are trying to learn now and how they are going about learning it.
- How our students learn: participants reflect on what opportunities modern students have that they did not.
- Transfer of learning: this is a review of the theories of transfer, and participants are asked to reflect on what students should already know when they come to class and what key knowledge they should leave with.
- Ground rules of peer review: the group discusses what good peer review entails.
- Ground rules of the seminar: the group discusses how they will work with absences and the submission of work for peer review.

Creating Learning Outcomes

- The facilitator leads a discussion of the distinction between goals and outcomes (e.g., Benander, 2009).
- Bloom's Taxonomy: participants use the language for learning outcomes outlined by this taxonomy to create or evaluate and revise the outcomes for the course to be redesigned. This can be done as a peer review session if all participants already have learning outcomes for their courses.

Assessment

- The facilitator introduces the following topics for discussion about assessment:
  - Timing of assessments
  - Types of assessment: multiple choice, essay, project
  - Formative versus summative assessment
  - Face-to-face assessment: conferences and office hours
  - The use of primary trait scales and rubrics
  - Online testing and surveys
  - Personal response systems

- Participants share personal experiences with these methods and offer suggestions for improvements.

Activities and Assignments

- The facilitator introduces the following topics about activities and assignments:
  - C-map, Blackboard organization
  - Instructional design—what is available
  - Discussion of the relationship of the activity to assessment
  - Use of active versus passive assignments (active assignments require that students engage with the material or practice skills learned in the course; passive assignments include things such as reading or watching videos to learn skills or content that they will apply later)
  - Reading as an activity
  - Points and motivation
  - Video as homework (YouTube and Google)
  - Discussions: large and small
  - Service-learning
  - Team-based learning
  - Problem-based learning
- Participants peer-review an activity that each has brought to the session.

Activities and Feedback

- The facilitator hands out a summary of some of Angelo and Cross's (1993) Classroom Assessment Techniques.
- The facilitator explains the model of self-regulated learning.
- The participants discuss types of feedback such as written comments, audio commentary, video commentary, and test scores/grades.
- The participants discuss how students will use feedback for quizzes or paper revisions, test retakes, or group revision/review.

Student Evaluations

- The facilitator introduces research findings on student evaluations.
- The facilitator presents different kinds of student evaluations for discussion:
  - Institutional forms

- o Additional test questions (e.g., asking an extra-credit question on an exam that asks students to identify the study method or course materials that most helped them prepare for the test)
- o Ratemyprofessor.com
- o Kansas IDEA forms
- o The Critical Incident Report: Brookfield (2006)

Classroom Management

- The facilitator introduces the following topics for participants to discuss:
  - o Responding to students
  - o Managing groups
  - o Dealing with emergencies
  - o Where teaching meets counseling
  - o College policies
  - o How to communicate expectations
- Participants peer-review each other's policy statements relating to these issues.

Representing a Course

- The facilitator presents the functions of the syllabus: as a legal document, as a record of the course, as a guidebook for the course, and/or as a teaching tool.
- The facilitator presents alternative syllabus organizations: the Learner-Centered Syllabus (Weimer, 2002), the Promising Syllabus (Lang, 2006).
- Participants peer-review each other's syllabi.

Creating and Sharing the Final Piece (in a Computer Lab)

- During the course of the seminar, participants have been updating their teaching e-portfolios with the items they have been working on such as the activities, assessments, student evaluations, and syllabi. In this last session, participants put the finishing touches on their e-portfolio websites and present their final reflective writing that introduces the items in the portfolio, the process of their redesign, and the final results of the revisions.
- Using the teaching portfolio rubric (see Appendix B), participants review each other's e-portfolios.

APPENDIX B
Sample Portfolio Assessment Rubric

Category	Poor	Acceptable	Good	Very good	Exemplary
Process	Merely lists changes made to the course	Describes changes made to the course	Analyzes how changes were made to course work	Applies seminar redesign principles in changing the course	Evaluates effectiveness of redesign changes to the course
Principles	Are not articulated as a reason for course redesign	Are generally explained as a reason for course redesign	Are discussed with examples as foundation for course redesign	Are integrated into course design as guiding structure with examples	Are integrated and explained how they serve as guide for future course design
Rationale	No explanation of rationale for course redesign given	General explanation of rationale for changes made in course redesign process	Explains specific reasons for changes made in course redesign process	Explains how changes made in course redesign are based on seminar redesign principles	Evaluates how well changes made in course redesign reflect seminar redesign principles
Plans for future	Does not discuss value of redesign or how it will be used in the future	Discusses general plan for using the redesigned course	Discusses specific uses for redesigned course	Tells how redesigned course will be integrated into larger program of studies	Tells how information from seminar will help with future course and program design
Grammar	Sentences confusing to readers	Consistent minor errors but do not interfere with meaning	Minor proofreading errors throughout	Few errors	No errors
Format	Confuses general readers	Accessible to general readers	Easily accessible to general readers	Focuses reader's attention on appropriate points	Focuses and enhances reader's understanding
Organization	Order confusing to general readers	Comprehensible to general readers	Logical transitions clearly signaled	Natural flow of ideas from one to another	Meaning enhanced by sophisticated structure

4

TIES THAT BIND

Enhancing Feelings of Connectivity With
an Adjunct Faculty Learning Community

Ronald A. Elizaga and Traci Haynes

The National Center for Education Statistics reports that student
enrollment in postsecondary institutions increased by 9% between
1989 and 1999 (Snyder & Dillow, 2011). By comparison, enrollment
at the college level increased in the decade that followed by a staggering 38%.
This increase was attributable partly to a recession-induced surge in enrollment at community colleges, as opposed to a flat enrollment trend at four-
year institutions (U.S. Census Bureau, 2012). A corollary to the enrollment
increase was a rise in the number of adjunct faculty members employed by
the nation's colleges and universities, which was even more of an issue at
two-year colleges, which tend to rely heavily on part-time instructors. For
instance, the number of adjunct instructional faculty at institutions of higher
education increased from 22% in 1970 to 48% in 2005 (Snyder & Dillow,
2011). At the community college level alone, a recent survey revealed that
adjuncts account for 70% of the faculty (American Federation of Teachers
[AFT], 2010).

Considering the decrease in full-time, tenure-track positions over this
same period, as well as current and expected budget constraints in education,
it is safe to assume that the percentages of adjunct faculty teaching at community college campuses nationwide will continue to rise. More generally,
the adjunct faculty member is an important fixture in the two-year college
landscape. As such, it becomes increasingly important that we find ways to
integrate part-time faculty members into their departments and colleges. In

this chapter we describe an adjunct connectivity faculty learning community (FLC), a group that strengthens the adjunct-department bond and provides part-time faculty with the tools they need for teaching success.

"Road Scholars"

While adjuncts represent the majority of higher education's instructional workforce, their relatively low professional status on campuses nationwide has been well documented. Many colleges pay adjuncts substantially less than tenure-track faculty for teaching the same courses, yet they afford them no health care, retirement, or other benefits. In addition, it is not uncommon for adjuncts to be without office space and receive little or no mentoring or guidance from full-time faculty in their departments. Many report that they typically arrive on campus, teach their classes, and then leave without ever interacting with colleagues. They are often retained on single-quarter or semester contracts, so they have no job security from term to term, let alone from year to year. Even long-term adjuncts are not protected from losing class assignments to newly hired full-time faculty. They have little choice in scheduling and are often appointed at the last minute. Adjuncts are handed courses and curricula that they have had little or no input in developing and are sometimes given little time to prepare. These factors prompt some to refer to the adjunct condition as the "dirty little secret" on America's college campuses. Adjuncts themselves are commonly referred to as "road scholars," "portfolio professionals," or "freeway fliers," which further illustrates that few envy a part-time instructor's life (Fenwick, 2002; Nutting, 2003).

Impact on Student Success

Overreliance on adjunct faculty can have an unfortunate impact on student success and performance, especially for first-year students. Recent research shows that students are more likely to drop out of college if gatekeeper (i.e., introductory) courses are taught by adjunct faculty (Eagan & Jaeger, 2008). Specifically at community colleges, students are less likely to return for their sophomore year when instructed primarily by adjuncts during their first year of college, which is discouraging considering the negative correlation between student graduation rates and percentage of adjuncts employed (Jacoby, 2006).

Clearly, student success is not solely dependent on the adjuncts themselves, but it is likely more related to an institutional culture that diminishes success for students of adjunct faculty members. Adjuncts often have no opportunity for interaction with their students outside of class and are offered little incentive to spend time on campus. In turn, students have less esteem for adjuncts because they perceive them as less involved and invested in the college. Adjuncts often have more e-mail correspondence with students than face-to-face contact outside of the classroom owing to time and space constraints. Community college students generally need more faculty support than do students at four-year institutions, yet there are few structures in place to support interaction with their adjunct instructors.

Adjunct Connectivity

Despite the difficulties inherent in the job, part-time faculty play an integral part in higher education. They present colleges the flexibility to offer courses at times that full-time faculty may not be available to teach, and allow departments the freedom to field courses that may ultimately have to be cancelled owing to low enrollment. Adjunct scheduling can accommodate fluctuations in student enrollment, or even replacement of full-time faculty who are temporarily assigned to other college responsibilities. Overall, adjunct faculty members can provide expertise, a passion for teaching, and real-world perspectives that serve as an important link to employment opportunities for graduates.

However, feelings of isolation persist. Richardson (1992) reports that "adjunct instructors are more likely than full-time faculty to feel an estrangement from the institution and a sense of isolation from other faculty members" (p. 29). In his anecdotal essays about life as an adjunct faculty member at a West Virginia Community College, Isaac Sweeney (2009) echoes this same sentiment as he writes about feeling like a ghost among the ranks of his full-time colleagues. The reported lack of connectivity makes providing rich opportunities for adjunct involvement an important goal to pursue that undoubtedly would benefit both the students and the instructors.

However, building community and collegiality within an academic environment is difficult when many adjuncts never see or have not even met their peers. In the aforementioned AFT (2010) survey, only 25% of adjunct respondents believed that conditions are getting better at their institutions, and 52% cited the importance of gaining a voice in departmental decisions.

Additionally, 13% felt that greater respect from full-time faculty is an important issue to address. Lyons (2007) stresses the need for adjuncts to have a sense of belonging to the institution and adequate recognition for quality work. Other scholars urged full-time faculty and administrators to include adjuncts in departmental meetings, seminars, mixers, research opportunities, and discussions of school policy (Gosink & Streveler, 2000). Institutions should improve mentoring programs for adjuncts and use surveys that offer adjuncts the opportunity to provide feedback and feel that their opinions were being heard (Lyons, 2007). Though the term *adjunct* might imply that part-time instructors merely serve as accessories to the academic community, the reality is that adjunct faculty members are responsible for a substantial share of the instruction of America's undergraduate college students, and feelings of adjunct connectivity to their department is essential to student success.

With this in mind, the Psychology Department at Columbus State Community College (CSCC) created an FLC to address adjunct connectivity. We felt that a learning community would be the best way to increase inclusion and encourage interaction and collaboration among all faculty members within the department. We recognized a wide range of training, interests, and expertise among the 12 tenure-track and approximately 35 adjunct faculty members who are employed each quarter, and we wanted to tap into that diversity within our own department. The goal of the adjunct connectivity FLC was to offer adjuncts an opportunity to collaborate with full-time faculty and other adjuncts to improve our department and the academic experiences of our students.

Comparison to Traditional FLCs

An adjunct connectivity FLC like ours differs from the more traditional style of learning community in that it is intradisciplinary. In other words, most FLCs at other institutions work toward reducing the campus by bringing in faculty members across departments. These cross-disciplinary groups would provide diversity in thinking by bringing together people from different fields. Our goal, however, was to address the isolation part-time faculty members might feel *within* a department. A departmental FLC still possesses diversity (e.g., educational background, teaching experience) but within the same discipline.

We considered our adjunct connectivity FLC a combination of a cohort-based and a topic-based FLC. Much like cohort-based FLCs, we targeted specific group members (i.e., adjunct faculty within the department) and their developmental needs. Yet we were also topic-based in that our goal was connectivity and student success. Nevertheless, like all learning communities, we offered a structured program that included a set curriculum, activities aimed at learning, and of course, community building. Further, the goals of an adjunct connectivity FLC are the same as those of most other learning communities: to increase faculty aptitude in classroom instruction, encourage collaboration among faculty members, and support the scholarship of teaching.

Our first attempt at an adjunct connectivity FLC at Columbus State resulted in much success. As expected, though, there were some anticipated accomplishments as well as unforeseen obstacles. In the following sections, we document the creation of our FLC and outline the things that worked for us and the challenges we had to address to help other institutions develop similar FLCs. We conclude with a one-year assessment and goals moving forward.

Things That Worked

When planning our learning community, we were proactive. At the outset, we identified specific objectives that were fundamental to a successful group (e.g., impartial facilitation, well-defined policies and procedures). Moving forward, there were other subtle decisions, such as departmental outreach, that also contributed to a successful endeavor. The following is a description of how we established an adjunct connectivity FLC.

Successful Facilitation

Like many organizations, the success of an FLC depends on its leadership. History tells us that groups may include highly skilled members who work toward brilliant ideas, yet are not immune to bad decision making (e.g., Bay of Pigs invasion, *Challenger* shuttle explosion). In particular, FLCs must especially defend against situations that lead to process loss, such as falling victim to groupthink—the tendency of members to value group cohesiveness and solidarity over good decision making (Janis, 1972). FLCs are especially vulnerable to this because they promote cohesiveness. In addition to a highly cohesive group, other indicators that groupthink may occur include (a) a directive leader who controls the discussions and makes his or her wishes known; (b) high-stress situations, such as the anxiety that arises when deadlines approach; and (c) a lack of a candor and a decision-making process that does not encourage alternate viewpoints (Janis, 1982; Stasser & Titus, 1985).

To make sure that all members felt they had an equal voice, we made sure the facilitators did not take a directive role in the group, but simply served as guides, and we minimized situations that would enhance the normative pressure to conform, while encouraging alternate ideas, for example, by using secret ballots (McCauley, 1989) or the "devil's advocate" technique (Hirt & Markman, 1995). We created an atmosphere of collegiality so that even part-time instructors felt comfortable participating. In sum, facilitators must keep in mind that it is a faculty learning *community*, and thus cannot be successful unless it allows proper and open communication. This is especially important since the specific goal of our FLC was to bring together adjunct and full-time faculty. It was paramount, therefore, that the full-time faculty members (as facilitators) did not contribute to the naturally created and often perceived divide between the two departmental factions.

Gaining Departmental Support

In addition to good leadership, FLCs need support from their department and its members. This is especially important in two-year colleges where the department includes both full- and part-time members, and each of these groups naturally has a different set of priorities. We are fortunate in our institution that the department as a whole is friendly and collegial. But in an institution as large as CSCC (we are the third-largest public institution of higher learning in Ohio), it is only natural that there will be some lack of connection, thus the need for our FLC. Milt Cox (2004), the pioneer of FLCs, suggests that the optimal group size for an FLC is 12 or so members, which, in our case, meant that many department members would be left on the outside looking in. We felt it was important, therefore, to make sure that we kept our FLC accessible to the rest of the department when possible.

One way we kept the department involved in our FLC was through constant updates and inclusion at every level. When pitching the FLC, we made sure that everyone knew that the ultimate goal was student success. Since a greater percentage of the classes at a community college are taught by adjuncts (for example, 56% of classes in the Arts and Sciences Division of CSCC are taught by adjuncts), enhancing their connectivity not only to the department but also to the college will improve the practice of teaching and, thus, student success. The wonderful thing about an adjunct connectivity FLC is that it meets the needs of almost everyone involved, which made gaining support quite easy. For instance, the learning community meets the needs of the college because it promotes student achievement; it appeals to the full-time members of the department because it offers an opportunity to work with colleagues on projects that further elevate the department; and it attracts adjuncts because it provides a bridge to the department beyond simply coming in to teach a class and then going home. We introduced our FLC at every relevant opportunity (e.g., chair meetings, departmental meetings, fliers and posters hung throughout the department, and e-mail invitations); to increase feelings of involvement, we solicited input from adjuncts and part-time faculty alike. For example, we informally solicited suggestions on issues within the department that could be addressed by an FLC project. In general, a successful FLC has support not only from within, but also from afar. Communication, therefore, is key.

Setting Policies and Procedures

As we designed policies and procedures, we followed the principles of inclusion and persuasion. To avoid the danger of a perceived hierarchy in which full-time faculty members were the leaders, and part-time faculty members simply the followers, we explicitly stated that all decisions would be made equally as a group, including the establishment of policies and procedures.

Even though things like participation and attendance are assumed in a professional setting, we outlined specific expectations for the group to leave no doubt. The following outline describes the policies and procedures that worked for our adjunct connectivity FLC. Again, the group made and agreed upon policy decisions at the first meeting.

1. *Frequency.* Because CSCC operated on the quarter system at the time, we decided to meet every two weeks until the end of the school year.
2. *Length.* Each meeting lasted for two hours in a conference room on campus.
3. *Compensation.* The college paid adjuncts hourly per the meeting rate, while full-time faculty received reassigned hours.
4. *Attendance.* The group expected attendance at every meeting. Of course, we did make concessions for unforeseen events. Nevertheless, we agreed that if a pattern of absenteeism became apparent, the

group would address the issue and consider it on a case-by-case basis. If attendance issues could not be resolved, then the group held the right to dismiss said members, thereby forfeiting future monetary compensation to them.

Curriculum

While establishing these policies and procedures, our group also decided on the type of curriculum we would follow throughout the academic year. Beyond the superordinate goal of connectivity, our more subordinate goals included investigations into best teaching practices and contributions to the department, both with the intended positive effect on student success. Therefore, we decided to split each meeting into two parts. The first half of every meeting was dedicated to best practice presentations. For every meeting, two members presented for a half hour each. We established the presentation schedule for the whole year at our first meeting. Presentations lasted approximately 20 minutes, followed by 10 minutes of discussion. We spent the second hour of every meeting discussing a group project related to student success that would be completed by the end of the academic year.

In retrospect, we were especially pleased with the curriculum component of the FLC. By providing a two-fold purpose—sharing best practices and group projects—we were able to develop connectivity through our shared love for teaching and also by undertaking projects that would contribute to the department as a whole. In addition, the two-part meeting style helped keep members engaged and discussions fresh. Everyone agreed that the best practice presentations were extremely helpful and insightful. No exact specifications were imposed on the presentations, as long as they were designed with the goal of student success in mind. Presentations ranged from specific teaching techniques that proved useful in the classroom to more broad theories on teaching.

One example of a teaching presentation was on visual auditory, read/write, and kinesthetic (VARK) learning styles (Fleming & Mills, 1992). Basically, the VARK model claims that students have preferred ways in which to learn information based on these four basic modalities. Visual learners best encode information through aids such as diagrams and overhead slides. Auditory learners encode information best through listening (e.g., lectures). Reading/writing learners obviously encode best via reading and writing down information. Finally, kinesthetic learners learn best through experience (e.g., projects, experiments). Another of the many helpful presentations was one on Bloom's Taxonomy (Bloom, Engelhart, Furst, Hill, & Krathwohl, 1956), which classifies learning objectives into different levels of processing, from the basic level of remembering to a deeper level of processing that requires more thorough evaluation. Through Bloom's Taxonomy, educators can better control the level at which they require their students to learn. Participants also made presentations specific to our college, such as tips on how to deal with student misconduct in the classroom and college resources (e.g., counseling services, public safety, the Writing Center).

In addition to all that we learned through the best practice presentations, we were equally proud of the project portion of the learning community. As our FLC comprised 10 members, we decided to split into two groups of five each to oversee one of two projects. Although splitting into two groups seems contrary to the goal of group connectivity, we decided that work would be more efficient, and the output greater, if members could focus their energies on either one of the projects. In that regard, we also made it a point to spend a few minutes at the end of each meeting for groups to share their progress and then allow for suggestions from other project members. The group brainstormed for project ideas over the course of two meetings. The first project was creating a digital adjunct guidebook listing resources and information relevant to adjuncts within our department. Different from the faculty handbook that was distributed by the college, this publication was specific to the department and outlined all things procedural and anecdotal that would help ease and enhance the experience of part-time faculty members. In essence, this guidebook included policies, procedures, resources, Web links, and phone numbers that an adjunct specific to the department would need to know. Accordingly, the handbook provided a way to extend feelings of connectivity to all adjuncts by reducing the divide and creating a tangible link to the department.

As our second project, our FLC created a resource group for first-generation college students. Students who are the first in their family to attend college face obstacles that other college students do not have to face (e.g., lack of family and peer support, ignorance about academic norms, nonacademic responsibilities). These obstacles are common at two-year, open-access colleges. Realizing that there were few organizations that specifically target this segment of our student population, our FLC created a support group and resource to help first-generation students better navigate an unfamiliar world. Through focus groups facilitated by FLC members beyond scheduled FLC meetings, we identified the needs of first-generation students and created the Generation One Trailblazers (GOT). Deficiencies in familial and peer support, feelings of being overwhelmed, and lack of procedural knowledge were among the many obstacles that first-generation students listed. To help, the GOT group, by way of the adjunct connectivity FLC, oversaw informational Web resources, coordinated peer support meetings and campus events, and established a network of faculty contacts that eventually grew beyond the Psychology Department and currently has representation in every department throughout CSCC's Arts and Sciences Division. Collectively, we organized meetings at which first-generation students could meet and socialize with each other while also getting answers to questions that other students might already know. For example, GOT students found it very helpful to hear about the differences in degrees (e.g., associate's versus bachelor's), resources for financial aid, classroom expectations, and even study tips. The GOT project was so popular that it gained autonomy from our FLC and is now a collegewide faculty organization, though still facilitated by FLC members. As a whole, the success of the FLC projects and the productivity of the group in such a short time prompted the dean to promote our FLC as a model for other departments throughout the college to follow in terms of adjunct connectivity.

Promoting Success

As our success became apparent, we wanted to plant additional seeds in the department to increase the number of applicants for the following academic year. When deciding on the due dates for our projects, we specifically had in mind the spring quarter department meeting, which would provide us with the largest audience to share our current success and promote interest for the next iteration of the FLC. We also presented a short amateur video that showed the fun of participating in the FLC. It included narratives from members about how the FLC experience not only enhanced adjunct connectivity to the department, but also contributed to their overall success as teachers. From our experience, any kind of promotion, whether traditional or creative, can only help to secure support as well as increase interest in future participation.

Challenges

With the success of our first attempt at an FLC, we were excited to get started with a new group as the next academic year approached. In the second year of the FLC, we met some new challenges with regard to the adjunct pool and the culture of a two-year institution.

Budget

Attempts to create and maintain an FLC in an environment of budget cuts is a challenge to which all academic institutions can relate. Add to that the inherent difficulties in an adjunct's work environment and work schedule, and the challenges become even more complicated. As stated in the introduction to this chapter, the reality of a part-time position is that adjunct faculty often find it difficult to feel completely invested, especially considering that it is not uncommon for them to divide their commitment among several institutions. This is not to imply that adjunct faculty members are not putting forth their best effort. They may simply hesitate to commit fully to an institution that does not commit fully to them. Nevertheless, there are creative approaches that departments or colleges can consider to address these challenges despite budget concerns.

Of course, it is much easier to plan and create an FLC when there is at least a minimal budget. If compensation is not possible, however, then the situation simply requires some resourceful adjustments. Among adjustments to consider are (a) meeting less often to reduce the sense of commitment; (b) meeting in more creative places (e.g., restaurants, bars) that may provide a livelier atmosphere than a conference room on campus; (c) placing more emphasis on project implementation for the full-time faculty members; (d) emphasizing the practical lessons for teaching; and (e) promoting the collegiality inherent in a learning community. Essentially, create an FLC that is practical enough to attract interest, but still engaging enough to promote connectivity. If monetary compensation is nonexistent, then facilitators must depend on a creative approach while also relying on the intrinsic motivation of the adjunct instructors.

Renewing Membership and Self-Selection

Another challenge an adjunct connectivity FLC might face involves membership renewal. Not only is refreshing membership yearly suggested in the learning community literature (Cox, 2004), but if adjunct connectivity is the goal, it would make little sense to limit membership to the same select group year after year. To avoid making outgoing adjunct members feel superfluous, one idea is to create an FLC "alumni" group whose members are invited, though not obligated (especially considering they are not likely to be compensated), to participate in new FLC activities.

An inevitable consequence, however, is a limited applicant pool owing partly to self-selection. As one rotation of the learning community concludes, this eliminates 7–10 members from the pool. Included in the remaining pool of adjunct applicants are those who were never interested in the first place. Extrapolating beyond the first year, more adjunct members will eliminate themselves via prior membership faster than new adjuncts who may be interested in the FLC are hired. As the pool of applicants shrinks with every year that goes by, it seems inevitable that participants in an adjunct connectivity FLC will come mostly from newly hired adjuncts. Nevertheless, this is in no way contradictory to the mission of connectivity. Instead, the adjunct connectivity FLC might simply evolve toward a focus on connectivity at the new-hire level, or it could be offered every few years to ensure enough interest.

Conclusions and Future Directions

Narrative data from our FLC members and others on the outside looking in show that an adjunct connectivity FLC was worthwhile and necessary, and increased connectivity between adjunct members and other members of the department. One main goal for the future is to establish better, more quantitative assessments of connectivity. Specifically, the facilitators of the adjunct connectivity FLC administered a survey to all adjunct members within the department to measure different aspects of connectivity (Appendix A). Through this assessment, we hope not only to gather information about adjunct feelings of satisfaction within the department, but also to correlate those measures with feelings of connectivity. In particular, we will compare the feelings of adjuncts in the group with the feelings of those who did not participate.

Concerning future directions, perhaps the FLC will focus more on new hires as a result of challenges stated in the previous section. Also, initial data from the survey show an interesting trend. Adjuncts as a whole indicated greater feelings of connectivity with full-time faculty members ($M = 3.2$), but less so with fellow part-timers ($M = 2.5$) on a Likert scale of 1 (not at all) to 5 (totally). Perhaps intuitively, one would think that adjuncts would feel a sense of connection and relate more with others who are at the same rank. However, each individual adjunct has more reason to interact with a full-timer (e.g., to ask questions, report grades, schedule classes), and full-time faculty are more likely to be found during business hours every day within the department. Adjunct faculty, on the other hand, often go straight to class, and then leave immediately afterward. In addition, there are fewer opportunities for adjunct faculty to fraternize beyond departmental meetings. Ultimately, solving this problem is the purpose of our learning community—to provide a forum in which adjunct faculty members can socialize and get to know one another, and at the same time work together to solve institutional problems and enhance their skills as instructors within the department.

In sum, an adjunct connectivity FLC provides part-time faculty with opportunities to become more involved with the department and overcome the sense of disconnection that is inherent in a part-time position. As institutions continue to grow, it is sometimes easy to forget that community colleges were established as a resource for the *community*. Specific to the community of instructors within the college, it seems beneficial to extend that sense of community to adjunct faculty in hopes that professional success within the curriculum of an FLC would extend to academic success for our students.

References

American Federation of Teachers (AFT). (2010). A national survey of part-time/adjunct faculty. *American Academic* (Vol. 2). Retrieved from https://www.aft.org/pdfs/highered/aa_partimefaculty0310.pdf

Bloom, B. S., Engelhart, M. D., Furst, E. J., Hill, W. H., & Krathwohl, D. R. (1956). Taxonomy of educational objectives: The classification of educational goals. *Handbook I: Cognitive Domain*. New York: Longmans, Green.

Cox, M. D. (2004). *Faculty learning community program director's and facilitator's handbook*. Oxford, OH: Miami University.

Eagan, M. K., & Jaeger, A. J. (2008). Closing the gate: Part-time faculty instruction in gatekeeper courses and first-year persistence. *New Directions for Teaching and Learning, 115*, 39–54. doi:10.1002/tl.324

Fenwick, T. (2002). Gypsy scholars: Careful dances outside the research machine. In S. Mojab & W. McQueen (Eds.), *Proceedings of the 21st Conference of the Canadian Association for the Study of Adult Education* (pp. 116–121). Toronto, ON: OISE/University of Toronto. Retrieved from http://www.ualberta.ca/~tfenwick/publications/PDF/64%20Gypsy%20Scholars.pdf

Fleming, N. D., & Mills, C. (1992). Not another inventory, rather a catalyst for reflection. *To Improve the Academy, 11*, 137–155.

Gosink, J. P., & Streveler, R. A. (2000). Bringing adjunct engineering faculty into the learning community. *Journal of Engineering Education, 89*, 47–51.

Hirt, E. R., & Markman, K. D. (1995). Multiple explanation: A consider-an-alternative strategy for debiasing judgments. *Personality and Social Psychology Bulletin, 69*, 1069–1086. doi:10.1037/0022-3514.69.6.1069

Jacoby, D. (2006). The effects of part-time faculty employment upon community college graduation rates. *Journal of Higher Education, 77*(6), 1081–1103. doi:10.1353/jhe.2006.0050

Janis, I. L. (1972). *Victims of groupthink*. Boston: Houghton Mifflin.

Janis, I. L. (1982). *Groupthink: Psychological studies of policy decisions and fiascoes* (2nd ed.). Boston: Houghton Mifflin.

Lyons, R. (2007). Deepening our understanding of adjunct faculty. In R. Lyons (Ed.), *Best practices for supporting adjunct faculty*. Bolton, MA: Anker Publishing.

McCauley, C. (1989). The nature of social influence in groupthink: Compliance and internalization. *Journal of Personality and Social Psychology, 57*, 250–260. doi: 10.1037/0022-3514.57.2.250

Nutting, M. M. (2003). Hiring of part-time university faculty on the increase. *Education Quarterly Review* (Statistics Canada, Catalogue no. 81-003-XPB), *9*(3), 9–14.

Richardson, R. C. (1992). The associate program: Teaching improvement for adjunct faculty. *Community College Review, 20*(1), 29–34. doi:10.1177/009155219 202000105

Snyder, T. D., & Dillow, S. A. (2011). *Digest of education statistics 2010* (NCES 2011-015). National Center for Education Statistics, Institute of Education Sciences, U.S. Department of Education, Washington, DC. Retrieved from http://nces.ed-.gov/pubs2011/2011015.pdf

Stasser, G., & Titus, W. (1985). Pooling of unshared information in group decision making: Biased information sampling during discussion. *Journal of Personality and Social Psychology, 48*, 1467–1478. doi:10.1037/0022-3514.48.6.1467

Sweeney, I. (2009). If colleges valued students, they'd value adjuncts. *Chronicle of Higher Education*. Retrieved from http://chronicle.com/article/Value-Students-Then-Value/48881/

U.S. Census Bureau. (2012). Retrieved from http://www.census.gov/hhes/school/index.html.

APPENDIX A
Adjunct Connectivity Assessment

*Please do not write your name on this form. All responses will be confidential and anonymous.

**Once you have completed this assessment, please place it in the box by the mailboxes and initial the checklist to indicate that you have completed it.

Instructions: Please indicate your answer to each question.

1	2	3	4	5
Not at all	Slightly	Moderately	Mostly	Totally

1. To what extent do you feel supported by the Psychology Department in your activities as an adjunct instructor at Columbus State?
2. To what extent do you feel a sense of overall community within the Psychology Department?
3. To what extent do you feel a sense of community with other adjunct instructors in the Psychology Department?
4. To what extent do you feel a sense of community with the full-time faculty in the Psychology Department?
5. To what extent do you feel that you, as an adjunct instructor, influence student learning?
6. To what extent do you feel that you, as an adjunct instructor, influence other departmental adjuncts?
7. To what extent do you feel you are effective in your role as an adjunct instructor in the Psychology Department?
8. How close do you feel to other adjunct faculty in the Psychology Department?
9. How close do you feel to full-time faculty in the Psychology Department?
10. How comfortable do you feel asking questions of other adjunct faculty in the Psychology Department?
11. How comfortable do you feel asking questions of full-time faculty in the Psychology Department?
12. How comfortable do you feel sharing ideas with other adjunct faculty in the Psychology Department?

13. How comfortable do you feel sharing ideas with full-time faculty in the Psychology Department?

14. To what extent do you, as an adjunct instructor, feel included in our two yearly departmental meetings?

15. To what extent do you, as an adjunct instructor, feel knowledgeable about existing departmental policies?

16. To what extent do you, as an adjunct instructor, feel knowledgeable about future departmental initiatives?

17. To what extent do you, as an adjunct instructor, identify with the Psychology Department?

18. To what extent do you, as an adjunct instructor, identify with Columbus State?

19. How important is it to you, as an adjunct instructor, to feel a sense of connection to the Psychology Department at Columbus State?

20. Please rate your overall satisfaction as an adjunct instructor in the Psychology Department at Columbus State Community College.

21. How many quarters (approx.) have you taught at Columbus State?
    _____ quarters

22. Do you teach at other institutions?   ___ Yes   ___ No

23. How long have you been teaching in the field of psychology?
    _____ years

24. Aside from teaching, do you work in the field of psychology?
    ___ Yes   ___ No

25. **Optional** (potentially identifying information): Were you a member of the 2011 Psychology Faculty Learning Community (PFLC)?
    ___ Yes   ___ No

Thank you for completing this survey! If you would like to make any additional comments, please do so in this space:

5

SELF-REGULATED LEARNING

Focus on Feedback

Charlotte Skinner

The Problem Faced by Two-Year Colleges

Despite the increase of program reforms targeting low retention and poor academic preparation in the past two decades, high attrition rates at two-year community, junior, and technical colleges remain a troubling statistic (Jones, 1986; Seidman, 1996; Summers, 2003). Individual faculty on the front lines at two-year colleges must cope with the problems that lead to attrition every day in their classrooms. Eavesdrop around the faculty water cooler at any two-year college, and you will certainly overhear their lamentations. These complaints, uttered by faculty of courses in all disciplines, from introductory to advanced, from general education to core courses of degree programs, share a common theme: students are falling short of instructor expectations. The specific problems may vary—lack of motivation, effort, and persistence; underdeveloped critical-thinking skills; transfer of learning deficits; or ineffective study habits—but the general woe is universal. If only students were more proactive, conscientious, and self-reflective, surely they would be more successful. By participating in a self-regulated learning faculty learning community (SRL FLC), instructors with these shared concerns can work collaboratively to develop strategies to promote productive behavior in students and improve their academic performance. Self-regulated learning is the process by which students set goals, monitor their performance, measure their success, and adjust their behavior accordingly. Faculty in an SRL FLC can learn to include specific exercises to help students work through the model explicitly and build the habit of self-regulated learning.

These problems are more prevalent at two-year colleges than at four-year institutions for several obvious reasons. Open admission policies at two-year schools are a significant contributor, but in addition, two-year schools have a larger share of commuter, employed, and first-generation college students, as well as students with familial obligations and financial concerns. Two-year colleges also have a greater percentage of students requiring remediation. Furthermore, while rates of remediation at four-year schools have decreased since the 1980s, they have remained fairly constant, and high, at two-year colleges (Rosenbaum, 2004). Since two-year college students spend less time on campus than their four-year counterparts, and have additional distractions and obstacles impeding their progress, it takes underprepared students longer to make up their deficits. The problem has only gotten worse in recent years, with enrollment growth at two-year colleges outpacing that of four-year schools. Enrollments at two-year colleges increased 5.3% from 2007 to 2008 and 7.9% from 2008 to 2009, while four-year college enrollments rose 4.3% and 6.4%, respectively (Snyder, 2008, 2009). In light of all these facts, two-year college faculty should not be surprised that students are not performing to their satisfaction. Finally, two-year colleges are more likely to offer smaller class sizes in support of institutional missions with a strong teaching emphasis. Therefore, on average, faculty at these institutions are likely to be cognizant of their students' success (or lack thereof) not only in the aggregate, but on an individual level as well.

What is the solution to the two-year college dilemma? Research shows that personal contact between campus employees and students is a key component of successful retention efforts (Jones, 1986). Additional studies reveal that instructors' behavior (or student perceptions of it) influences student engagement (den Brok, Levy, Brekelmans, & Wubbels, 2005; Skinner & Belmont, 1993; Wentzel, 1997). Since two-year college students spend less time on campus outside of their classes, it is reasonable to suggest that reform efforts that are anchored in the classroom will reach a greater number of students than efforts outside of class. Some faculty may balk at targeting study skills in their courses, as they preciously reserve their time for "covering content." The improvement of students' study habits and the presentation of course content need not be mutually exclusive, however. Instructors can learn to integrate student success strategies into activities directly related to the curriculum without sacrificing content. Teaching interventions composed of SRL strategies allow faculty to target students' learning and study skills in the classroom, making efficient use of student time. Simultaneously, instructors can embed these strategies in course goals and course content, thereby using instructional time efficiently.

Faculty interested in establishing an FLC that focuses on SRL should begin by consulting the research literature to educate themselves on the subject and meeting to brainstorm classroom interventions. The instructors in our college's SRL FLC first practiced self-regulated techniques in their own personal lives to effect such change as reducing soft drink consumption, managing house cleaning chores, and finding time to engage in scholarly activity. These personal experiences provided faculty with an understanding of the SRL process and better equipped them to incorporate SRL strategies in their teaching and to instruct students in their use.

Research on SRL

Across a variety of disciplines and pursuits, those recognized as experts in their field of study, such as athletes and musicians, possess and engage in common thoughts, beliefs, and behaviors in their quest for excellence (Cleary & Zimmerman, 2001; Hallam, 2001). These specialists are likely to be aware of their strengths and limitations and how they learn most effectively. Consequently, their extensive practice is characterized by purposeful and reflective actions. They set goals, plan and implement a course of action, evaluate the outcome, and make adjustments as needed to attain their goals. Furthermore, they possess a high level of confidence in their ability to accomplish a task effectively, which provides the necessary motivation for them to persist.

Researchers discovered that academically successful students of various ages, from elementary school children, to adolescents, to college students, and across a variety of subjects, also shared similar motivational thoughts and strategic actions (Pintrich & De Groot, 1990; Zimmerman & Bandura, 1994; Zimmerman & Martinez-Pons, 1990). One's level of *self-regulation* is the extent to which one exhibits monitoring and proactive behaviors when performing a task (Zimmerman, 2002). Self-regulated learning consists of the cognitive, motivational, and behavioral processes that take place before, during, and after one's performance of specific learning tasks (Nicol & Macfarlane-Dick, 2006). In practice, it consists of three cyclical phases: forethought, including assessing past performance and goal setting; performance of the task, including identifying and employing appropriate strategies and monitoring one's progress; and evaluation, including self-reflection (Zimmerman & Cleary, 2006). Each phase flows continuously into the next.

A key component of the SRL process is *self-efficacy*, one's belief in his or her capacity to complete a task successfully (Zimmerman & Cleary, 2006). "Self-efficacy . . . focus[es] on personal ratings of performance success in task domains" (Zimmerman, 1990, p. 9). This belief influences motivation, the perceived value of a task, persistence, and attributions about the controllability of success or failure. All of these, when possessed in high levels, perpetuate adherence to the SRL cycle. Continued adherence to the SRL cycle and the integration of self-evaluation along the way inform self-efficacy. In this way, one's level of self-regulation and one's self-efficacy are intertwined (Dweck, 2000; Garcia, 1995). Several studies have shown the interdependence of self-efficacy and self-regulated behavior. This means that instructors should spend time building confidence in addition to including activities to build SRL. For example, an investigation by Zimmerman and colleagues (as cited in Zimmerman & Cleary, 2006) showed that social studies students with more academic confidence earned higher grades, and they were more likely to set challenging academic goals. A review of several additional studies also shows a link between self-efficacy and goal setting, a self-regulated skill (Schunk, 1990). A study of fifth, eighth, and 11th graders revealed a correlation between their self-perceptions of verbal and mathematical efficacy and their use of self-regulated strategies (Zimmerman & Martinez-Pons, 1990). A path analysis study showed that college freshmen with higher levels of writing self-efficacy earned higher grades on writing assignments and also exhibited self-regulated behavior (Zimmerman & Bandura, 1994). Two additional studies, one on primary students' arithmetic skills and the other on female adolescents' writing, each showed that "those that self-monitored had higher self-efficacy beliefs and performed higher on tests of the skills involved than those that did not self-monitor" (Zimmerman & Cleary, 2006, p. 61). Exploring this literature in an SRL FLC can persuade participants to use SRL techniques.

The role of self-monitoring and feedback in general are critical components of the SRL cycle. *Self-regulation* has been defined as "self-generated thoughts, feelings, and actions that are planned and cyclically adapted based on performance *feedback* [emphasis added] to attain self-set goals" (Zimmerman & Cleary, 2006, p. 56). Whether generated internally through self-monitoring or externally from teachers or peers, feedback on learning effectiveness influences self-efficacy and self-regulation (Zimmerman & Cleary, 2006; Zimmerman & Martinez-Pons, 1990).

Any student, even the most inefficient learner, can develop self-regulating skills if modeled appropriately (Glenn, 2010; Nicol & Macfarlane-Dick, 2006; Zimmerman, 2002). Instructors can create opportunities for students to practice self-regulation processes such as goal setting, self-monitoring, and strategic planning. When students see that performance is linked to strategy use and not inherent ability, their self-efficacy and achievement improve (Zimmerman, 2002). Instructors can further enhance students' SRL development by providing timely performance feedback to students, and then prompting them to demonstrate that they understand the feedback (Hudesman, Moylan, & White, 2008). Frequent feedback can develop students' self-regulatory processes and self-efficacy and, ultimately, promote academic achievement (Nicol & Macfarlane-Dick, 2006). Teachers should create opportunities for students to reflect, generate their own feedback, and adjust as a result (Nicol & Macfarlane-Dick, 2006). An SRL FLC will help instructors identify opportunities for providing feedback and for developing exercises for reflection.

The SRL Model

Our group started with individual faculty participating as part of a federal grant from another institution, and our membership grew until we evolved into a collegewide collaborative FLC. University of Cincinnati Blue Ash College's (UCBA) SRL FLC originated from a 2006 invitation from a research team at the City University of New York (CUNY) to join several schools in a three-year study on SRL funded by a grant from the U.S. Department of Education's Fund for the Improvement of Postsecondary Education. What distinguished the investigators' endeavors from reform efforts that had fallen short at other institutions was the premise that initiatives to promote persistence and academic achievement must require subjects to think about and reflect on their own learning processes (Hudesman, 2006). The research team advocated the use of the SRL model as the instrument of change in its interventions, teaching instructors to use SRL methods in their classes.

Initially, the research team in New York provided the structure, materials, and timing of the projects. Each participant selected a minimum of one course to target and identified an area of concern (e.g., students not completing the required reading prior to class) to serve as the focus of his or her SRL intervention. The members of the FLC group were presented with the following model (figure 5.1) during their orientation by the research team (Hudesman et al., 2008, p. 4):

FIGURE 5.1
Self-regulated learning

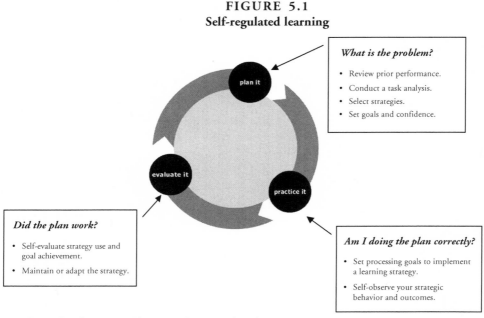

From Hudesman et al., 2008. Reprinted with permission.

This model provided the framework for each member's intervention. Following the training and prior to the start of the term, each member completed a long-term planning sheet, including goals and measurable outcomes. (A copy of this form is included in Appendix A.) Each instructor was assigned a member of the New York City staff who monitored progress, provided guidance, and offered feedback. The SRL coaches stayed in touch with the instructors regularly throughout the entire process via e-mail, phone, on-site visits, and videoconferencing.

The FLC's focus evolved over time and was modified based upon feedback from the participants. In the first two years, trying to implement all three phases of the SRL model (forethought, practice, evaluation) effectively in the classroom without significantly increasing workload or sacrificing course content was proving to be a challenge. In true SRL fashion, we simplified our efforts to follow educational psychologist and SRL project co-principal investigator Zimmerman's Golden Rules (Hudesman et al., 2009):

1. Give students fast, accurate feedback about their performance.
2. Make the students demonstrate that they actually understand this feedback.

This streamlined approach made implementation easier on participants and students alike.

Implementation

Our SRL FLC consisted of faculty from dental hygiene, English, mathematics, nursing, psychology, and sociology. Several participants' SRL interventions shared the goal of improving student performance on assessments, such as exams, papers, and nursing patient care plans. Some of the strategies that instructors used to promote improvement included increasing the number of drafts and/or revisions of an assessment, modeling a particular skill more often, and illustrating both exemplary and unsatisfactory implementations of the skill.

Another common goal was to develop students' ability to evaluate the quality of their work and assess their own learning. To do so, FLC instructors implemented ways for students to reflect on their current study/work practices through journaling or discussion, or with follow-up questions after exams to identify effective study strategies. Some faculty asked students to predict their own scores, indicate confidence levels regarding their own ability to complete an academic task, or demonstrate that they evaluated their work against established criteria. Other FLC participants allowed students to self-select from an instructor-generated list of options for meeting course requirements rather than mandating a single assignment. In all cases, the predominant feature of the interventions was an increase in the frequency of feedback provided to the student and additional opportunities for students to generate their own feedback.

Planning Recommendations

If faculty wish to initiate an SRL FLC at their college, they should articulate its goals and their expectations of participants before recruiting members. They should consider the possibility that participants' experiences will be of interest to other faculty. In fact, the SRL FLC may choose to establish itself as a research group, fully intending to disseminate its results to a wider audience, through presentation or publication. In such a case, data would likely need to be collected. Materials collected by the SRL FLC at our college in support of our hypothesis that our SRL interventions would improve student learning included pre- and postintervention grades, student and instructor survey results, and samples of student work. Instructors conducting research on student performance must consult and comply with institutional review board (IRB) research requirements in the early stages of launching the FLC.

The leader or organizing committee establishing an SRL FLC should be selective when recruiting instructors to participate. The ideal participants are learner-centered faculty with some experience making changes to their teaching, assessing the effectiveness of those changes, and modifying as necessary. Good candidates should have higher than average rates of instructor self-efficacy, the belief in one's ability to improve student learning. To measure how much influence instructors believe they have on student motivation and persistence, gauge their answers to such questions as, "How much can you do to keep students on task on difficult assignments?" and "How much can you do to motivate students who show low interest in schoolwork?" (Hudesman et al., 2008, p. 6). Of course, a solid work ethic would be an obvious benefit as well. The leader or organizing committee should take these characteristics into consideration.

Because of the large time investment required, ideally the college should reward participants with a stipend; however, this FLC could function without participant funding. As in all FLCs, the facilitator ideally would need some released time from teaching responsibilities. Funding would also help keep participants committed to the project throughout its duration.

Establishing an SRL FLC will require several individuals to accomplish the following tasks: become resident "SRL-experts"; acquire funding (if desired); investigate IRB research requirements; plan the FLC's activities for the academic term; and recruit, train, and coach participants. It would be very helpful to create a website or wiki complete with a reference area of SRL resources and individual pages or folders for participants to post intervention plans, SRL class materials, and progress reports. If dissemination of results is a goal of the FLC, any data collected to support (or reject) research hypotheses should be stored in a secure, central location. As the FLC grows in size, consider selecting a data coordinator or statistical analyst to organize, analyze, and interpret the data.

FLC facilitators need to be knowledgeable about designing SRL research projects to guide new, and possibly inexperienced, members in designing interventions, complete with appropriate short- and long-term goals and measurable outcomes. In addition, the facilitators must be able to provide constructive feedback to FLC members on their plans and actions before, during, and after implementation.

Prior to the start of the academic term, FLC participants' responsibilities would include attending a kick-off session on SRL led by the facilitator; designing an intervention plan complete with goals and measurable outcomes; perhaps submitting prior grade distributions of the SRL target course to establish a benchmark; and complying with any IRB requirements. A sample form to assist in planning an SRL intervention is included in Appendix A. Participants submit their plans to the FLC facilitator or coach who reviews individual plans and offers feedback.

During the term, FLC members' tasks may include completing a progress report two to three times per term summarizing activities, results, adjustments, and students' grades to date; conducting a peer observation of the teaching of another in the group; and collecting three to five samples of student work from each SRL activity. The progress reports keep participants accountable, focused, and on track. A sample log form is included in Appendix A. It is recommended that the FLC meet two or three times during the term to discuss progress to date and to receive feedback from the facilitator and the rest of the group. The peer observations are opportunities to receive feedback on SRL methods in practice and to observe students engaging in SRL activities at the same time. If scheduling conflicts arise, consider videotaping one SRL-targeted class of each FLC member and critique it at a group meeting. By capturing the SRL discourse between instructor and student, these recordings can also be an excellent source of qualitative data to support the FLC's research.

At the conclusion of the academic term, participants submit their students' final course grades and their final logs summarizing results of the term, including whether stated goals were met. If not, what changes will be made the next time? This is a fundamental activity of the FLC to encourage instructors to engage in their own SRL cycle in their classes. It is a time to reflect on which efforts were effective and what modifications need to be made to those techniques that may have missed the mark. Which assessments or activities will be used again, and which will be adjusted or even abandoned? These reflections inform the planning of the SRL intervention for the next academic term, when the cycle begins again.

After completing a minimum of two academic terms of interventions, the incoming cohort of SRL instructors can share its results at a faculty development workshop at the college. Workshop participants are potential SRL FLC recruits for the upcoming year. At our college, when colleagues saw the presentation of the initial group's SRL work, they were encouraged to join because the interventions seemed relevant and the data looked persuasive. This should provide the necessary confidence and motivation for SRL FLC graduates to disseminate their findings to a wider audience through conference presentations and publications.

Effects of the FLC

Participation in an SRL FLC has a positive impact on teaching and learning. Teaching improves as faculty learn to monitor, evaluate, and adjust their pedagogical practices. Members also benefit from the interdisciplinary collaboration of the group. Furthermore, additional faculty are educated when SRL FLC participants share their research and experience with a wider audience. The effects of an SRL intervention on students are equally beneficial. Students discover that SRL skills have more of an influence on their academic success than natural ability has. Subsequently, they become more proactive, deliberate, and self-reflective learners, which leads to improvement in their self-efficacy and academic performance.

Faculty Benefits

Participants become more systematic about improving their teaching. Instructors found that by systematically testing and modifying methods, and recording their effectiveness, they could effect change in their classrooms and participate in scholarly teaching by sharing their results. Monitoring progress and maintaining a record lead to more useful results. For example, faculty may have a vague sense of how students performed on an assignment overall based upon perceptions while grading. By looking at class performance on specific components of the assignment, faculty can determine whether that conclusion is, in fact, valid. By sharing these detailed results with students, instructors provide them with individualized, targeted feedback. Similarly, faculty can collect data to show that a particular assessment or activity is effective, instead of simply assuming it is. Sharing this evidence with students provides them with the rationale for the activities in a course and can also encourage them to work harder.

Faculty learn to see disappointing student performance as an opportunity for improvement. Faculty should not be discouraged if their plans do not produce perfection immediately. In fact, expect interventions to undergo several iterations before instructor goals are met. The strategies, techniques, and assessments that emerge after repeated modifications will become a permanent part of one's pedagogical toolbox.

In the first two years of the CUNY SRL project, when instructors fell short of their stated goals, they adapted their plans (after all, instructors were engaging in the SRL cycle as well), so that by the third year they were seeing more promising results. For example, initially one participant, a math instructor, included time management activities (scheduling homework and study time) that students viewed as additional work with little added value. Then she modified her SRL intervention to activities that were tied to course content, for example, selecting and completing specific practice strategies that contributed to students' grades. She observed a significant decrease in student resistance and an increase in both the effort students exerted on the task and the value students attributed to the task.

Another benefit to faculty is that they become more creative in using activities to solve student performance problems. The interdisciplinary community can provide ideas that an instructor may not encounter in his or her discipline. Modifications that multiple instructors in our SRL FLC applied to their interventions included making directions and grading criteria for assessments more explicit and introducing additional opportunities for students to practice a particular skill. Instructors report that these efforts led to improved quality of student work, an increase in student engagement, and a decrease in incomplete work.

By the conclusion of the project, the overall CUNY grant group, which included our college's FLC, found that 39 faculty implemented SRL methods in over 75 classes and affected almost 3,000 students across the six sites, a marked increase over the original proposed targets of 30, 60, and 1,800, respectively (Hudesman, 2010). Furthermore, six months after the project ended, a vast majority (at least 85%) of faculty involved found the SRL methods valuable enough to continue using them even after the grant ended.

Student Results

With increased exposure to SRL methods, students became aware that their academic success was less dependent upon inherent ability and more related to self-regulation and self-efficacy. They realized that they had more control over their academic success than they once thought, which empowered them. Resistance turns into persistence. The SRL instructors in our FLC report that students not only welcome the increased feedback, but even solicit it.

As a result of the SRL intervention used by a participant who was a psychology professor, performance improved. She targeted student improvement on research papers through the use of self-ratings, worksheets, and increased feedback. Two specific aspects of the paper that she targeted included developing students' effective use of scholarly resources and their ability to apply the concepts they learned in class to the paper. The percentage of students earning a B or better on her grading criterion of "summarizing scholarly articles" rose from less than 25% to about 70% over two years.

Students also demonstrated improvement on the psychology concept application section of the paper. This type of improvement is consistent with other findings that test SRL interventions. For example, across six schools, researchers observed approximately a one-half letter grade increase in course grade distributions from pre- to post-SRL intervention (Everson & Isaac, 2010).

Another benefit to students is that they develop a better attitude toward the class and their own effort. For example, a dental hygiene instructor surveyed the students about her class activities. Across two quarters, 76%, and then 90%, of the students indicated that they found predicting test scores, identifying study techniques, and then reflecting on the preparation to be valuable. One hundred percent of the students indicated that they took the initiative to review missed exam questions prior to the final exam and said that it helped their final exam preparation.

Students benefited from the opportunities to be more responsible for their progress through practice. An SRL math instructor designed a menu of out-of-class activities for students to practice concepts and receive feedback on their progress. Students could select a combination of their choosing to earn credit in the course, and there was a relationship between the number of these activities the students completed and their exam grades. For example, in her Intermediate Algebra course, in two quarters, the average first exam and final exam grades of those students who completed at least the minimum required number of these activities were significantly higher than the corresponding exam averages of those who did not complete the minimum required number of activities. The students who were willing to put in the extra time performed better on the exams.

Conclusion

Participation in the SRL FLC resulted in a positive and long-lasting impact on instructors and their students alike. By creating opportunities and providing the structure for students to practice self-regulated behavior, such as strategic planning, and monitoring and evaluating their own performance, instructors shift some of the responsibility for learning from themselves to their students. This allows faculty to use their limited time more strategically and efficiently. More important, students become more active, effective learners and are better prepared for lifelong learning.

References

Cleary, T. J., & Zimmerman, B. J. (2001). Self-regulation differences during athletic practice by experts, non-experts, and novices. *Journal of Applied Sport Psychology*, *13*, 185–206. doi:10.1080/104132001753149883

den Brok, P., Levy, J., Brekelmans, M., & Wubbels, T. (2005). The effect of teacher interpersonal behaviour on students' subject-specific motivation. *Journal of Classroom Interaction*, *40*(2), 20–33. Retrieved from http://www.compact.org/resources/service-learning-resources/publishing-outlets-for-service-learning-and-community-based-research/journal-of-classroom-interaction/949/

Dweck, C. S. (2000). *Self-theories: Their role in motivation, personality and development*. Philadelphia: Psychology Press.

Everson, H. T., & Isaac, S. (2010). Final evaluation report, *Disseminating the self-regulated learning model in high school and college*, supported by the Fund for the Improvement of Post-Secondary Education (FIPSE). New York: U.S. Department of Education, Center for Advanced Study in Education, Graduate School & University Center, City University of New York.

Garcia, T. (1995). The role of motivational strategies in self-regulated learning. *New Directions for Teaching and Learning*, *1995*(63), 29–42. doi:10.1002/tl.37219956306

Glenn, D. (2010, February 7). Struggling students can improve by studying themselves, research shows. *Chronicle of Higher Education*. Retrieved from http://chronicle.com/article/Struggling-Students-Can/64004/

Hallam, S. (2001). The development of metacognition in musicians: Implications for education. *British Journal of Music Education*, *18*, 27–39. doi:10.1017/S026505170100012 2

Hudesman, J. (2006). *The dissemination of the self-regulated learning model to improve student performance in high schools and colleges, FIPSE grant proposal*. New York: CUNY Graduate School and University Center.

Hudesman, J. (2010). *The dissemination of the self-regulated learning model to improve student performance in high schools and colleges, FIPSE grant final report*. New York: CUNY Graduate School and University Center.

Hudesman, J., Moylan, A., & White, N. (2008). *SRL handbook*. New York: CUNY Graduate School and University Center.

Hudesman, J., Zimmerman, B., Flugman, B., White, N., Moylan, A., & Crosby, S. (2009). *The dissemination of the self-regulated learning model to improve student performance in high schools and colleges, FIPSE grant materials*. New York: CUNY Graduate School and University Center.

Jones, S. W. (1986). No magic required: Reducing freshman attrition at the community college. *Community College Review*, *14*, 14–18. doi:10.1177/009155218601400203

Nicol, D. J., & Macfarlane-Dick, D. (2006). Formative assessment and self-regulated learning: A model and seven principles of good feedback practice. *Studies in Higher Education, 31*, 199–218. Retrieved from http://www.tandf.co.uk/journals/carfax/03075079.html

Pintrich, P. R., & De Groot, E. V. (1990). Motivational and self-regulated learning components of classroom academic performance. *Journal of Educational Psychology, 82*, 33–40. doi:10.1037/0022-0663.82.1.33

Rosenbaum, J. E. (2004, Spring). It's time to tell the kids: If you don't do well in high school, you won't do well in college (or on the job). *American Educator.* Retrieved from http://www.aft.org/newspubs/periodicals/ae/spring2004/rosenbaum.cfm

Schunk, D. H. (1990). Goal setting and self-efficacy during self-regulated learning. *Educational Psychologist, 25*, 71–86. doi:10.1207/s15326985ep2501

Seidman, A. (1996). Retention revisited: RET = E Id + (E + I + C)Iv. *College and University, 71*(4), 18–20.

Skinner, E. A., & Belmont, M. J. (1993). Motivation in the classroom: Reciprocal effects of teacher behavior and student engagement across the school year. *Journal of Educational Psychology, 85*(4), 571–581. doi:10.1037//0022-0663.85.4.571

Snyder, T. D. (2008). *Mini-digest of education statistics, 2007* (NCES 2008-023). Washington, DC: National Center for Education Statistics, Institute of Educational Sciences, U.S. Department of Education.

Snyder, T. D. (2009). *Mini-digest of education statistics, 2008* (NCES 2009-021). Washington, DC: National Center for Education Statistics, Institute of Education Sciences, U.S. Department of Education.

Summers, M. D. (2003). ERIC review: Attrition research at community colleges. *Community College Review, 30*(4), 64–84. doi:10.1177/009155210303000404

Wentzel, K. R. (1997). Student motivation in middle school: The role of perceived pedagogical caring [Abstract]. *Journal of Educational Psychology, 89*, 411–419. doi:10.1037//0022-0663.89.3.411

Zimmerman, B. J. (1990). Self-regulated learning and academic achievement: An overview. *Educational Psychologist, 25*, 3–17. doi:10.1207/s15326985ep2501_2

Zimmerman, B. J. (2002). Becoming a self-regulated learner: An overview. *Theory Into Practice, 41*, 64–70. doi:10.1207/s15430421tip4102_2

Zimmerman, B. J., & Bandura, A. (1994). Impact of self-regulatory influences on writing course attainment. *American Educational Research Journal, 31*, 845–862. doi:10.2307/1163397

Zimmerman, B. J., & Cleary, T. J. (2006). Adolescents' development of personal agency: The role of self-efficacy beliefs and self-regulatory skill. In F. Pajares & T. Urdan (Eds.), *Self-efficacy beliefs of adolescents* (pp. 45–69). Charlotte, NC: Information Age.

Zimmerman, B. J., & Martinez-Pons, M. (1990). Student differences in self-regulated learning: Relating grade, sex, and giftedness to self-efficacy and strategy use. *Journal of Educational Psychology, 82*, 51–59. doi:10.1037/0022-0663.82.1.51

APPENDIX A

SRL Planning and Monitoring Documents

LONG-TERM GOAL SHEET (PLANNING FORM)

Instructor: _____

Subject area/course title: _____

Project Focus	What is the target of your intervention? What change are you trying to create overall in your students (e.g., "I want to improve my students' ability to edit for grammar")?
Feedback Goal	1. Describe the assessment tool you will be using (e.g., quizzes, response papers, essays, etc.). 2. How many of these assessments will you do during the project? 3. Describe what kind of feedback you'll give students on these assessments. 4. Describe what students will *do* with your feedback.
Measurable Goal	In terms of improving your grade distribution, what is your overall measurable goal? *Optional*: What is your goal in terms of improvement in student performance at the middle and end of the semester/quarter?
Baseline for Measurable Goal	Please attach or e-mail your grade distribution from the last time you taught this class.

From Hudesman et al., 2009. Reprinted with permission.

SELF-MONITORING LOG FOR INSTRUCTORS

Name:
Log submission date:
Log time period:

1. Just to review, please briefly describe the overall goal and the measurable goal for your SRL project. (Please be sure to include any changes you've made as the semester/quarter has progressed.)
2. Please briefly describe what kind of assessment you're using in your class (e.g., quizzes, writing assignments, etc.). Be sure to include how many times you've used this assessment so far this semester/quarter.

3. Now please describe the feedback you're giving your students on each assessment and describe the ways in which students are using your feedback.
4. Both overall and in terms of your goal, what seems to be working and not working about your SRL project? What adjustments will you make?

From Hudesman et al., 2009. Reprinted with permission.

6

ADDRESSING CRITICAL THINKING IN TWO-YEAR COLLEGES

Sarah Cummins-Sebree and Frank Wray

Two-year colleges embrace a wide variety of students—both students who were not accepted into traditional four-year colleges, and students whose scores meet traditional entrance requirements but who choose a two-year college for various reasons. Just like our four-year college counterparts, faculty at two-year institutions want students to succeed in their educational endeavors. This means we would like our students not only to master the course content of the discipline we teach, but also to develop critical-thinking skills that go beyond rote memorization of material. For example, a psychology professor wants her students not only to memorize Freud's defense mechanisms but also to apply those terms to everyday behavior they see and critique them. What faculty too often find is that some students are capable of rote memorization but seem to have difficulty in taking the content to the next level. This becomes a frustrating experience for faculty, who have been trained to reason more deeply about their discipline, and for students, who struggle when faced with this new type of thinking.

Inherent in this problem is that institutions of higher learning (whether four-year or two-year) are not simply extensions of high school. College-level work requires more complex reasoning skills; in particular, we expect students to reach all levels of Bloom's Taxonomy (see Anderson & Krathwohl, 2001, for a revised model). In the revised version of Bloom's Taxonomy, the hierarchy of cognitive skills has at its base *remembering*, followed by *understanding, applying, analyzing, evaluating,* and *creating.* Some consider *analyzing, evaluating,* and *creating* to form a single category referred to as *problem solving.* At each level the form and complexity of cognition not only increases, but builds from previous levels. For example, to be able to *create* a novel psychology research study, a student needs to be able to do the lower levels of cognitive skill: *remember* the key components of a research study, *understand* what goes into those components, *apply* those components to this novel research study, *analyze* what methods have and have not worked in the past based on a literature review, and *evaluate* the best previous methods before creating a new version of the study.

When it comes to students entering most four-year institutions, there is a reasonable expectation that they should bring with them at least a moderate level of complex reasoning skills. These students, after all, have taken courses in high school that are supposed to prepare them for the demands of college. When it comes to students entering many two-year institutions, however, this is not always a reasonable expectation. Many have not taken college preparatory classes and may have gotten through their basic courses through simple rote memorization of facts. These students have not been taught how to think critically about the content they are learning, nor have they been prepared for the fact that college requires a higher level of thinking than they are used to.

Let's consider our two-year institution as an example. At University of Cincinnati Blue Ash College (UCBA), one-third of our incoming students test into at least one developmental English course, and two-thirds test into at least one developmental math course based on placement test scores. A common refrain from first-quarter freshmen can be heard in classes all over campus after their first major college test: many express with surprise that memorization is not sufficient to earn good grades on tests. Until this point, many students have not been required to think critically about the material they are learning.

This is a significant issue in both the college classroom and the workplace. Recent surveys indicate that business managers and human resource personnel are quite disappointed in the level of critical thinking exhibited by college students entering the workforce (Taylor, 2010). They may have a basic understanding of what is required for the job (e.g., basic principles of accounting for a tax firm), but their ability to apply information to novel situations, create new solutions to old problems, adequately critique the status quo to look for improvements for the company, and synthesize a variety of important information to find the best solution to a single problem is lacking. We must help students develop critical-thinking skills to make them competitive in the job market, whether that happens directly upon graduation from the two-year college or upon graduating from the four-year program to which they transferred. Thus, it is imperative that two-year institutions consider the development of critical-thinking skills as a core mission in the education of their students.

But what is critical thinking? How do we measure it? Is this a skill that can be developed and applied in a variety of contexts, or is it best fostered within a particular discipline? How should we structure our courses and/or assignments to foster it? In fact, there are no easy answers, and these questions led to the development of our critical thinking and assessment (CTA) faculty learning community (FLC). The University of Cincinnati system denotes critical-thinking skills as a core competency, and surveys suggest that schools are not promoting the development of critical thinking in ways that might better prepare students for the job market. For this reason we are committed to improving critical thinking, and this commitment led to the formation of the CTA FLC. In its first year, our CTA FLC focused on defining critical thinking in our separate disciplines, examining interdisciplinary crossover of critical thinking, and measuring critical thinking more accurately. What we found at the time was that defining and measuring critical thinking is a complicated and often debatable endeavor.

Defining and Assessing Critical Thinking

In general, there are two camps when it comes to defining critical thinking—the domain-general camp and the domain-specific camp. Those who adhere to the domain-general camp suggest that critical thinking is an underlying metacognitive skill that can be used in multiple situations involving a variety of content knowledge (e.g., Halpern, 1998). This perspective promotes instituting a basic critical-thinking course at colleges and universities, such as those seen at the University of Phoenix and California State University. This philosophy is also the basis of standardized critical-thinking tests, such as the California Critical Thinking Skills Test (CCTST) and Watson-Glaser Critical Thinking Appraisal (Bers, 2005); one of the most widely used standardized critical-thinking tests is the Critical Thinking Assessment Test (CAT), which is supported by the National Science Foundation. This tests students on a wide range of critical-thinking skills needed to solve problems in the real world (Center for Assessment & Improvement in Learning, Tennessee

Technological University, 2012). Based on the domain-general perspective, students who have developed critical-thinking skills, then, should be able to apply any new information they have learned to novel situations, effectively critique a variety of sources (e.g., written, visual media), and synthesize multiple pieces of information to solve complex problems, regardless of the topic at hand.

Within the domain-general camp, researchers have identified several particular types of thinking skills. These skills include (a) self-regulation (Combs, Cennamo, & Newbill, 2009); (b) use of declarative and procedural knowledge with metacognition to solve problems (Kurfiss, 1988); and (c) analysis, inference, reflection, and evaluation (Jones, Dougherty, Fantaske, & Hoffman, 1997). Self-regulation (Combs et al., 2009) involves a variety of behaviors deemed necessary to be a good critical thinker capable of generating and evaluating new ideas to solve problems; one needs to be able to plan the process by which the problem must be solved, monitor progress made toward solving the problem (what is working, what is not), and evaluate the resulting solution to the critical-thinking problem. Critical thinking entails combining metacognitive skills, such as reflecting on what knowledge one does and does not have and determining what is needed to solve a problem. This includes both declarative knowledge (content, such as definitions and other factual information) and procedural knowledge (how to solve critical-thinking problems) (Kurfiss, 1988). Jones and colleagues conceive of critical thinking similarly (1997). In their definition, thinkers break down the components of a problem, reflect on the presence or absence of valid information pertaining to the problem, and evaluate the possible outcomes of a given critical-thinking problem.

In particular, Paul and Elder's domain general model (2008) presents critical thinking as a combination of skills, standards, and traits.

> Critical thinking is, in short, self-directed, self-disciplined, self-monitored, and self-corrective thinking. It requires rigorous standards of excellence and mindful command of their use. It entails effective communication and problem solving abilities and a commitment to overcoming our native egocentrism and sociocentrism. (Paul & Elder, 2008, p. 2)

The elements of thought are the building blocks of basic reasoning. The thinker considers features such as purpose, assumptions, and point of view. Intellectual standards are characteristics that convey quality. The thinker is encouraged to seek clarity through elaboration, to explore problems deeply, and to be precise by using specific details. Regularly using the standards and elements cultivates intellectual traits—for example, Intellectual Autonomy and Fairmindedness. This type of framework could be applied to any discipline and demonstrates the flexibility of applying domain-general definitions to a variety of critical-thinking activities in various courses.

From the domain-general point of view, institutions can assess critical thinking in a variety of ways. To save time and money and to have data to report changes in critical thinking, colleges can administer a variety of standardized tests, as mentioned previously, many of them using multiple-choice questions. For those who are wary of multiple-choice tests, essay questions, complex research projects, and debates are good options in basic critical-thinking courses that expose students to a variety of topics (i.e., those designed around a loosely based topic, such as a "Developing Logical Thinking" course) with the ultimate goal of developing critical-thinking skills that cross domains.

Those who adhere to the domain-specific camp suggest that critical thinking can occur only in areas in which the student has substantial background knowledge (e.g., Abrami et al., 2008). Willingham (2007) argues that students need to have a deep knowledge of content so that they do not rely on surface characteristics when trying to solve problems. He notes that cognitive psychology has shown that we tend to rely on surface characteristics of problems rather than looking for the underlying components that are at the heart of those problems. Think back to a math class and how the regular math problems for homework seemed easier than the word problems (e.g., evaluating rates for a bank loan). We have a tendency to focus on the aspects of the word problems that do not tell us much about the underlying mathematical concepts required to solve them. As we develop a more in-depth knowledge base in math, those word problems get easier because we can focus on the core components of the problems, without being distracted by information that is less important. But gaining that knowledge in math is not going to help a student think critically about the implications of, for example, a change in party control of Congress, as that would require deeper content knowledge of how Congress operates, its responsibilities outlined in the Constitution, and a history of these types of situations. In other words, a student who has a well-established knowledge base in math may be able to make critical comparisons about which bank loan out of four options will cost the least amount of money in the long run, but not about the confluence of factors that lead to deadlocks in our government.

The domain-specific perspective suggests that a better way to promote critical thinking in college students is to have faculty implement critical-thinking tasks in their specialty courses; that is, instead of creating a one-size-fits-all general course on critical thinking, faculty should strive to incorporate critical-thinking exercises that emphasize the use of discipline-specific course content. This philosophy underlies the attitude taken by the University of Cincinnati. When we assess students' critical-thinking skills, we report data on critical-thinking assignments within content courses. We assess these assignments consistently with a basic primary trait assessment grid, constructed around a five-point scale. The faculty modify the assessment grid and criteria to fit their own critical thinking assignments. In this way, we fall in line with other universities that view critical thinking as dependent on domain-specific knowledge and applications.

For those in the domain-specific camp, then, defining critical thinking at the institutional level is complex. Each discipline has its own definition or set of skills that it may consider to be critical thinking. These skills do overlap, but there are also some differences. For example, in English, critical thinking might include rhetorical awareness, while in psychology, instructors emphasize the logic of the scientific method. A CTA FLC can be beneficial for colleges following the domain-specific camp of critical thinking. In the absence of a standardized multiple-choice test, the FLC can allow them to review assessment data that take into account the diversity of disciplinary definitions. Additionally, in the absence of a collegewide class on the topic of critical thinking, instructors across disciplines can share ideas for developing classroom activities that promote critical thinking.

Implementation

Determining how to teach critical thinking in one's course and the college can be challenging, and developing appropriate and engaging critical-thinking activities can be time-consuming. Though many education-based and discipline-specific websites have links to sample critical-thinking activities (e.g., Merlot, an online digital objects repository, or American Psychological Association, respectively), faculty often want assignments that fit well with their teaching style, course goals, and student learning outcomes. Searching for already established assignments that promote the level and type of critical thinking one is hoping students will develop can take hours; creating assignments from scratch can also be time-consuming, and an instructor may be unsure about whether the created assignment is going to promote critical thinking in the way he or she wants. Thus, determining what critical thinking is and how to measure it can be a daunting undertaking, indeed.

Often, though, there are other faculty in one's department or college who find themselves in the same boat: they want to assist their students in developing critical-thinking skills, but do not know where to start or are hoping that others in their college have some good ideas they can share. This is where a CTA FLC can help those faculty develop or determine a framework to promote critical thinking in students and, subsequently, design or choose activities and assessments to meet their goal.

When forming a CTA FLC, there are a variety of aspects one must consider. How big should the group be? How often should it meet? What are the FLC's products? For example, the FLC might be designed to review class assignments only. It might create a path for research on critical thinking that contributes to the scholarship of teaching and learning. The FLC might compile and analyze data that can inform the college about the potential for a collegewide critical-thinking program. Each institution's goals and product may differ depending on its unique missions and the needs of its faculty.

Based on our experiences, we suggest creating an interdisciplinary group that meets at least twice during each academic term; by having individuals from different disciplines, participants can learn how various areas of study define *critical thinking*. Furthermore, these discussions can lead to brainstorming about designing critical-thinking activities for different disciplines. A facilitator should be chosen to lead the group and provide some level of structure; thus the facilitator should be organized and able to help the group identify clear objectives.

The backbone to any successful FLC is support. This support can come in many ways: financial, administrative, and collegial. While it is ideal to have all three, the realities of budgets, buy-in, and motivated faculty can limit successful implementation of a CTA FLC. At UCBA we are fortunate to have support on all three levels. Facilitators receive a modest stipend, and a small amount money is allocated to the FLC for books, a speaker, or materials. In addition, FLC participation is viewed as significant professional development, which factors into decisions about reappointment, promotion, and tenure. A CTA FLC cannot be achieved without the support of the faculty. Faculty need to be convinced of the value of the CTA FLC and recognize that the time they spend in the group will pay dividends for both their students (in their development of critical-thinking skills) and themselves (in professional growth in their educational practices).

To recruit participants, the facilitator will need to advertise the group and actively invite a few well-respected faculty to participate. Pamphlets, fliers, and e-mails provide descriptions, objectives, and meeting times. We advertised our preset, established meeting times through those notices. The preset meeting times may limit the number of participants who sign up, but we have found that, logistically, this arrangement is much more conducive to planning a successful yearlong FLC.

Once a meeting time has been chosen, ground rules need to be established for participation. Helpful ground rules could include statements about commitment (a) to attend the meetings; (b) to provide a supportive atmosphere for sharing activities and student performance data; and (c) to provide encouraging peer reviews of materials participants develop. Within the discussion, usually two categories of participants emerge: those who want to attend the meetings and are enrolled to affect teaching and learning (what Richlin and Cox [2004] would call scholarly teaching), and those whose participation is a combination of scholarly teaching and producing scholarship. Participants should identify their goal because it affects the FLC's activities; for example, having a group interested in producing scholarship may mean taking time to review institutional review board (IRB) procedures for gaining approval to collect student data for future presentations and publications. A research-focused group might create an annotated bibliography and focus on data collection and publication outlets, whereas a teaching-focused group might discuss methods and schedule classroom observations.

The facilitator should establish a way to provide articles and documents for the community to discuss once the FLC begins and make sure that each member has access to them. A community in the college's technology management system (e.g., Blackboard) or a wiki can allow all participants to access materials and make peer comments on the various CTA assignments faculty would like to have reviewed.

Once the basics of participation are out of the way, the group can focus on reviewing literature on critical thinking so that it might guide the construction of their own critical-thinking activities. The literature involves research articles centered on theoretical approaches as well as practical examples of classroom activities (e.g., Combs et al., 2009). For example, our CTA FLC has reviewed Halpern's (1998) article on the four components of critical thinking (dispositions, skills, structure training, and metacognitive monitoring) and how they might be applied across domains; we discussed what aspects of this model instructors could affect. We felt that we could teach our students the steps of critical thinking and offer them multiple activities for practice. However, we were more skeptical that we could develop their disposition to want to engage in more cognitively complex tasks, especially in our short, 10-week quarters.

As another example, our group read and discussed a chapter in Brook-field's (1987) *Developing Critical Thinkers* to see what more we could do to become good facilitators in our students' critical-thinking development; group members took away from this suggestions for how we can structure our teaching environment and interactions with students to support their growing critical-thinking skills.

Those participants whose goals center on scholarly teaching should be encouraged to share critical-thinking activities they are either creating or using in the classroom. In our group, participants typically e-mail the activity out to the CTA FLC members a week before our meeting. In the meeting the group reviews and discusses the activities. Often, participants find the peer review to be the most illuminating part of the FLC because they hear perspectives outside of their disciplines. These perspectives frequently help participants improve their activity for the classroom. For example, one participant noted, "Over the course of the academic year, I created a defined lesson plan, which, based upon a number of suggestions from FLC members, now challenges my students to alternative ways of thinking and reflection." Another noted, "I found the peer review especially helpful as it made me look at my learning activities from a very different perspective! I saw an immediate change in both the learning and reaction from my students after using my changed classroom activity!"

With each new quarter or semester, participants can continue with peer reviews of their critical-thinking assignments. Participants who also engage in the scholarship of teaching and learning can get feedback on their study design as well. An example of this kind of change took place when an FLC participant presented a research project that involved the use of case studies in the classroom. While the researcher was well-versed in case study design, he was less experienced in research design. Comments from his peers showed the researcher how to add relevant quantitative data to his research.

Late in the academic year, the facilitator can organize a venue for presenting the critical-thinking projects to the larger faculty. We held a critical-thinking fair that included classroom research presentations, roundtables for discussion of critical-thinking issues, and posters that displayed classroom activities. Not only does a venue of this sort help nonparticipating faculty reflect on their own critical-thinking activities, it also allows participants to be recognized by their peers. Participants are able to practice presentations that they may take later to national or international teaching conferences. The facilitator coordinated a program schedule. Our Critical-Thinking Fair cost very little to implement. We reserved a room on campus, e-mailed promotional materials among faculty, and served simple refreshments.

Other Models

Other institutions of higher learning have CTA FLCs, and they vary in their structure and function. For example, the University of Louisville has a selective process in populating its CTA FLC (University of Louisville, 2008). Selected participants receive a $1,000 stipend, complimentary books and publications, teaching documents, coaching, and a certificate of completion. Instead of our focus on classroom interventions that may follow any of a variety of models, participants at the University of Louisville receive support in the use of the Paul and Elder critical thinking framework (referenced previously), instructional design, and assessment principles.

Ferris State University (2010) has three levels of CTA FLCs that train faculty to be more expert in critical thinking. Participants receive a $500 stipend for completing each level and a certificate of completion after achieving the third level. As an example, the participants in level I at Ferris State have as objectives to (a) be familiar with critical-thinking terminology; (b) be able to use basic critical-thinking concepts in instructing the content of one's classes; (c) be able to use various activities in class to focus students on the value of thinking critically; and (d) possess a basic portfolio of tactics to teach critical thinking in one's classes and activities.

While these two institutions offer financial incentives for participation in CTA FLCs, it is possible to run the FLC with a very small budget. Facilitators should receive some sort of incentive or release time to handle the increased workload, and some funding for books or speakers would be helpful. The Critical-Thinking Fair used a small amount of money for refreshments and advertising, and costs associated with printing posters were covered by the administration. But dedicated faculty could run this type of FLC with little or no budget.

A CTA FLC may rely on new participants to maintain energy and interest. It takes some energy on the part of the facilitator to vary activities to encourage participants to stay in over a year. If a facilitator sees a decline in attendance and participation over the course of a year, it is important for him or her to remain in contact with the participants to let them know that the core of the group can continue to peer-review activities for them, even if their attendance is sporadic. As popular and rewarding as CTA FLCs can be, overriding institutional priorities can lead to waning interest in some years, so the facilitator must be flexible and offer support to those who find themselves unable to contribute at the level that was originally expected.

Benefits to Faculty

A structured CTA FLC benefits faculty in several ways. In particular, it directly benefits their teaching and, consequently, student learning. Some examples of peer-reviewed activities in our CTA FLC include the following:

- Students in a biology class use the analogy of a metropolitan area to better understand cell structure and function. Students divide up into groups and teach each other the different components of the cell. Once completed, they are put in to new groups, and must take the cellular components and find an equivalent analog to the infrastructure of a metropolitan area.
- Students use discussion forums on the course management system to compose critical-thinking questions related to the course content. The faculty member modeled how to write critical-thinking questions that coincided with the content. Students then submitted their critical-thinking questions in a discussion board. All questions had to cover a different component of the content. The instructor then used a certain percentage of the questions in subsequent exams.
- A nursing instructor uses case studies to help nursing students understand components of their board exams. The instructor expanded the questions associated with established case studies, and students were required to use research to inform their answers and confer with one another.
- A psychology professor uses behavior modification contracts to improve student independence and success. The faculty member changed an existing activity by modeling what would be considered independence and success in the classroom. Then, students created behavior modification contracts to give them more ownership of their learning.

- A composition instructor helps students recognize assumptions in ethnography research. The faculty member introduces students to the idea of underlying assumptions in written and spoken language. In doing so, she increases students' ability to recognize such assumptions in their ethnography research and reduces the time she needs to meet with students individually to clarify these things.

All of these activities were sharpened in the FLC's peer-review process. This process also allows participants to see what their colleagues are doing in their classrooms and gives them ideas for new assignments in their own. One FLC participant explained the usefulness of peer review in an unsolicited letter:

> The UCBA *Critical Thinking Learning Community* also offered me a more formless, indefinable experience, which was the process of working with cross-discipline faculty members who were themselves thinking critically, mentoring, and modeling ways in which to create, explore, and examine the ideas brought to the group. As it turns out, it was the *process* of reflective examination and critical thinking that may have been the best aspect of this wonderful learning community.

Another faculty member pointed out the social benefits and how the FLC helped to convey the institution's expectations for critical thinking:

> The learning community provided an environment that was both encouraging and intellectually stimulating. Because this was my first year at UC–Blue Ash, this learning community was instrumental in acquainting me with some of my colleagues outside of my own department and introducing me to many of our institution's expectations for its faculty and students.

Faculty who participated in the CTA FLC benefited in other ways as well. Those participants who focused on the scholarly teaching aspect of the learning community were able to present their classroom practices at our Critical-Thinking Fair. This gave them a line on their curriculum vitae (CV), allowed them to discuss their work with colleagues, and gave them collegewide recognition. Those participants who engaged in scholarship of teaching and learning (SoTL) projects within the CTA FLC presented their research findings at a variety of teaching and learning conferences. FLC participants have remarked on the community's value in their professional lives.

One said, "Having a carrot [dissemination venue] at the completion of the faculty learning community provided me with a goal that I, otherwise, would not have considered investing the time." Another said, "Improving my teaching and simultaneously adding a professional development element to my CV made this experience very worthwhile and a pleasant experience."

Another benefit to faculty is that their participation produces concrete changes in their classroom that improve student learning. Clearer directions and revised activities allow students to focus more on higher-level thinking and avoid getting bogged down by confusion over minor details. Several participants revealed that simple clarification of their assignments through the peer-review process was invaluable and helped reduce student confusion. Thus, students are given better assignments that promote critical thinking, which should lead to critical-thinking development on their part as they move through the course.

In a CTA FLC, research, review of scholarly teaching methods, and peer review of critical-thinking activities provide different avenues for faculty to find their comfort level within the complex topic of critical thinking. When the results of these practices move to the classroom, faculty are transmitting their knowledge about critical thinking to their students. When we see students grow in their critical-thinking skills, we can be confident that we are doing what we need to do as educators to move them beyond rote memorization to the ability to problem solve and create in more advanced ways.

References

Abrami, P. C., Bernard, R. M., Borokhovski, E., Wade, A., Surkes, M., Tamim, R., & Zhang, D. A. (2008). Instructional interventions affecting critical thinking skills and dispositions: A stage one meta-analysis. *Review of Educational Research, 78*(4), 1102–1134. doi:10.3102/0034654308326084

Anderson, L. W., & Krathwohl, D. R. (2001). *A taxonomy for learning, teaching, and assessing: A revision of Bloom's Taxonomy of educational objectives.* New York: Longman.

Bers, T. (2005). Assessing critical thinking in community colleges. *New Directions for Community Colleges, 130,* 15–25. doi:10.1002/cc.192

Brookfield, S. D. (1987). *Developing critical thinkers: Challenging adults to explore alternative ways of thinking and acting.* San Francisco: Jossey-Bass.

Center for Assessment & Improvement in Learning, Tennessee Technological University. (2012). *Critical thinking assessment test.* Retrieved from http://www.tntech.edu/cat/home/

Combs, L., Cennamo, K., & Newbill, P. (2009). Developing creative and critical thinkers: Toward a conceptual model of creative and critical thinking processes. *Educational Technology, 49*(5), 3–14. Retrieved from http://dialnet.unirioja.es/servlet/revista?codigo = 4006

Ferris State University. (2010). *Faculty center for teaching and learning: Critical thinking faculty learning community.* Retrieved from (http://www.ferris.edu/htmls/academics/center/events/2010spring/Critical.htm

Halpern, D. F. (1998). Teaching critical thinking for transfer across domains: Dispositions, skills, structure training, and metacognitive monitoring. *American Psychologist, 53*, 449–455. doi:10.1037/0003-066X.53.4.449

Jones, E. A., Dougherty, B. C., Fantaske, P., & Hoffman, S. (1997). *Identifying college graduates' essential skills in reading and problem solving: Perspectives of faculty, employers, and policymakers.* University Park, PA: U.S. Department of Education.

Kurfiss, J. G. (1988). *Critical thinking: Theory, research, practice, and possibilities.* ASHE-ERIC Higher Education Report (no. 2). College Station, TX: Association for the Study of Higher Education. Retrieved from http://www.eric.ed.gov/ERICWebPortal/detail?accno-ED304041

Paul, R., & Elder, L. (2008). *The miniature guide to critical thinking: Concepts and tools.* Dillon Beach, CA: The Foundation for Critical Thinking Press.

Richlin, L., & Cox, M. (2004). Developing scholarly teaching and the scholarship of teaching and learning through faculty learning communities. *New Directions for Teaching and Learning, 97*, 127–135. doi:10.1002/tl.139

Taylor, M. (2010, September 12). Schools, businesses focus on critical thinking. *Wall Street Journal.* Retrieved from http://online.wsj.com/article/SB10001424052748703882304575466100773788806.html

University of Louisville. (2008). *Faculty learning community on critical thinking.* Retrieved from https://louisville.edu/ideastoaction/aboutlc/flc-ct

Willingham, D. T. (2007, Summer). Critical thinking: Why is it so hard to teach? *American Educator*, 8–19. Retrieved from http://www.aft.org/newspubs/periodicals/ae/summer2007/index.cfm

7

ASSESSMENT INCOGNITO
Design Thinking and the Studio Learning FLC

Joanne Munroe

"Why Won't This Work in Your Classroom?"

The engineering professor sat in her office looking curiously at the invitation she had just received. The new campus studio learning space was having an open house, and the flier about it grabbed her attention. It pictured the studio filled with brightly colored chairs, new kinds of interactive media, and floor-to-ceiling whiteboards that appeared to be covered with drawings, writings, and concept maps. The college eLearning team had issued the invitation, which referenced the work of the studio learning faculty learning community (FLC), but there was no mention of new technology training workshops as she would have expected. It was hard to understand what the space and the open house were all about.

As she scanned the flier, she noticed the Lego blocks pictured in the lower left-hand corner and tried to make the connection with the photo of a teacher in the center of the page. She was writing a challenge on the whiteboard wall: "Why won't this work in *your* class?" The engineering professor paused, reread the invitation, and tried to decide whether attending would be worth her time.

The "Why won't this work" question set an experimental tone that invited the professor to meet the challenges hinted at in the flier. While she did not use eLearning strategies in her engineering classes, she did use Legos twice a week in hands-on problem-solving activities with students, and she trusted the research and case studies she had read on using physical models to illustrate concepts. The flier mentioned "design thinking," so she googled it, and Stanford University came up as the first hit. Stanford had a design thinking program and something called the d.school. Exploring the design program and d.school websites gave her a pretty good idea of how design thinking might fit her discipline. According to the d.school website (Stanford University Institute of Design, 2012), design thinking is a creative problem-solving process that offers a

> methodology for innovation that combines creative and analytical approaches, and requires collaboration across disciplines. This process—which has been called design thinking—draws on methods from engineering and design, and combines them with ideas from the arts, tools from the social sciences, and insights from the business world.

Furthermore, the website explained that the d.school offered classes using design thinking to help students "learn this process together, and then personalize it, internalize it, and apply it to their own challenges." While she remained highly skeptical that innovation and creativity could be taught, she was more concerned that a focus on design thinking would be a waste of her time. She did not understand how it would be applicable to the design of her classes and her role as an educator. Her community college students were struggling with basic math skills. This was not Stanford. How could design thinking help her to cover her content? Who else had tried this?

The professor wanted to know more. Ironically, while she would not allow Wikipedia citations in work her students produced, she started there. It seemed as if the only way she could keep up with changes in the teaching and learning literature was to start with these quick Web searches. Even as she did this, she felt misgivings about not using more traditional scholarly methods. This made her start thinking about what the rush toward online education was doing to her profession. Were the eLearning team in the new studio space and the FLC trying to push faculty into online teaching? She did not think she was holding her students back from twenty-first-century learning opportunities, and she doubted that online teaching and instant Internet answers were promising solutions to the deteriorating quality of higher education. Now she was being invited to play with new technologies in a studio space.

She glanced at the invitation again and focused on the term *Assessment Incognito*. She was responsible for mapping her department's outcomes for an upcoming accreditation, so maybe a visit to the studio space would be useful. The FLC participants claimed that design thinking could help reframe assessment, and they challenged her by saying that design thinking would work in college classes. They had asked her to show that it would not; she would go and check it out. Game on!

What Is Studio Learning?

The studio learning FLC at Tacoma Community College helps participants like this fictional engineering professor research teaching and learning by using principles of design, sometimes referred to as studio thinking. Our FLC meets in a specially designed studio learning space, which helps to facilitate the work of the group. Our work involves designing new, innovative solutions to solve the tensions between traditional academic approaches to learning and new, less traditional ones. An effective studio learning FLC can teach participants a systematic way to approach creative thinking and problem solving. Many times, the design process results in innovative classroom changes.

During the design thinking process, participants give and receive frequent feedback. The process of constant assessment could change the way teachers give feedback in their classes and solicit feedback about their teaching from their peers. Thus, the innovative redesign that happens in a studio learning FLC can help change the culture of teaching and learning at a two-year college. The title of this chapter is "Assessment Incognito" because a studio learning FLC trains participants to use constant assessment as they are designing and producing work. Assessment is no longer a scary evaluative process, but rather a way to help the design move forward in a way that allows for playful experimentation. In the context of brainstorming and collaborating, assessment happens incognito.

The fictional engineering professor is a composite character who embodies the skepticism about change and the bias toward traditional teaching methods that we see in pockets of nearly every two-year college. More important, though, the story of the composite professor models one of the primary strategies taught and practiced in a studio learning FLC: storytelling as a method of communicating problems that need to be solved. We begin the design thinking process by talking to colleagues both within and outside the group and looking for the institutional or classroom problems that need solutions. We gather these problems and create a composite that we write as a case study, a story that brings to life the teaching problem, concern, or misconception we need to solve. Writing this story forces us to better understand the cause of the problem or the source of the concern or misconception, the need for a solution, and, of course, the people we're designing for. This step in the creative process cultivates empathy, a crucial element in design thinking. To design an effective solution, we must understand our audience. In other words, in a studio learning FLC, we strive to become the flexible, critical thinkers we would like our students to be. To that end, we study and practice techniques that prepare us to identify needs, focus on human values, and create empathy for our colleagues' or our students' concerns.

What is the design thinking problem embedded in the story of the composite engineering professor? It is messy and multifaceted like real-world problems. At one level, the instructor is debating the usefulness of learning a design process. At another level, she is skeptical about the push toward online teaching. Additionally, she is entrenched in traditional ideas about research and knowledge discovery, but simultaneously recognizes that she engages in the kind of instant research the Internet can provide. This case study was created within the studio learning FLC and led to discussions about the group's purpose and an exploration of the false distinctions between online and face-to-face teaching. Ultimately if a studio learning FLC took this example through the entire design process, it might result in real classroom change, for example, revised research assignments that encouraged students to evaluate a variety of Internet sources. It might result in peer mentoring surrounding design thinking, or it might result in face-to-face instructors using some of the helpful principles of online course design, for example, alignment and unit-level learning outcomes.

An emerging theme from our FLC is that our students need new skill sets to navigate the world. Technology is ubiquitous. Students constantly use their digital devices for their own everyday research and problem solving. To ignore that in a face-to-face classroom misses an opportunity and can create the perception that the professor or the discipline is completely outdated. Furthermore, Bergquist and Pawlak (2008) assert that new technologies are catalysts for new ways of thinking. Traditional educational approaches assume that knowledge is stable and does not change much over time. Twenty-first-century learning requires nimble responses and the ability to keep up with, participate in, and contribute to the creation of information technology spaces that are altered and reshaped by participants. The distinctions between the practices used in face-to-face and online education are not entirely useful then. Thomas and Seely Brown (2011), Brown (2009), and

Littman and Kelley (2005) discuss the importance of using studio spaces to foster a culture of innovation. Information age thinking is more participatory; therefore, we cannot count on being taught or trained in how to use each new tool, medium, or communication mode. Our students are not reading manuals or memorizing when they are interacting online. In other words, they are learning by participating. A studio learning FLC can teach participants a process that helps them to identify, analyze, transform, and use organic, inquiry-driven processes to teach skills like innovation and creativity. The FLC work prepares participants to mentor peers and students and to train them more formally for their increasingly active roles in seeking and integrating new information. It has the added benefit of giving them a supportive community in which to test these ideas and methods and to bring them into public discussion, making what Polyani (2009) describes as "tacit knowledge"—those hidden assumptions that experts or skilled practitioners take for granted—explicit and available for use in the transfer to formal instruction.

In addition to exploring the skills students need for the digital age, a studio learning FLC attempts to model the types of learning that are now more typical of the modern way problems are approached. With Ito and colleagues (2009, 2010), Jenkins (2009), Thomas and Seely Brown (2011), and Davidson and Goldberg (2010), we see that new, more participatory forms of learning have accompanied the changes in the World Wide Web and the ways we interact with information and with others. As the growing body of work in this area indicates, more and more learning is taking place in informal settings, and the lines between academic and everyday contexts and classroom and peer-based social learning are becoming blurred. Like Jenkins (2009) and Thomas and Seely Brown (2011), our FLC works from the assumption that knowing how to retrieve, judge, analyze, and synthesize information; knowing how to enter a conversation in which diverse voices are represented; knowing how to cocreate new ideas; and knowing how to learn and how to evaluate what is learned in and outside of class are the skills eLearning teaches.

Technology does not solve every problem at the two-year college, and our FLC does not see technology as a one-stop solution. In fact, based on what Cuban (2001) found in his work, *Oversold and Underused: Computers in the Classroom*, we know that putting technology in the classroom does not mean that faculty actually use it. Furthermore, the wrong technology integrated for the wrong reasons may not be the best answer. Instead, participants in a studio learning FLC use design thinking to decide how to select and use the right tool, strategy, or technique in the right teaching and learning context. Sometimes that tool is a smartphone, and sometimes it is a flipchart and a set of Lego blocks. The focus is on finding novel solutions without worrying about whether the tool is a traditional one or a new, digital one.

In our experience, there are deep misunderstandings about teaching and learning responsibly with technology, and we see proponents of face-to-face classes and online classes talking past one another as they argue over traditional versus digital tools rather than considering teaching and learning strategies. The literature indicates that new virtual forms of education may threaten the structures and roles in higher education, but there are ways of designing spaces and experiences that allow us to focus on deep and meaningful collaborations that will see us through these challenges (Bergquist & Pawlak, 2008; Doorley, Witthoft, & Hasso Plattner Institute of Design, 2012). Our diverse group, made up of educational technologists, information systems professionals, and faculty, is the perfect group to take on the task of debating these issues and generating innovative solutions that consider the needs of a variety of constituents. An effective studio learning FLC will work best when all of these groups are represented as participants because then they have to communicate and engage with one another's ideas as they work through the steps in the design process.

These steps are many. In our FLC, we begin by listening for problems or issues within the institution, and we look for common themes. We work together to write a fictional story that embodies these themes, and this exercise forces us to begin to empathize with the concerns behind the problem or issues at hand. We go beyond the reading, thinking, and reflecting that are typical of many professional development activities. Before we design trainings or prescribe solutions, we listen carefully to create experiences and activities that take into account both the outcomes desired and the needs of the person for whom we are designing. In the FLC, we are training together to develop the habits of mind we can use for problem solving and course design.

Why Use Studio Learning in the Two-Year College Setting?

Our expectations of students sometimes reveal a hidden irony. For instance, we ask them to work collaboratively in peer groups, to present their work in all stages, to accept our feedback and use it for improvement, and to make and learn from errors, sometimes in very public settings, but we seldom do these things ourselves. We accept as common knowledge characteristics of the successful twenty-first-century learner, but we sometimes fail to invest time and effort to learn to teach these skills. In a world where access to knowledge is changing by the minute, we must keep up to teach our students and ourselves. How do we do that?

To teach critical literacy and the ability to lean into and flex with the cultural and intellectual shifts all around us, we need to learn new technologies as well as new teaching and learning techniques. Not only do we need to know how to design and deliver courses in our disciplines that are based on and designed around adult learning principles, we also have to admit that while the technological changes are the most obvious to us, and the easiest to complain about, the real shifts seem to be in the ways of thinking brought about by technological innovations.

Some professors are unsettled by the idea that traditional teaching methods are losing favor, but the shift away from authoritative expertise and fixed knowledge has a positive side. Our studio learning FLC explores the connections and possibilities inherent in a world where our ideas are out in the public domain almost as soon as we think them. When we can model, present, copy and paste, mash up, sample or build three-dimensional, interactive gesture-based simulations, all while communicating with a colleague down the hallway or halfway around the planet through Skype, our methods need to change. If we are going to teach these strategies, we need to explore them ourselves. But how do we do that? Who has the time?

What Does the Studio Learning FLC Do That Makes a Difference?

The studio learning FLC was initiated at Tacoma Community College as a way to help instructors model, design, deliver, and assess learning activities with students in mind, and to begin these processes by creating a space for participants to learn and think in public. For the purposes of this chapter, thinking in public means creating some sort of object or demonstrating a product that allows another person to review it and provide feedback. For example, a participant might show a learning object in VoiceThread, and FLC peers would give comments on how to improve it.

Ideas about play are central to our design process, both to inspire creativity and to help us extract lessons we can use in our classrooms. A number of researchers have identified the importance of play in creativity and developing higher-order thinking (deFreitas & Maharg, 2011; Huizinga, 2008; Ito et al. 2009, 2010; Piaget, 1962; Sutton-Smith, 2001; Winnicott, 1999). We use role-play and video game activities to study assessment techniques that make it safe to risk making mistakes in front of our peers when we are learning something entirely new. This experience helps make us more open to feedback about our designs and helps us to empathize with our students' anxieties about trying something completely new in a class. We are studying what we learn when we are immersed in play, and we are using what we learn to inspire our work in designing learning experiences for others.

Our studio learning FLC follows a protocol developed by Stanford's d.school. The d.school's "bootcamp bootleg" design thinking toolkit (Hasso Plattner Institute of Design, 2010) provides a framework for organizing our meetings and our outcomes. In each of our bimonthly meetings we focus on one or more of the d.school "mindsets" that are necessary for design thinking:

1. "Show Don't Tell": This mindset asks participants to make concrete representations of their ideas, for instance, with storyboards, pictures, diagrams, or even Play-Doh.
2. "Focus on Human Values": This mindset requires empathy. When a participant is empathetic, that person adjusts his or her design ideas with the audience in mind.
3. "Embrace Experimentation": In this mindset, we do not view our work as a finished product but rather as a work in progress. We create drafts of products, give feedback on them, and continually revise them.
4. "Be Mindful of Process": This mindset asks participants to keep the end goals in mind. For example, we use a backward design process that focuses on what students should be learning.
5. "Craft Clarity": In this mindset, we identify topics for investigation by starting with messy, ill-formed problems. By beginning with open-ended questions about problems that need solutions, we come to understand the things we still need to learn about the topic.
6. "Bias Toward Action": This mindset keeps the process active. We are encouraged to try out ideas—not simply talk about them. In this way, we put ourselves in the position of students, trying new things with little experience.
7. "Radical Collaboration": This mindset assumes that when diverse groups come together, design thinking is enriched. A group that includes faculty, eLearning specialists, and instructional designers offers varied viewpoints about helpful solutions to potential problems.

These mindsets inform the d.school's design thinking protocol, and we have adapted the following for our FLC: "empathize," "define," "ideate," "proto- type," and "test" (Hasso Plattner Institute of Design, 2010, pp. 1–5). Follow- ing the sequence and using the mindsets, we collect issues for study from the college as well as work through the d.school's suggested activities. Any col- lege starting a studio learning FLC might start with consulting the d.school resources for a framework and agenda ideas.

How Is the FLC Work Changing Our Practice?

For many of us who were trained in academic disciplines, the bias toward action identified in the d.school approach presents the biggest hurdle, and in our FLC we design activities that have us jumping right in and trying things. We introduce messy problems and set tasks without defining parame- ters to see how each group of three or four uses the resources in the studio space: whiteboards, technology, art supplies, or games. Whatever the ques- tion, the groups create products or demonstrate solutions, and then report out in some fashion that allows everyone to interact with the ideas.

In one such experiment, one group used the whiteboard walls to give visual form to its ideas. It presented from the space where its members had drawn concept maps on the walls. Another group projected onto the interac- tive whiteboard screen from iPads after creating a Google document, and a third group went "low tech" and used paper and pencil and an appointed speaker who stood and summarized results verbally without any visual aids. Participants use different tools to solve the same problem at this stage. These experimental sessions in our FLC are very different from the targeted work- shops on tools and techniques that eLearning support teams usually request, and our studio learning FLC work opens a dialogue about how instruction changes in flexible spaces like our studio. We use the studio space to learn to use what is around us to develop personalized instruction techniques that connect to different learning preferences.

We study games that are intentionally built around informal learning outcomes, and we use activities with Kinect *Rock Band* and *Dance Central* video games to test the ideas presented in studies of gaming (deFreitas & Maharg, 2011; Gee, 2007, 2010; Ito et al., 2009; Jenkins, 2006, 2009; McGonigal, 2010). We use the game's formative assessment to investigate the power of immediate or delayed feedback to teach skills and to motivate a learner intrinsically or extrinsically toward improved performance. By studying our own experience as participants in the games and making connections, we design our classroom assessments for learner engagement.

We are not looking for literal transfer to classroom activities (we are not going to use *Guitar Hero* in class). Rather, we are looking for ways we can re-create engagement experiences, and after playing one of these games together, we find that we view assessment with fresh eyes. We all risk looking foolish or less than accomplished in front of our peers, and we are learning from failure without having to live with real-world consequences.

Looking at how we learn in games helps us to appreciate the investment, engagement, and full presence involved in learning. We recognize the ways immediate, real-time feedback helps us to move to the next level of performance. This allows us to appreciate the power and the speed of solutions when multiple minds and bodies are working together. In addition, we open up possibilities, and, in a debriefing, we look at the ways the disciplines in the performing and visual arts use this method of real-time critique to improve learning every day.

The FLC sessions always end in plenary mode with these guiding questions: "How could you use this in your class?" "Why wouldn't it work?" In these summing up sessions, we discuss outcomes, compare results, and plan future sessions during which we will address the remaining questions.

How Does the Studio Space Help?

The flexible nature of the studio space encourages the search for multiple solutions to a single problem, and we use strategies to introduce play as a technique that makes it safe to get things wrong. Because of our node chairs, we can quickly reconfigure into groups of four. The art supplies, the games, and the technology allow us to try out, discuss, and revise the possibilities of new teaching and learning techniques in ways that make sense to us in the moment. The activity and the different ways in which faculty approach problems present a microcosm of what happens in a classroom, where students have different learning needs and different approaches to problem solving. As we investigate the literature about designing learning spaces (e.g., Oblinger, 2006), we focus consciously on creating environments that allow us to decide in the moment what tool fits what task for active, participatory learning. Our studio-based learning activities provide real-world examples and open dialogues about creating flexible, networked learning spaces. These experiences provide the nonteaching professionals in the group the opportunity to look for concerns and challenges about implementing new techniques in existing spaces with current institutional resources.

In our ideal, flexible space, facilitators are free to circulate, join groups, and observe the ways in which the groups use the studio space as they work. In this way, they are practicing classroom skills and giving feedback in the moment. We assign roles within the FLC so that, by the end of the session, each participant will have taken a co-facilitator role.

Symbolically and practically, the chairs selected for the studio space facilitate creativity. They move with the participants as they join new conversations and activities. Selected in four bright colors, specifically to make the combinations and recombinations of assigned groups more efficient, the node chairs suggest that this is an active space. With their moveable table-tops, they form common working surfaces when two to four of them are wheeled together. Our experiments with assigning and managing group work based on chair colors have inspired demonstrations of new group-learning techniques. Their self-contained mobility invites interaction, encouraging participants to make the space work *for* and *with* them, rather than forcing participants to accept the limitations of the room's design.

Experiencing the ease of movement inspires experimenting with strategies such as reinventing new groups every few weeks to reshuffle learning teams and maximize scaffolding as described by Vygotsky (1978). While at this point in the life of the FLC, we have moved beyond conversations about chairs, interactive touch televisions, iPad docking stations, and wall-to-wall whiteboards, the availability of these items remains an important component in the studio approach. For groups starting a studio learning FLC, we recommend at least a dedicated space with movable chairs, whiteboards, art supplies, and a variety of technology.

How We Recruited Members and Funded Our FLC

The membership in the studio learning FLC is drawn from across campus roles and responsibilities. Each of the FLC members has made a yearlong commitment to come together twice a month for two hours to contribute assignments, activities, and sweat equity to change the face of teaching and learning on the campus. The members of the community were recruited based on commitments to innovation, assessment, technology, scholarship of teaching and learning, and, for some, "geeking out."

This FLC was strategically planned using the learning communities literature (Cox & Richlin, 2004; Cox, Wentzell, & Richlin, 2009). Specifically, at Tacoma Community College, we began with one learning community on social media and participatory learning, investigating the questions that eventually became foundational in the studio learning FLC. We recruited the participants based on their reputations as thought leaders, their roles in the campus community, and their reach to influence faculty, students, and programming. In addition, we wanted faculty and nonfaculty professionals at the same table talking about the rapid changes in the teaching and learning environment. While we began with an informal recruitment process that required only a short written interest and commitment statement, this year we are instituting a formal application process.

Our FLC program began with funding for one community with seed money ($5,000) from one competitive statewide grant. The grant process was part of a systemwide pilot modeled on the Ohio Learning Network and the success of Miami University's FLC model. Tacoma Community College's eLearning Department, which is self-sustaining, is entrepreneurial, and operates as a community of practice, got institutional buy-in based on winning the competitive grant process.

The eLearning Department matched the state funds, and the FLC program adapted the Miami University (Cox, 2004) model to our two-year context. In our practice, we incorporate and assess all 30 components described in the FLC literature (Cox, 2004). The pilot grant was written to include the purchase of ebooks and refreshments for off-campus meetings, and in the second year, we added a technology request for iPads. The technology and reading materials loaded on the e-readers became property of the state, on loan to the FLC participants, and no stipends or release time were offered (even for facilitators). Faculty and nonfaculty professionals participated for the learning opportunities and the sense of community we created, and there was no attrition. Faculty participants used the strategies they were learning in the community in their classrooms and the eLearning Department funded travel to a Lilly conference to present results. Another budget item to consider would be the costs of sending facilitators to Lilly conferences or FLC conference training sessions.

We have used Facebook and other social media to connect the larger college community with our promising practices, and, in terms of finding and leveraging funding sources, the techniques we learned in our social media FLCs have served us well in equipping our studio space. In addition to keeping connected through the use of Facebook group sites, we posted references to the literature on play and studio learning there. In addition, we said we needed games to complete our FLCs strategic plan, and a nonprofit donated them to us. We would encourage other FLCs to explore the potential of using social media sites both for networking and as a way to add collaborative time and space for their learning communities.

The studio learning FLC was proposed in part to develop and assess strategies taken up by other related FLCs at the college. The development of the studio learning FLC necessitated the acquisition of a permanent studio space. When we consider whether this studio learning FLC would function well without a dedicated studio space, we think it would not. The environment is integral to the creativity and collaboration of the group. Initially, some of the meetings were held at restaurants. While participants typically enjoy off-campus meetings, the food, and the social atmosphere, the studio learning FLC participants *asked* to move our meetings from the restaurant setting back into the studio where we could play. We have established a sense of community, and the space is novel and exciting.

Our Outcome: Using FLCs as Scalable, Sustainable Professional Development

The studio learning FLC has built a permanent play space focused on assessment and innovation. The studio approach is tied to the college mission and vision statements and to Tacoma Community College's strategic plan. Additionally, the studio learning FLC is the lynchpin in a new FLC program for sustainable, scalable faculty development in eLearning. Our Tacoma Community College vision statement emphasizes documenting student learning, innovation and excellence, and the creation of inclusive community. We can do these things though our responsible integration of technology across the curriculum. In acting upon that vision, next year the eLearning Department will begin supporting three face-to-face learning communities per year. The professional development activities offered through eLearning will continue to emphasize teaching responsibly with technology, and giving real-time feedback in a way that encourages students to take risks. Our studio learning FLC is using design thinking to address institutional challenges that are new to both teachers and students.

Tacoma Community College uses learning communities to build a culture of peer mentorship and inquiry into teaching and learning practices. This approach leaves us better prepared to address faculty concerns about keeping up with technology, concerns like those of the engineering professor whose story set the context for this chapter. The design approach taken by our studio learning FLC can be applied to her current questions as well as her future ones. The existence of the new studio space, equipped with state-of-the-art technology, modular furniture, and whiteboard walls, is evidence that learning communities and design thinking are permanent fixtures on our campus. But this is just the beginning of improving our practice. Watch us "level up." Game on!

References

Brown, T. (2009). *Change by design: How design thinking transforms organizations and inspires innovation*. New York: Harper Collins.

Bergquist, W., & Pawlak, K. (2008). *Engaging the six cultures of the academy* (2nd ed.). San Francisco: Jossey-Bass.

Cox, M. (2004). Introduction to faculty learning communities. *New Directions for Teaching and Learning, 97*(1), 5–23.

Cox, M., & Richlin, L. (2004). Building faculty learning communities. *New Directions for Teaching and Learning, 97*(1).

Cox, M. D., Wentzell, G. W., & Richlin, L. (2009). Recognizing the strength and fragility of learning communities: A message from the editors. *Learning Communities Journal, 1*(2), 1–3.

Cuban, L. (2001). *Oversold and underused: Computers in the classroom*. Cambridge, MA: Harvard University Press.

Davidson, C., & Goldberg, D. (2010). *The future of thinking: Learning institutions in a digital age*. The John D. and Catherine T. McArthur Foundation Reports on Digital Media and Learning. Cambridge, MA: MIT Press.

deFreitas, S., & Maharg, P. (2011). *Digital games and learning*. London: Continuum.

Doorley, S., Witthoft, S., & Hasso Plattner Institute of Design at Stanford University. (2012). *Make space: How to set the stage for creative collaboration*. Hoboken, NJ: John Wiley & Sons.

Gee, J. P. (2007). *What video games have to teach us about learning and literacy* (2nd ed.). New York: Palgrave MacMillan.

Gee, J. P. (2010). *New digital media and learning as an emerging area and "worked examples" as one way forward*. The John D. and Catherine T. MacArthur Foundation Reports on Digital Media and Learning. Cambridge, MA: MIT Press.

Hasso Plattner Institute of Design at Stanford. (2010). *d.school Bootcamp Bootleg*. Retrieved from http://dschool.stanford.edu/wp-context/uploads/2011/03/bootcamp Bootleg2010

Huizinga, J. (2008). *Homo ludens: A study of the play element in culture*. New York: Routledge.

Ito, M. (2010). *Hanging out, messing around, and geeking out: Kids living and learning with the new media.* Cambridge, MA: MIT Press.

Ito, M., Horst, H., Bittani, M., boyd, d., Herr-Stephenson, B., Lange, P. G., Pascoe, C. J., & Robinson, L. (2009). *Living and learning with new media: Summary of findings from the digital youth project.* The John D. and Catherine T. MacArthur Foundation Reports on Digital Media and Learning. Cambridge, MA: MIT Press.

Jenkins, H. (2006). *Convergence culture: Where old and new media collide.* New York: NYU Press.

Jenkins, H. (2009). *Confronting the challenges of participatory culture: Media education for the 21st century.* The John D. and Catherine T. MacArthur Foundation Reports on Digital Media and Learning. Cambridge, MA: MIT Press.

Littman, J., & Kelley, T. (2005). *The ten faces of innovation: IDEO's strategies for defeating the devil's advocate and driving creativity throughout your organization.* New York: Doubleday.

McGonigal, J. (2010). *Reality is broken: Why games make us better and how they can change the world.* New York: Penguin.

Oblinger, D. (Ed.). (2006). *Learning spaces.* EDUCAUSE. Retrieved from http://www.educause.edu/learningspaces

Piaget, J. (1962). *Play, dreams & imitation.* New York: W. W. Norton.

Polyani, M. (2009). *The tacit dimension* (reissued ed.) Chicago: University of Chicago Press.

Stanford University Institute of Design. (2012). *d.school. Our point of view.* Retrieved from http://dschool.stanford.edu/our-point-of-view/

Sutton-Smith, B. (2001). *The ambiguity of play.* Cambridge, MA: Harvard University Press.

Thomas, D., & Seely Brown, J. (2011). *A new culture of learning: Cultivating the imagination for a world of constant change* (self-published).

Vygotsky, L. S. (1978). *Mind in society: The development of higher psychological processes* (14th ed.). (M. Col., V. John-Steiner, S. Scribner, & E. Souberman, Eds.) Cambridge, MA: Harvard University Press.

Winnicott, D. W. (1999). *Playing and reality.* New York: Routledge.

8

SMART CONNECTIONS
Transfer of Learning and First-Year Student Success

Ruth Benander, Robin Lightner, and Gene Kramer

A basic premise of higher education is that students transfer the knowledge from one course not only to other courses, but also to the workplace after graduation. However, there is much anecdotal evidence that students are unaware of the need to transfer learning. Many students have tunnel vision and compartmentalize their learning, believing it is relevant only to the class in which it is taught. Hallway conversations among our faculty reveal a good deal of frustration over students' inability to transfer what they learn across classes. When these conversations came up at our college, we complained, for example, that students who completed a math course that teaches graphing are unable to graph in chemistry class. Other students in a history class claimed never to have learned about citation format when it was clear that they had finished the English composition sequence that emphasized it. With frustration about these seemingly obvious instances of transfer, we grew increasingly concerned about students' ability to transfer material to more distant contexts—clinical settings, the office, or other aspects of their lives outside of school.

To address the problem of our unmet expectations about transfer of learning, a group of 11 faculty from different disciplines in our two-year college formed a faculty learning community (FLC) that we called "Smart

Authors' Note: We would like to acknowledge the contributions of the following faculty members who participated in this faculty learning community with the authors: Melinda Greer, Beverly Knauper, Mary Kaye Scaramucci, Charles Emenaker, Stefanie Bethuy, Diana Becket, Marlene Miner, and Andrea Kornbluh.

Connections," referring to the goal of having students make cross-course connections with the material they were learning. We studied the background literature together, gathered data in several studies (about attitudes toward transfer, knowledge and learning beliefs, how content transferred, and student reflections on what they thought transferred). Finally, we developed some interventions to strengthen students' abilities to transfer what they learn. This chapter describes our group's activities and suggests ways that other colleges might create a similar FLC that can educate faculty on the research about transfer and ultimately affect how students use what they learn in their other courses and beyond the classroom.

To start a transfer FLC, an interested faculty member might find like-minded colleagues by asking about whether their transfer expectations are met and if they would be interested in researching causes and solutions. An interdisciplinary FLC allows for discussions that can reveal discipline-specific ways of thinking, so transfer FLCs should be created with discipline diversity in mind. Middendorf and Pace (2004) describe how conversations about student bottlenecks in learning can be overcome as faculty explain their own discipline-specific thought processes: "This step is difficult because faculty have to dissect their own innate thinking" (p. 5). This type of FLC could be formed to meet larger college goals and initiatives in which transfer plays a big role, such as improving student retention, improving the first-year experience, or writing across the curriculum.

Transfer of Learning in the Literature

As we began to explore our frustration with students' lack of transfer and our questions about the topic, we learned that there is a rich body of evidence that addresses the problem of students not using what they know in other classes. An FLC on this topic should start with an exploration of the literature, and this section provides an overview and references to research studies that inform transfer.

Transfer of learning is the application of skill and knowledge learned in one context to another context (Cormier & Hagman, 1987). Transfer of learning is multifaceted. It can happen at different levels—for example, low road transfer refers to a skill that has become automatic (Salomon & Perkins, 1989). It usually requires repeated practice and is relatively easy to apply in new contexts. Some examples of low road transfer are being able to tie different types of shoes, or using the different types of keyboards on various electronic devices. High road transfer is much more elusive. It is the intentional, mindful abstraction of a concept for application in a new context. In other words, the learner seeks the key elements from a concept that are general enough to apply to other situations. High road and low road transfer refer to the content of what transfers from one context to another. In mathematics classrooms, a goal is to make a skill become a low road skill. However, this can cause the classroom to become a forum for low road transfer at the cost of high road transfer. For example, in a math course, if students are only required to perform the algorithms asked in the same manner they have been exposed to, they may know how to calculate the problems, but they will not apply the algorithms in novel situations. Many students do remember how to solve linear equations because they are asked to perform the skills from pre-algebra through calculus and beyond.

Another facet of the transfer of learning is the similarity of the learning situation to the application situation (Barnett & Ceci, 2002). Near transfer occurs when the tasks presented are in very similar contexts, so there is not much conscious effort on the part of the learner. Some examples of near transfer would be being able to find the windshield wiper controls in a Ford, and then being able to find them in a Honda, or being able use a mobile phone and a tablet. Far transfer occurs when the leaner is required to use a skill in a new and seemingly dissimilar context. For example, far transfer would be driving an automatic transmission Ford and a manual transmission Honda, or being able to use a word processor on a personal computers versus a tablet. In the case of far transfer, the larger concepts may be the same, but application of the concepts will be quite different in the local contexts. One of the problems we face as educators is that we worry only about how the students perform in our class, which is teaching for near transfer, when our goal should be to promote far transfer with a focus on the next course for which our course is a prerequisite. Understanding this distinction helps us to recognize how difficult the tasks are that we are asking of our students, and it encourages us to be more explicit about our practice opportunities (e.g., Halpern & Hakel, 2003).

The fundamental dimensions that appear to underlie effective transfer are described as the "pillars of transfer" (Alexander & Murphy, 1999), which include subject-matter knowledge, general cognitive and metacognitive strategies, and motivation of the learner. Metacognitive strategies deal with knowing what or how a student comes to learn and how he or she structures knowledge. Metacognition comprises students' awareness of what they know and how they know it. This includes accurately monitoring their learning, recognizing how they study best, and being able to change this strategy as demanded by the situation. The self-regulated learning (SRL) literature addresses the components of metacognitive processes (Pintrich, 1995; Zimmerman, 2000) and suggests several opportunities for instructors to intervene to build the skills of monitoring, adjusting from feedback, and assessing.

Some recent research suggests that the design of tests and assignments affects how well students will transfer what they learn. For example, Rohrer, Taylor, and Sholar (2010) report that children benefited from testing practice, even if the children were asked to do difficult application problems after the testing practice. Similarly, in a study on promoting critical thinking, students were able to recall information more accurately and problem solve more creatively when they experienced instruction that allowed collaboration and less-structured rehearsal of the information they needed to learn (Lizarraga, Baqueado, Mangado, & Cardelle-Elawar, 2009).

Other research examines instructional methods (e.g., Case & Gunstone, 2002; DeCorte, 2003); metacognitive processes (Pressley, Van Etten, & Freeborn, 1998); and self-regulation (Winne & Hadwin, 1998); however, little attention has focused on the attitudinal components of transfer. Pea (1987) discusses how attitudes about what is an appropriate context for a certain skill will strongly influence its transfer. He offers the example of Brazilian street children who can do calculations when they are selling merchandise on the street, but when they get to school, they are unable to do basic math (p. 644). Pea suggests that attitudes about what can be learned and where it is appropriate to apply certain knowledge are culturally determined. He urges teachers to focus on helping students become more metacognitively aware so they can use their knowledge more effectively for transfer. McCombs and Marzano (1990) agree that attitudes are key to the self-regulation models affecting metacognition. Before a student can be metacognitively aware, he or she must believe that it is possible and desirable.

Once students have the predisposition to be aware of their thinking processes, they need to have appropriate skills to retrieve, incorporate, and apply new knowledge. Practice at retrieval promotes long-term retention and transfer (Halpern & Hakel, 2003; Karpicke & Blunt, 2011). Learners need to generate responses with minimal cues, repeatedly over time, with varied applications. Students should repeat the procedure in varying contexts and at different times to create more networks for retrieval. This was illustrated in one study finding that when students collaborated with colleagues at their new workplace, they were better able to transfer their learning from school to work (Nielsen, 2009). The act of rehearsing the knowledge with each other, and then performing the tasks in formal assessments, helped them retain and apply the knowledge better. These findings corroborate the assertions of Graesser, Person, and Hu (2002), who describe ways that instructors could promote deep versus shallow learning, including reciprocal teaching, asking challenging questions, and one-on-one tutoring.

Another example that emphasizes how practice can affect retrieval in different settings examined students who reviewed a reading task (Karpicke & Blunt, 2011). Afterward, the students rehearsed the information in a new manner, free writing what they remembered. They retained the information more accurately than students who either just read the article a second time or who made concept maps while consulting the reading. Other studies show that students transfer material better when they rehearse the material in their own words (deWinstanley & Bjork, 2002). Other areas of research relevant to transfer of learning include instructional practices, rehearsal techniques, collaboration, and active learning strategies.

When planning an FLC about transfer of learning, the group should spend some time studying the relevant background literature in educational psychology or cognitive science. The time spent on background literature is vital not only to gain understanding about the concepts, but also to create grounded interventions to improve student learning. Discussion groups might start their investigation of this topic with practical, accessible, and research-based books such as *Why Don't Students Like School? A Cognitive Scientist Answers Questions about How the Mind Works and What It Means for the Classroom* by Daniel Willingham (2009) and *How Learning Works: Seven Research-Based Principles for Smart Teaching* by Susan Ambrose and colleagues (2010). Becoming informed about the literature on transfer of learning helps the participants plan for other activities their FLC might find useful. Perhaps the group would decide to research transfer attitudes further or the current state of transfer at its institution. The group might decide to try some transfer-promoting classroom activities and report on their success. The group might even find that delving into the literature and discussing the implications provides a rich enough experience for the FLC.

Implementing a Transfer of Learning FLC

When creating a transfer FLC, it is important to consider the basic elements of effective FLCs: recruitment, structure, timing, and funding. Recruitment is the first crucial component to the success of an FLC because committed people must be brought together who will continue to meet. The structure of the FLC needs to frame the task appropriately to support the momentum of the group's goals. Timing of the meetings must accommodate both the schedules of the group members and the requirements of the FLC's tasks. Finally, finding funding to support those tasks often requires a combination of institutional support and FLC member creativity to be successful.

Logistics

Recruitment

The problem of transfer of learning interested two members at our college, and they sent out informal e-mails to ask whether any other faculty were interested in participating in a transfer of learning FLC at a weeklong faculty retreat/summer institute.

Timing

In year one, the group attended the weeklong institute to do intensive research, focus the problem, and develop a research plan to be enacted over the following year. After that, the group met once each month to work on several research projects. In year two, this group had another weeklong retreat/institute to work on creating modules for content classes to address transfer skills. Members continued to meet in the following year to create materials that could be used in the classroom. Although a number of different timing models would work for this type of group, we believe the intensive week of study at the beginning was an effective way to create momentum on the topic.

Structure

This FLC was, perhaps, the most informally conceived of all the FLCs discussed in this volume since it was an entirely spontaneous event, not initiated by any formal process, nor responsible to any reporting entity. Quite simply, a group of faculty came together to identify a classroom problem, learn about cognitive science, conduct research about the group's questions, and create materials that would be helpful in teaching their classes. Though a leader called the meetings and helped the group to formulate its own goals and next steps, the projects arose organically from exploring the topic, rather than following a facilitator's preset agenda.

Funding

Participants in our group received $2,000 each in faculty development funds for travel and resources, such as books and speakers. This level of funding was helpful for several of the members who presented the group's research results at conferences, and for others who attended conferences to learn more about educational research on transfer. This group could function without funding, provided a facilitator was willing to schedule meetings and serve as a discussion leader.

Our FLC Activities

The work of our transfer FLC was strongly influenced by the general assumptions of higher education as well as the specific mission of our open access, two-year institution. We worked with issues of college readiness, attitudes toward transfer, metacognition, knowledge transfer from course to course, and barriers to transfer. Finally, we applied what we had learned from our research to better understand what skills we could teach that might support transfer.

Understanding Transfer Challenges

Two-year colleges present an interesting context for the study of transfer. Because many of our programs are technical, the assumption that we are preparing our students directly for the workplace is strong. In addition, we struggle with prerequisites as we review and revise our programs. If being "ready for English composition" is a prerequisite for courses in the natural sciences, behavioral sciences, and humanities, then this is a specific expectation of transfer. But what do we expect to transfer, and is it actually working?

Some assumptions we make about transfer include that students bring knowledge from other courses, like prerequisites, into the courses we are teaching. However, the amount of time between courses in a series also seems to be important. At our college, in an assessment of English Composition completed in 2003, we found that of the 330 students who started the English Composition series in the fall, only 100 took the three courses in the sequence consecutively that year. In fact, one student completed English Composition I in 1981, and then waited more than two decades to take English Composition II. Sequences are a problem in other disciplines as well. For example, we have long waiting lists for clinical practice programs. By the time students reach their clinicals, some have difficulty remembering the anatomy and physiology information they need because they took that course so long ago. This is a typical problem in two-year colleges, as students step in and out of their programs, sometimes waiting years before finishing up courses in a sequence.

We are also working with a population that may not be transferring very much knowledge from their high school experiences. At many two-year schools, students take a significant number of developmental courses, completing or repeating high school material. Particular skills seem difficult to transfer. In an English Department assessment of effective writing using yearlong portfolios at our college, for example, we found that over the course of a year, students seemed to do very well in demonstrating practical writing skills such as improving editing and using texts in their research papers. However, they did not do as well with more abstract concepts such as critical thinking and rhetorical awareness. It was also clear from these portfolios that the students who stayed with the same instructor over the course of the series showed more improvement over time. Instructors at two-year colleges need to be particularly mindful of the effects of timing on transfer of learning when they schedule, as many of our students dip in and out of school, or return after years to finish a program.

These findings from the English Department, together with our research in this FLC, highlighted the importance of course sequencing and instructor consistency. We realized how difficult transfer is and how the skills of transfer need explicit support beyond just wanting and expecting it to happen. Other colleges interested in a transfer FLC could look at transfer performance systematically across sequences as we did here to get an understanding of what specific skills students struggle to transfer and to begin institution-wide discussions about promoting them.

Additionally, the FLC could examine other barriers to transfer that might be institution-specific. Our FLC did this as a way to identify what transfer was and what might impede it. Transfer seemed to be most instructors' goal, and yet from anecdotal evidence, our students were not doing it. One of the studies this FLC completed was a survey of faculty and students concerning their attitudes about transfer (Lightner, Benander, & Kramer, 2008). In surveys, students reported that they did not readily perceive the need to transfer knowledge from one course to the next, while faculty surveys indicated contrastingly higher expectations for this transfer. Students also reported that they often perceived individual instructors' demands as idiosyncratic and not demands that other instructors would share. For example, while one instructor might stress the format of an essay, another might emphasize organization over format. Both want good essays, but it seems to students that what a "good" essay is varies from instructor to instructor. Students can come to believe that using the rules from one class in another may be counterproductive. This inhibits transfer of learning. From this study, it was clear that instructors need to make their expectations clear, but they must also articulate how their expectations are shared by other instructors and other courses to help make the connection for students that transfer is not only expected but also beneficial. Surveying faculty and students about transfer expectations might be an enlightening activity for an FLC beginning to investigate this topic.

In addition to getting a picture of attitudes, we tested how much students remembered from the course immediately preceding the one in which they were enrolled to answer the following questions. Do students learn important content from their prerequisites, and does their level of learning match instructors' expectations? Students were given a pretest on the first day of class in the second course of a three-course series. These pretests were based on the final exam the students had taken at the end of the course they had just finished. The average scores for the pretests were compared and sorted according to whether the students were new to the course, or whether they had taken the preceding course with the same professor. The average scores for each category are listed in figure 8.1. The study included 18 biology students, 32 chemistry students, 82 psychology students, and 31 math students.

The same pattern appeared for each discipline. Continuing with the same professor over the entire series of courses may help to promote transfer. As part of the study, the correlation between the pretest data and final grades was computed for both psychology and mathematics. The correlation

FIGURE 8.1

Percent of correct answers on a review of material covered in prerequisite courses with the same professor and with a different professor

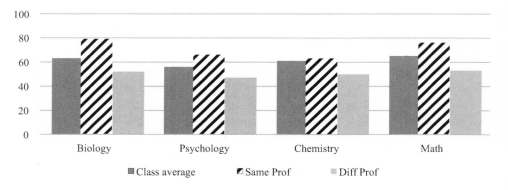

between the pretest scores and students' final class average was $r\,(29)\,=\,0.61$ for the students in the mathematics course and $r\,(79)\,=\,0.67$ for psychology. Students who were more successful in transferring knowledge from one course to the next were also, not surprisingly, more successful in the course. This may be because students are able to see the connection between the first course and the second, or it may be because the instructor knows what she covered in the first course and is assuming that students have the specific background information that she expects. Either way, the students perform better in the second class with the same instructor. An FLC at another institution could encourage pretests to communicate transfer expectations with students or to check on assumptions about what students are transferring in. Furthermore, if the FLC discusses these types of data, instructors are reminded about their often overly optimistic assumptions about what students bring with them from previous classes.

Addressing Transfer-Related Skills

In addition to this research showing that faculty need to make their expectations of transfer explicit, and that practice of the same skills in different contexts can promote transfer, this FLC created a series of activities designed to help first-year students practice basic academic skills across the disciplines. We created these activities because, if faculty in different disciplines had access to short, easy-to-assign and -grade activities, they might incorporate them more readily into their content courses. Then students would be exposed to the same skills in different contexts, increase their use of metacognitive strategies, and perhaps see the connections among their courses. The FLC participants created a series of exercises and compiled them into a handbook from which instructors could choose an assignment that would address the skill required at the moment. Some of the activities included basic academic skills that challenge first-year students—for example, citation format (see Appendix A), defining the discipline (see Appendix B), and graphic representation of the textbook (see Appendix C). Having identified the skills list, the group divided the skills, and each member created a quick activity to address it. The group members agreed on a template to structure each activity for the class, and each activity took no more than 10 minutes of class time. In some cases, the activity can be given as an online assignment or as homework so that class time need not be used. To reinforce and emphasize the importance of the activity to students, it might be effective to award points to the assignment.

Students responded positively to these exercises, particularly when the instructor explained why they were important. For example, in the time management activity, students often commented that they watched too much TV, and they thought they might be able to change that. In a math course, using the graphic text module helps students connect the material from various sections and chapters. Many students remarked that it made them look at the big picture, not just at an individual skill. In a psychology class, students commented after completing "Defining the Discipline" that they were surprised that so much of psychology is not just about mental illnesses or that they had not realized that psychology overlaps so much with biology.

Institutions starting a transfer FLC might be interested in our modules in the appendices, or they might take on the task of creating a workbook of such modules for the skills that meet the students' needs at their own colleges.

Other Changes to Teaching

This FLC could enhance teaching in several important ways. We created the handbook of study skills modules for instructors to use in content classes. Additionally, we designed activities to emphasize the relevance of our concepts to future classes, and we addressed differences in the terminology we used to describe assignments across disciplines. For example, a history instructor expects analysis in a "summary paper," whereas a social scientist expects merely an overview. As a result of these discussions, the participants in the FLC became much more explicit about assignment expectations. In classes, FLC participants ask their students to rehearse concepts in a number of formats with various examples. We remind students of the connections with both previously covered and forthcoming material. Finally, we are more realistic about what we think students are bringing in from other places. Because of this, we state our specific prerequisite expectations, and we offer opportunities for students to remediate when these expectations are not met. For example, students who have difficulty with the technology expectations in a course watch an online video tutorial; students who do not do well on a pretest are given chapters from the previous class's textbook to review.

Suggested Activities for a Transfer FLC

Just discussing the challenge of transfer of learning can move a college forward in terms of the way instructors teach, as they focus on skills that result from classes, rather than just lists of topics and definitions. In addition to these discussions, here are several activities that a transfer FLC might consider to help students.

- Discuss books in cognitive science related to metacognition and transfer—for example, Ambrose et al. (2010) and Willingham (2009).
- Create a college survey of students and faculty about where they expect to use course material or what were their greatest difficulties with transfer of learning.
- Share and compare language in writing assignments. Create a document for students to help them understand disciplinary explanations and writing conventions. Share and compare rubrics.
- List and share instructor expectations for skills and knowledge transferring into and out of courses.
- Explore options for building student metacognitive competence—for example, create monitoring and reflection exercises.
- Hold a concept-mapping session among faculty to explore linkages across disciplines and options for cross-disciplinary guest lecturing and sharing resources among content courses. For example, psychology and anatomy both cover the brain. History and English both spend time on documenting resources. Math and sociology both focus on interpreting correlational data.
- Take the Epistemologic Belief Inventory (Schraw, Bendixen, & Dunkle, 2002) and give it to students to explore beliefs about knowledge that will affect transfer. Examine differences between faculty and students, and across disciplines.

Conclusion

Transfer of learning is central to the mission of most colleges. The success of this FLC lay in the individual members' commitment to the research process. The benefits included presentations and publications as a result of the collaborative research as well as practical course materials to use in the classroom. In addition, as a result of this research, all members of the FLC continue to follow the recommendations of making transfer explicit, making references to how material will be used in other courses, providing early assessments to help students retrieve knowledge from previous courses, and providing multiple opportunities to practice skills in different contexts.

References

Alexander, P. A., & Murphy, P. K. (1999). Nurturing the seeds of transfer: A domain-specific perspective. *International Journal of Educational Research, 31,* 561–576. doi:10.1016/S0883-0355(99)00024-5

Ambrose, S. A., Bridges, M. W., DiPietro, M., Lovett, M. C., & Norman, M. K. (2010). *How learning works: Seven research-based principles for smart teaching.* San Francisco: Jossey-Bass.

Barnett, S., & Ceci, S. (2002). When and where do we apply what we learn? A taxonomy for far transfer. *Psychological Bulletin, 128*(4), 612–637. doi: 10.1037/0033-2909.128.4.612

Case, J., & Gunstone, R. (2002). Metacognitive development as a shift in approach to learning: An in-depth study. *Studies in Higher Education, 27*(4), 459–470. doi:10.1080/0307507022000011561

Cormier, S. M., & Hagman, J. D. (1987). *Transfer of learning.* San Diego: Academic Press.

DeCorte, E. (2003). Transfer as the productive use of acquired knowledge, skills, and motivations. *Current Directions in Psychological Science, 12*(4), 142–146. doi:10.1111/1467-8721.01250

deWinstanley, P. A., & Bjork, R. A. (2002). Successful lecturing: Presenting information in ways that engage effective processing. *New Directions for Teaching and Learning, 89,* 19–31. doi:10.1002/tl.44

Graesser, A. C., Person, N., & Hu, X. (2002). Improving comprehension through discourse processes. *New Directions in Teaching and Learning, 89,* 33–44. doi:10.1002/tl.45

Halpern, D., & Hakel, M. (2003, August). Applying the science of learning. *Change,* 36–41. Retrieved from http://www.jstor.org/stable/40165500

Karpicke, J., & Blunt, J. (2011). Retrieval practice produces more learning than elaborative studying with concept mapping. *Science, 331,* 772–774. doi:10.1126/science.1199327

Lightner, R., Benander, R., & Kramer, E. (2008). Faculty and student attitudes about transfer of learning. *Insight: A Journal of Scholarly Teaching, 3,* 58–66. Retrieved from http://www.insightjournal.net/Volume3/FacultyStudentAttitudes TransferLearning.pdf

Lizarraga, M., Baqueado, M., Mangado, T., & Cardelle-Elawar, M. (2009). Enhancement of thinking skills: Effects of two intervention methods. *Thinking Skills and Creativity, 4,* 30–43. doi:10.1016/j.tsc.2008.12.001

McCombs, B., & Marzano, R. J. (1990). Putting the self in self-regulated learning: The self as agent in integrating will and skill. *Educational Psychologist, 25,* 51–69. doi:10.1207/s15326985ep2501_5

Middendorf, J., & Pace, D. (2004). Decoding the disciplines: A model for helping students learn disciplinary ways of thinking. *New Directions for Teaching and Learning, 98,* 1–12. doi:10.1002/tl.142

Nielsen, K. (2009). A collaborative perspective on learning transfer. *Journal of Workplace Learning, 21*(1), 58–70. doi:10.1108/13665620910924916

Pea, R. D. (1987). Socializing the knowledge transfer problem. *International Journal of Educational Research, 11*, 639–663. doi:10.1016/0883-0355(87)90007-3

Pintrich, P. (1995). Understanding self-regulated learning. *New Directions for Teaching and Learning, 63*, 3–12. doi:10.1002/tl.37219956304

Pressley, M., Van Etten, S., & Freeborn, G. (1998). The metacognition of college studentship: A grounded theory approach. In D. J. Hacker, J. Dunlosky, & A. C. Graesser (Eds.), *Metacognition in educational theory and practice* (pp. 347–366). Mahwah, NJ: Lawrence Erlbaum and Associates.

Rohrer, D., Taylor, K., & Sholar, B. (2010). Tests enhance the transfer of learning. *Journal of Experimental Psychology: Learning, Memory, and Cognition, 36*(1), 233–239. doi:10.1037/a0017678

Salomon, G., & Perkins, D. (1989). Rocky roads to transfer: Rethinking mechanisms of a neglected phenomenon. *Educational Psychologist, 24*(2), 113–142. doi:10.1207/s15326985ep2402_1

Schraw, G., Bendixon, L., & Dunkle, M. (2002). Development and validation of the Epistemic Belief Inventories (EBI). In B. Hofer & P. R. Pintrich (Eds.), *Personal epistemology: The psychology of beliefs about knowledge and knowing* (pp. 261–276). Mahwah, NJ: Lawrence Erlbaum and Associates.

Willingham, D. T. (2009). *Why don't students like school? A cognitive scientist answers questions about how the mind works and what it means for the classroom.* San Francisco: Jossey-Bass.

Winne, P. H., & Hadwin, A. F. (1998). Studying as self-regulated learning. In D. J. Hacker, J. Dunlosky, & A. C. Graesser (Eds.), *Metacognition in educational theory and practice* (pp. 277–304). Mahwah NJ: Lawrence Erlbaum and Associates.

Zimmerman, B. J. (2000). Attaining self-regulation: A social-cognitive perspective. In M. Boekaerts, P. R. Pintrich, & M. Zeidner (Eds.), *Handbook of self-regulation* (pp. 245–262). San Diego: Academic Press.

APPENDIX A
Citation Format Quick Skills Bite

Objectives

- To help students understand that there are different documentation styles.
- To acquaint students with two common documentation styles.

Materials

- Articles used in "Two Kinds of Sources" activity
- Two index cards
- Sample entries for various documentation styles

Time

- In-class explanation: 10–15 minutes
- Out-of-class activity: 10–15 minutes
- Discussion: 15 minutes

Outline

- Have students bring the two articles they found for "Two Kinds of Sources" activity.
- Hand out index cards.
- Ask about students' experience with documentation.
- Explain the documentation style of your discipline.
- Give the assignment.

PROCEDURES AND ACTIVITIES

Explanation

Have students take the two articles they found, the scholarly journal and the popular article. (Hand out two index cards per students.) Ask students if they are familiar with what a citation format is. Ask who is currently taking English Composition or has already taken it. Ask anyone who raises his or her hand what citation format(s) he or she learned in English Composition (the answer should be MLA or APA). Explain what citation format you use in your discipline. Show the students where the information for a citation format is located on the first pages of the journals they did in the last assignment. Explain why it is important to follow the specific format of your discipline.

Assignment

Use one index card for each article. Have students write the citation for each article in MLA format on one side of the card. On the other side of the index card, have them write the citation for each article in the citation format appropriate to your discipline. Tell students to use their English Composition handbook or to find the citation style online. (Faculty may refer to the sample entries attached, but students should be asked to locate this information.)

Product: For each student, you will have two index cards, one for each article, with the MLA citation on one side and the discipline-specific citation on the other side.

Suggestions for Further Integration

- A week before a research paper is due, ask for the citation page. Have peers compare and proof each other's citation pages.
- Have students search for three articles that interest them. Have students write an annotated reference page.

APPENDIX B
Defining the Discipline Quick Skills Bite

Objectives

- To help students examine what they already know about the discipline.
- To have students learn more about the discipline.

Time

- In-class activity: 15–20 minutes
- Out-of-class activity: 30–60 minutes
- Discussion: 15 minutes

Outline

- Brainstorm descriptions of the discipline.
- Distill responses.
- Give the assignment.
- Discuss the researched descriptions.

PROCEDURES AND ACTIVITIES

Explanation

This activity should be done in weeks one or two of the quarter. Ask students what they think your discipline is about. Write their responses on the board. Distill these responses into a brief description. (You might have to bite your tongue a bit during this initial part of the exercise.)

Take-Home Activity

Ask students to go on the Internet using both websites through Google and the library. Ask them to look at different sites that relate to your discipline, and at .com, .org, and .edu sites. (You may need to explain how these types of sites differ.)

Ask students to write a two- to three-sentence description of the discipline. When they hand them in, compare them to the descriptions the students came up with when you initially asked the question. You might coach them to a description you are comfortable with.

Suggestions for Further Integration

- Ask for an outline of specialties in your discipline.
- Ask students to write a reflection on how their perception of the discipline has changed based on the initial definition, their research, and the ensuing class discussion. Have them outline how their view has changed.

DEFINING THE DISCIPLINE WORKSHEET

Look at the different Internet sites that relate to the discipline of _____.
Find and list the title (one of each) of the three types of Internet sites.

?.org _____

?.com _____

?.edu _____

Based upon the classroom group activity and what you find on the websites, write a two- to three-sentence description of the discipline of _____.

APPENDIX C

Graphic Representation of the
Textbook Quick Skills Bite

Objectives

- To make students aware of how knowledge is presented and organized in the course text.
- To make students aware of how they can use the various forms of information presented in the text.

Materials

- The course text

Time

- In-class quiz: 10 minutes
- Out-of-class activity: 30 minutes
- Discussion: 10 minutes

Outline

- Give an overview of chapter organization in the text.
- Demonstrate how to graphically represent the information organization.
- Have students outline a chapter of the text and indicate how they can use the different forms of organization.
- Conduct follow-up discussion of how the chapter they outlined can be used for the day's discussion and for the upcoming test.

PROCEDURES AND ACTIVITIES

This activity should be done in week one or two of the quarter. Have students take out their primary text for the class. Explain how you expect them to use the text with reference to lectures, discussions, and tests in this class.

Explanation

Textbooks present different kinds of information in different ways. Among the many ways information can be presented are headings, subheadings, boxes, graphs, and sidebars. You read and use this information in different ways. Explain how you expect the different kinds of information to be used for lectures, labs, or tests.

Writing Assignment Option

For the next class meeting, make a graphic representation of the different kinds of information available in the assigned reading. It can be done by hand, in PowerPoint, or in Word. You can collect the assignments, or you can ask that they be posted as attachments on your Blackboard site in a discussion board designated for these outlines.

Group Activity

In small groups discuss how individuals used the text to prepare for the day's activities. Discuss how the information in the chapter might be used to prepare for the next test. Have small groups share their pictures of the chapter.

9

LEARNING TECHNOLOGY IN A COMMUNITY

Design Your Own Spring Break

Rhonda Berger and Patrick Nellis

An online speech instructor greets her class several times each week with a personalized video and screencast review of an assignment, a reminder, or sometimes just, "Hello, I hope all is well." An English instructor has created animated characters to deliver reminders about deadlines and other course news. Another professor meets his class a couple of times each semester for virtual field trips in the 3D online world called Second Life. Twitter, blogs, *Jeopardy!* games, and interactive websites are becoming commonly used tools for faculty in many face-to-face and online classes.

What do all these instructors have in common? They are all searching for engaging ways to enhance instruction for today's students, and they have participated in a short-term technology faculty learning community (FLC) at Miami Dade College (MDC), called Design Your Own Spring Break. This FLC was designed to equip faculty with current technology tools, empower them to use these tools to improve teaching, and build a supportive community for technology exploration. The FLC can be modified easily and reproduced at other two-year colleges and can be used as a vehicle for advancing technology, collegiality, and student learning. This FLC provides an opportunity for faculty to propose projects using new technologies to enhance instruction and get the time, tools, and support needed for creating learning innovations. It provides a respite and a renewal of sorts as participants learn, engage with one another, and experiment with new technologies in a nonthreatening and supportive atmosphere. Instructors who participate typically display a renewed enthusiasm for being in the role of learner and have a desire to continue to explore and learn. As one member said after participating in the first seminar, "Now I want to improve, advance, and implement my new skills, after which I want to 'return to the well' for a wider range of content and skills."

When the technology FLC was first designed, it was conceptualized as a seminar; however, the structure, emphasizing faculty support and control, as well as the embedded peer collaboration and support, helped transform this annual event into an FLC. Faculty members who have participated have continued to support each other and provide innovative technology leadership. This kind of community and reciprocal mentoring is at the heart of any well-run FLC—even a short-term one.

This technology FLC has demonstrated to the organizers that a successful faculty development program to encourage and facilitate the adoption of instructional technology is not built around a one-size-fits-all model. The themes that have emerged from our post-FLC surveys convince us that individualization matters. Participants in the FLC remarked on a variety of essential characteristics, including choice and a customized learning experience based on skill level; time, tools, and technical assistance; and recognition and support from the institution and colleagues.

Review of Literature

It has been nearly 15 years since Terry O'Banion (1997) published his manifesto on *A Learning College for the 21st Century*, which called for community colleges to meet the new demand for anytime, anyplace modes of instruction and learning. Two-year colleges are still struggling to realize this vision. These colleges are the point of access to higher education for those who need it most: minority, low-income, and first-generation college students, and workers in need of training for new skills. O'Banion called for the two-year college to create a new model of education, "one that incorporates the best practices and philosophies of its past with the expanding base of new knowledge about learning and technology" (p. 47). Recently, the U.S. Department of Education (2010) called for "applying the advanced technologies used in our daily personal and professional lives to our entire education system to improve student learning," (p. v). Community colleges, in particular, bear an enormous responsibility for meeting this goal because we educate half of all college students in the country—and our half is the group most in need of technological skills, in part because of limited access in their homes and previous school experiences. As the League for Innovation documented in its study, *Access in the Information Age: Community Colleges Bridging the Digital Divide* (de los Santos, de los Santos, & Milliron, 2001), the community college is the best hope for our workforce to gain access to the jobs available in the new knowledge- and technology-based economy. The challenges addressed by a technology FLC include how to use technology to teach content and familiarize students with new digital learning tools. For most of our faculty, the technology FLC provides an exciting professional learning opportunity, and it can do this for faculty at other two-year institutions hoping to implement a similar FLC.

Two-year colleges across the country are adjusting to the wide-ranging changes that information technology is bringing to teaching and learning, and a new educational landscape is emerging. Professors from all disciplines are scrambling to learn new tools and to understand the changes technology is bringing to their disciplines. In a review of faculty development programs around the country, Moore, Fowler, and Watson (2007) identified several best practices for supporting and encouraging participation in faculty development that leads to change: implementing adult learning practices; offering incentives to participate; delivering workshops; using colleagues and peers; and providing ongoing support. These practices, combined with an atmosphere of trust and rewards for risk taking, will enable necessary and transformational changes to take place.

In addition to these features of effective faculty professional development, Yilmazel-Sahin and Oxford (2010) found that technology development models that integrate faculty choice and involve faculty directly in planning and implementing are the most effective in a broad comparative analysis of various studies and programs. While most research focuses on one model or a specific example of faculty development, this study organized seven faculty development models for integrating instructional technologies into three broad categories: workshops, mentoring, and university-school collaborations. According to these researchers, mentoring models and collaboration models were the most effective because they (a) involve faculty in the planning and implementation and choosing the technology skills to be acquired; (b) increase the comfort levels in using technology in their courses; (c) allow participants to develop skills at their own pace; and (d) offer individualized assistance and support.

The heavy investment in infrastructure to support the addition of instructional technology has not always translated into transformative educational models. This type of major overhaul is needed to meet the changing needs of today's students. Many faculty remain resistant to change. In addition, early adopters (EAs) and those identified as mainstream technology users need training and support (Zayim, Yildirim, & Saka, 2006). Initial theories of acceptance and rejection of technology in education help explain reluctance to using technology, even today. EAs favor revolutionary change, have a strong technology focus, and are seen as visionaries and risk takers (Rogers, 1995). Mainstream faculty (MF), on the other hand, favor evolutionary change, are problem-oriented, and are seen as conservative and risk avoiders.

In a study that classified faculty training needs by their technology competence, Zayim and colleagues (2006) found that EAs and MF have different needs in training and support. MF prefer formal training, while EAs prefer working with outside professionals and studying advanced topics. The EA group is more likely to consist of junior assistant professors in the 20- to 40-year-old age range who have significantly higher self-efficacy for computer use. Both EA faculty and MF in this study listed lack of reward structure and training opportunities as barriers to adoption, and the MF group listed lack of training at a slightly higher rate. The EA group was more likely to value outside resources such as outside consultants or vendor training, and the MF group rated one-on-one help as the most valuable. Both Baby Boomers and Gen-Xers populate higher education's existing faculty ranks, and they have different needs and different expectations for training and support for instructional technology. The technology FLC addresses this diversity of needs and expectations by offering a program that can be tailored to any skill level.

Other institutions have also developed successful technology FLCs. Moore, Moore, and Fowler (2005) report that at Virginia Tech, the Faculty Development Institute has provided a continuous cycle of development and support at various levels for more than a decade. While early development consisted of programs to introduce technologies and reduce faculty anxiety, more recent programs address instant communication, social networking, and Web resources for use in classes. Participants gave positive feedback about the use of faculty facilitators and the important role they play in the overall success of the FLC. Beyond the technical help from the professional support trainers, faculty peers helped each other sort out ways to use technology to deepen learning. Faculty contributions to the institute included examples and personal narratives about implementation (Moore, Moore, & Fowler, 2005). Our FLC at MDC has had similar positive results because of our use of faculty facilitators who not only deliver training but also assist in the development labs, helping participants transform the new technology skills into instructional modules. Previous attendees often return as facilitators, adding a peer support richness to the technical assistance structure, thus transforming our short-term Design Your Own Spring Break experience into a collaborative FLC.

Learning to meet the needs of today's technology-savvy students entails a pedagogical shift that requires reexamining the faculty role. While some technology FLC participants embrace becoming learners as they discover and apply new instructional technologies, others need more guidance, training, and encouragement. Moreover, increasing expectations of faculty without providing them with adequate training and support can lead to poor results. The University of South Carolina's Center for Teaching Excellence surveyed 197 faculty members and found that providing a variety of seminars, workshops, online and one-on-one trainings, and communities of practice all were valued, though this varied by individual (Crews, Miller, & Brown, 2009). The survey revealed barriers and challenges that included time constraints for preparing new lectures that integrate technology and for learning new technology to implement it effectively, and lack of knowledge about new and available technologies. A well-designed technology FLC addresses many of the challenges identified in this review of literature by providing dedicated time for faculty to learn and develop a technology project of their choice, technology training and support during the event, and an ongoing community of practice centered around shared technology interests or disciplines.

Faculty Development and the Mission of the College

Faculty development is central to the two-year college teaching mission, and this is true at MDC. The college invests in faculty training and seeks to spur creativity and innovation in teaching. Providing professional development for faculty is a crucial element in the MDC Strategic Plan, and professional development is also included in the faculty contract as a requirement to maintain faculty rank or to progress toward promotion. One of the areas in which faculty development is quite needed is the realm of technology, including, but not limited to, instructional design for online delivery methods. In 2002 the Learning Innovation initiative at MDC, a faculty-led program to support innovation at the college, recommended an intensive, project-based learning opportunity for faculty to occur during the week between spring and summer terms, and this began our technology FLC.

Design of FLC

In 2003 MDC created the Design Your Own Spring Break Technology FLC. This FLC assisted faculty at various levels of expertise to complete a project of their choice and to receive the necessary training and one-on-one assistance during an intensive, collaborative experience.

In the years since, more than 240 participants have successfully completed the technology FLC and created a variety of projects that have enhanced instruction at the college. Last year we offered 28 workshops and three development labs to serve 31 faculty members who participated in the community. Five trainers and seven lab technicians provided the one-on-one assistance as faculty designed their own training and development schedule. The sessions focused on new technologies such as lecture capture, virtual worlds learning opportunities, interactive online lessons, and collaborative Web 2.0 technologies. The event culminates each year in a showcase on the fourth day during which participants share their learning and projects with each other, department chairpersons, and other academic leaders. Facilitators request audience feedback on each session in the showcase, which is eventually given to each presenter. One showcase participant said, "It is always amazing to watch the transformation of each faculty member from the often timid learner during the seminar to the confident and newly empowered instructor once they are on stage demonstrating their project."

Any two-year college interested in designing a short-term technology FLC should consider participants' interests and needs. In our FLC, choice is central, from the initial project proposal through workshop selection and development time. Participants apply and propose a project that must be completed during the FLC and implemented by the following fall semester. When applying, faculty assess their current technology skill level and list the training they think they will need to complete their project. See Appendix A for a sample application form. An instructional designer reviews each project to ensure that it can be completed. Each year, FLC facilitators select 30 applicants, giving priority to first-time participants and attempting to balance campus and discipline representation. After that, selection is by lottery.

Early FLC cohorts included many participants who defined themselves as "technologically challenged," and projects were designed to meet their skill levels. These simple projects often included templates and easy-to-use tools. Projects have changed over the years, but the structure and the support for all skill levels continue. Participants are required to complete the training (including from three to 12 hours of workshops) and the original project that was proposed, but most far exceed their own expectations and incorporate many other technologies as they are exposed to new tools and share ideas with colleagues. Participants typically are enthused and eager for more opportunities to learn new skills. An early participant in our FLC said, "The seminar was amazing! It provided me the opportunity to explore the latest technologies available at that time and ways to incorporate them into my curricula. I can only imagine what types of things are available now!"

Once selections are made, the technology team and FLC facilitators review the project and design the schedule. Since the technology FLC is held during spring break, when classes are not in session, computer labs and other facilities are usually available. We reserve five computer labs and install special software to support the training and development requests. In addition, we hold concurrent training sessions in three labs on days one and two, and reserve day three for project development, with optional workshops as needed. Each hour-long workshop is hands on, with the focus on software, demonstration, and some guided instruction. After that, participants move to one of two development labs to get more practice and one-on-one assistance from the lab technicians. Last year, 28 workshops were held on a variety of Web 2.0 and interactive Web technologies. (See Appendix B for a sample of each day's schedule.) The hosting campus's support is crucial to assist with software installation and other technical support.

The culminating event of the week is the showcase. Participants present a short demonstration of their project, focusing on what they learned and how they will incorporate the project and new skills into instruction. In the first FLC cohort, the faculty members were asked to showcase their projects in small groups in different rooms. However, it soon became evident that the design of the showcase needed to change to one large event as participants were anxious to see and share their projects with everyone. Sharing accomplishments during the showcase continues to be a highlight of the event. Invitations are sent to other faculty, chairpersons, and academic leaders at the college. Each year this event has grown and has become an ever more popular venue for sharing and celebrating teaching and learning. Often the chairperson wants more faculty in his or her department to see what was presented at the showcase, so many FLC members present their projects again at departmental meetings.

Projects

In the earliest days of the FLC, many projects consisted of the faculty member's first Web page and links to resources on the Web for their students.

Others used the animation tools in PowerPoint and learned how to create interactive presentations that went way beyond sliding bullets. Other Power-Point projects included the creation of *Jeopardy!* games and other interactive game-show-style activities on topics such as writing skills, biology, math, and more. Participants created animated and multimedia presentations on a range of topics, from famous plays, symbolism, and parabola equations in the real world, to Cannibal Island, an interactive task-based project that predated the television show *Survivor*. Recent seminars have focused on emerging and Web 2.0 technologies. Five examples of technologies that participants have used recently are described in the following sections.

Web 2.0 Technologies

One recent participant set a goal to explore collaborative and other emerging technologies that would work for her English as a Second Language (ESL) students. She explored a variety of tools and created several projects, including a humorous Xtranormal video that introduces students to the speech lab requirements with the use of animated characters. "This is something I cover over and over in class. Now I will send it out to be viewed as homework. I'll be curious to know if two cartoons saying the same thing I go over and over might hold their attention more," she said of the video. She also created a Jing screen capture orientation to her course in the learning management system used at the college.

Lecture Capture

Several participants have used the Panopto lecture capture software to capture video, PowerPoint, and/or screen images. One professor created a lecture on memoir writing focusing on the book *Tuesdays with Morrie*. She uses this lecture in her face-to-face, blended, and fully online courses. Students can view it as many times as needed and use the search function to review certain topics as they prepare to write their own memoirs. She has noticed improved scores on test answers related to this lecture.

SoftChalk Interactive Web Pages

The last technology FLC introduced SoftChalk, an authoring tool for developing engaging online content. This software allows faculty to create content and exercises that can be embedded in online lesson pages or uploaded to the learning management system grade book. Online learning material developed using this tool can be used to supplement classroom work or for distance-learning courses. SoftChalk provides an engaging way to present lessons and a variety of tools to create practice activities to reinforce retention, including puzzles, drag-and-drop activities, matching, and more. FLC projects using this authoring tool included a lesson on medical errors for medical students; an interactive tutorial on American Psychological Association (APA) style developed by a librarian; and activities for language learning with immediate feedback.

Second Life

Many colleges have created their own space or island for exploring and using this 3D virtual world for instructional purposes. Miami Dade College has created MDC Island, which consists of virtual classroom space, meeting areas, and learning tools. A faculty librarian created an activity to introduce visitors to the Sistine Chapel, all connected to the MDC Island. She also created a field trip kit to help visitors to our island transport to Vassar College's Second Life version of the Sistine Chapel and provided information and resources such as notecards and YouTube videos. Vassar College's realistic 3D reproduction of the Sistine Chapel is a popular Second Life destination. The 2010 participant commented about the benefit of this technology: "[I]n some ways [it is] better than visiting the real thing because in Second Life you can actually fly and get a real close-up view of the painting."

Tablet and Mobile Computing

The FLC has helped faculty develop ideas for using iPads, tablets, and other mobile devices. Participants use SoftChalk and other tools to develop lessons using these devices. The FLC facilitators realize that this is a growth area and will require attention for future FLC cohorts.

Evaluation

The technology FLC has expanded technology-based teaching innovations across the college. This model has proven to be a reliable vehicle for professional development. The overall quality of the seminar was rated as "excellent" by 95% of last year's participants. Most either strongly agreed (91%) or agreed (9%) that they were able to demonstrate expertise in at least three new technologies and apply new skills in a learning module. Incorporating feedback from peers, discipline experts, and technology coaches into their final projects was seen as significant by 86% of the respondents. Although data have not been collected on overall effectiveness of the FLC on student learning directly, many faculty have reported improved performance as a result of something they learned or created. One FLC participant, a biology professor, said, "I also created an assignment in VoiceThread for my students. After starting to use this assignment to teach students about different types of cells, their grades on this specific component of the course have improved."

Recognition for the MDC technology FLC was not simply institution-wide. The *Chronicle of Higher Education*'s 2010 Great Colleges to Work for Survey named MDC and indicated that the technology FLC was one of the reasons the college received high marks (Mangan, 2011). Internal endorsements as well as external recognition promote the FLC and make sure that the college commitment to the FLC remains strong.

Resources Needed

Whereas many other types of FLCs can be implemented fairly inexpensively, a technology FLC will require considerable resources. The FLC's biggest expense is connected to personnel. The key features of the experience are the extensive training, instructional design, and technical support. MDC assigns all technical training and design staff in its College Training and Development Department to the weeklong technology FLC. Our FLC requires three to four trainers/instructional designers and seven lab technicians to staff three concurrent workshop tracks and three development labs. Additionally, other trainers have been hired for two or three training sessions when special expertise is required. Technical personnel at the campus often assist with software installation and other support, including any network or media issues that might arise. We have found that the best participant-to-support personnel ratio is 3:1. Another expense is compensation for the members, who receive $500 for their participation. Lunch and breaks are also required for participants and personnel for the week. The final showcase session usually includes coffee and continental breakfast for participants and guests. Any college adapting this FLC will have to have sufficient lab and space facilities—for example, we use five labs to allow for concurrent sessions and breakouts.

This model could be adapted and a similar FLC built on a smaller scale at a lower cost. Faculty facilitators and media support personnel could be asked to volunteer, and fewer projects and participants could also cut down on costs of training, stipends, and food. As long as faculty can propose and create their own learning path, get the time and support needed, and work together, this vibrant FLC could work in a scaled-down format.

Community Building: Recognition and Support

One of the unexpected outcomes of this project was the informal FLCs that occurred during the event and continued beyond the seminar. On the first day, small groups of four to five participants with similar projects meet with an instructional designer who assists in recommending a training plan. During the seminar, faculty spend many hours together in the labs and often group together and seek each other out for assistance and support because the labs are also divided up by project type. This cross-disciplinary interaction often is cited as a seminar highlight. One participant responded, "It [the cross-disciplinary interaction] is vital; it's very helpful to see what other instructors have already tried and what worked or did not work well; it is also helpful to hear suggestions from colleagues about what tools/methods work best in their classrooms." Another participant added, "I always welcome the opportunity to meet and hear from faculty teaching in other disciplines. I teach ESL, and talking to my colleagues in the disciplines helps me get a sense of what my students will be facing after they leave our ESL program. I also hear from them about how our former students are doing in their programs."

Another facet of the community created by participation is the spread of the culture of technology collaboration beyond the participants. Members often finish the FLC and become technology leaders in their departments and continue to share their enthusiasm and technology skills with their colleagues. One such participant said, "Now, thanks to the seminar, I am a member of the technology committee, and we are organizing a symposium for our colleagues. Also I have shared a lot of information in the science retreat." Members of the FLC often become informal trainers for their peers and teach others how to use some of the innovative learning technologies they have discovered. "I have taught many of my colleagues how to use Delicious.com. Overall I think this experience really helps keep faculty up to date regarding technology. Technology moves very quickly so it is important for faculty to share with each other what they know. It helps us all stay 'updated.' "

Closing Thoughts: Spring Break as a Pilgrimage

A short-term technology FLC creates a temporary community that is outside of the normal college work structures. Faculty members are freed from their regimented schedules, and they leave their roles as teachers in order to become learners again, able to follow their own vision for new ways to use technology to engage students. In many ways the experience approximates the anthropological concept of "communitas," which denotes a temporary sense of community outside the normal social structure in which participants enjoy an equality that is not present in daily affairs (Turner, 1974). For instance, during this FLC, normal roles are reversed as faculty become students, and all participants interact as equals, without concern for degree, rank, discipline, or other status markers. The instructional designers and lab technicians are the guides on this faculty pilgrimage to find new ways to teach, which is ultimately a quest for renewed interest and commitment to the profession. It would be hard to imagine sustaining a long career as a two-year college professor without opportunities like the technology FLC to create a time out of the normal structure—a time to learn instead of teach. The formal showcase event that provides the endpoint to the journey follows all of the normal academic presentation rituals and allows faculty to share their vision for new teaching techniques in their own courses, display what they have brought back from the pilgrimage to invigorate their practices, and reenter the everyday college structure of teaching and learning.

References

Crews, T. B., Miller, J. L., & Brown, C. M. (2009). Assessing faculty's technology needs. *EDUCAUSE Quarterly, 32*(4). Retrieved from http://www.educause.edu/EDUCAUSE + Quarterly/EDUCAUSEQuarterlyMagazineVolum/Assessing FacultysTechnologyNee/192969

de los Santos, G. E., de los Santos, J. A., & Milliron, M. D. (2001). *Access in the information age: Community colleges bridging the digital divide.* Mission Viejo, CA: League for Innovation in the Community College.

Mangan, K. (2011, July 24). Some colleges earn and A+ in career development. *Chronicle of Higher Education.* Retrieved from http://www.chronicle.com/article/Three-Colleges-Earn-an-A-in/128299/

Moore, A. H., Fowler, S. B., & Watson, C. E. (2007, September/October). Active learning and technology: Designing change for faculty, students, and institutions. *EDUCAUSE Review, 42*(5), 42–61. Retrieved from http://www.educause.edu/EDUCAUSE + Review/ERVolume422007/EDUCAUSEReviewMagazineVol ume42/161905

Moore, A. H., Moore, J. F., & Fowler, S. B. (2005). *Faculty development for the net generation.* (D. G. Oblinger, & J. L. Oblinger, Eds.) Educause. Retrieved from http://www.educause.edu/Resources/EducatingtheNetGeneration/FacultyDevelopmentfortheNetGen/6071

O'Banion, T. (1997). *A learning college for the 21st century.* Phoenix, AZ: American Council on Education and Oryx Press.

Rogers, E. (1995). *Diffusion of innovations.* New York: Free Press.

Turner, V. (1974). *Dramas, fields and metaphors: Symbolic action in human society.* Ithaca, NY: Cornell University Press.

U.S. Department of Education. (2010). Transforming American education: Learning powered by technology. Washington, DC: U.S. Department of Education. Retrieved from http://www.ed.gov/sites/default/files/netp2010.pdf

Yilmazel-Sahin, Y., & Oxford, R. L. (2010). A comparative analysis of teacher education faculty development models for technology integration. *Journal of Technology and Teacher Education, 18*(4), 693–720.

Zayim, N., Yildirim, S., & Saka, O. (2006). Technology adoption of medical faculty in teaching: Differentiating factors in adopter categories. *Educational Technology & Society, 9*(2), 213–222.

Design Your Own Spring Break 2010

Application due by _____

Technology-Enhanced Lesson

First Name	Last Name
Department	E-mail
Chairperson (for Showcase Invitation)	

Campus:

Lesson or Project Title:

Lesson Description (Describe what the lesson entails and what technology will be used to enhance this lesson.):

Lesson Objectives (Please list two or three objectives.):

At the end of this lesson, my students will be able to . . .

Lesson Assessment Plan (How will you assess the students' learning of the lesson? Although this may not be part of the actual project, the application needs to indicate how the learning will be assessed.):

Which of the MDC Learning Outcomes does your lesson plan address?

What Course Competency will your lesson plan address?

How will the project benefit student learning?

Describe type(s) of technologies the lesson needs (How will the seminar expand your learning in terms of applying technology skills in instruction?):

Training Plan (What skills [workshops] do you need to learn to complete the project?):

Check your current technology level. Necessary prerequisite skills will depend on the scope of the project. All skill levels are welcome.

I have basic Web skills.	I have created a Web page.	I use e-mail with students.
I use the Internet with students.	I use PowerPoint in my class.	I use graphics software.
I use ANGEL.	I have created a podcast.	I have used Second Life.
I have used social media (Blog, Wiki, Twitter, Facebook) application(s) in my instruction—for example:	I have created interactive activities for students using Studymate, Hot Potatoes, or other applications.	I have used Panopto, Lecture Capture, or other screen capture applications.

Other technology skills:

If you have created a Web page, please provide the Web address:

Have you attended a Spring Break Seminar before?

Have you attended more than once before?

APPENDIX B
Sample Schedule of Supporting Workshops

Day One			
8:30 am–12:15 pm	Introduction Demonstrations Individual Consultations		
12:15 pm–1:00 pm	Lunch		
	Room 1	Room 2	Room 3
1:00 pm–2:00 pm	Interactive PowerPoint	SoftChalk 1	Jing Screen Capture
2:15 pm–3:15 pm	Instructional Games	SoftChalk 2	Lecture Capture 1
3:30 pm–4:30 pm	Prezi Presentations	Twitter in the Classroom	Lecture Capture 2
Day Two			
8:45 am–9:45 am	Learning Objects 1	Softchalk 1	Lecture Capture 1
10:00 am–11:00 am	Learning Objects 2	Softchalk 2	Second Life Overview
11:15 am–12:15 pm	Finding Free Images	Xtranormal	Camtasia
12:15 pm–1:00 pm	Lunch		
1:00 pm–2:00 pm	Finding Podcasts	Google Docs	ANGEL Assessments
2:15 pm–3:15 pm	Web 2.0	Google Sites	StudyMate Games
3:30 pm–4:30 pm	Prezi Presentation	Free Tools	YouTube Channels
Day Three			
8:45 am–9:45 am	Optional iPad Demo		
8:45 am–4:30 pm	Development Lab	Development Lab	

10

THE TEACHER SCHOLAR
INQUIRY GROUP

Building a Teaching Commons Among
Two-Year and Four-Year Faculty

Ellen Lynch and Margaret Cheatham

> What is fascinating is that as you analyze that teaching . . . you see that it isn't just someone who has mastered a set of teaching tricks, it's not just process. And it's not just someone who has a deep knowledge of the subject matter. Neither one of those is sufficient. What we see in great teaching is the masterful intersection of the two. Someone who really understands the subject deeply and understands how exquisitely complex it is to make your knowledge accessible to the knowing processes of those who do not yet understand. (Shulman, 1989, p. 11)

How frequently do faculty members have opportunities to engage in meaningful discussions about teaching? All too often conversations about pedagogy occur sporadically as one instructor stands in the office doorway of another or during the last few minutes before a committee meeting is to begin. While there is no doubt that informal, unscheduled exchanges with colleagues can be valuable, they rarely permit the time or space we need to engage in truly significant conversation that leads to the transformation of one's instruction.

Traditionally, faculty members have gone about their planning and implementation of teaching with few formalized opportunities to discuss their practices, concerns, and questions with colleagues outside or even within their own discipline. Lee Shulman (2004), former president of the

Carnegie Foundation for the Advancement of Teaching, describes his naïve assumptions about the professoriate as a new faculty member. His expectations were that his life as an instructor would include interaction with others as part of a community, both inside and outside the classroom, and that as a researcher, his time would be spent in isolated scholarly pursuits. In fact, he found quite the opposite to be true:

> We experience isolation not in the stacks but in the classroom. We close the classroom door and experience pedagogical solitude, whereas in our life as scholars, we are members of active communities: communities of conversation, communities of evaluation, communities in which we gather with others in our invisible colleges to exchange our findings, our methods, and our excuses. (p. 140)

Shulman further contends that it is this pedagogical solitude, or the separation of our teaching lives from our scholarly lives in which our questions and practices are discussed and evaluated by colleagues, that has led to greater value or reward being attached to research and less to teaching. Moreover, because teaching has remained a private activity to some degree, few established procedures or processes exist for providing faculty with forums for in-depth, protracted discussion of teaching practices and how these affect their students' learning, or for sharing ideas with peers whose own pedagogical practice might be enriched by this information (Huber & Hutchings, 2005).

As we consider the implications of this isolation and the need to move discussions of teaching into the realm of what Shulman (2004) calls "community property," many questions arise. For example, given the significant time constraints most faculty experience, how do we find the time to engage in meaningful conversation about scholarly teaching over time? How can we promote the perspective that teaching is a scholarly endeavor worthy of our examination, evaluation, and reflection? How can we ensure that these discussions encourage self-reflection and ultimately lead to transformation of our teaching?

It is a developing sense of pedagogical solitude experienced by the authors of this chapter and like-minded colleagues, as well as the desire to engage in deep thinking about scholarly teaching, that led to the formation of a unique faculty learning community at our institution—the Teacher Scholar Inquiry Group (TSIG). For us, TSIG has become our "pedagogical oasis in the desert" and what Huber and Hutchings (2005) have called a "teaching commons."

Review of the Literature

> When educators pursue inquiry in the company of students and colleagues, they begin to create a "teaching commons" on their campus—a set of interconnected forums where conversations about learning take place, where innovations in curriculum and pedagogy get tried out, and where questions and answers about education are exchanged, critiqued, and built upon. (Huber, 2008, p. 2)

The Teaching Commons

According to Ernest L. Boyer's (1990) landmark report, *Scholarship Reconsidered: Priorities of the Professoriate*, teaching is viewed in the academy as a routine activity, an addendum to the "real" work of the faculty member—scholarship. Boyer asserts, however, that teaching is a scholarly endeavor, and as such, it is the responsibility of professional educators to engage in rigorous discussion and study of the quality of their pedagogy and its impact on their students' lives.

Shulman (2005) identifies ambitious goals for those who are working to transform thinking about the value of teaching:

> to build knowledge about teaching and learning in the classroom; to transform our education institutions so that they support and encourage a scholarly approach to improvement; to invent new forms of documentation that better represent the intellectual work of teaching; to develop models of classroom inquiry that balance concreteness with the possibility of generalization; and to advance visions of what's possible for student learning that matters. (p. vi)

While these ambitions may appear somewhat daunting, Shulman contends that progress toward achieving these goals can be made by supporting smaller initiatives as an institution works toward building its own teaching commons over time.

Huber and Hutchings (2005) first coined the term *teaching commons* to refer to a conceptual space in which "communities of educators committed to pedagogical inquiry and innovation come together to exchange ideas about teaching and learning, and use them to meet the challenges of educating students for personal, professional, and civic life in the twenty-first century" (p. x). The teaching commons can be thought of more narrowly as small groups of faculty on one campus who meet to discuss and systematically investigate questions surrounding pedagogy, and more broadly, as the global community of teacher scholars who conduct this work and engage in conversations at conferences and contribute the results of their inquiry through presentations, publications, and websites (Huber, 2008). The teaching commons also facilitates and supports the scholarship of teaching and learning (SoTL) in which faculty engage in systematic study of their teaching and student learning and share the outcomes of their inquiry with colleagues. In short, the teaching commons supports the development of teaching in higher education as a discipline worthy of discussion, scholarly investigation, and critique in the same way that the "academic commons" supports efforts in scientific, disciplinary-based research (Huber & Hutchings, 2006).

Faculty Learning Communities and Faculty Inquiry Groups

One of the many challenges those seeking to establish a teaching commons on campus face is to identify how best to provide a framework that supports faculty discussion and investigation of questions related to teaching and learning. Huber & Hutchings (2005) suggest that as part of the development of the teaching commons, "structures and occasions are needed to bring people together on campus for sustained, substantive, constructive discussion about learning and how to improve it" (p. 119). While there is no single method or approach for providing these opportunities, a robust body of literature on faculty learning communities (FLCs) and faculty inquiry groups (FIGs) does exist that can inform the process.

Faculty Learning Communities

The value of faculty learning communities to support scholarly teaching, SoTL, and student learning has been discussed in-depth by Cox (2001). The manner in which FLCs are implemented and managed on each campus may differ; however, there is general agreement about what constitutes such a group. According to Beach and Cox (2009), faculty learning communities include "8–12 faculty (and, sometimes, professional staff and graduate students) engaged in an active, collaborative, yearlong curriculum focused on enhancing and assessing undergraduate learning with frequent activities that promote learning, development, SoTL, and community" (p. 9). The authors further identify two basic types of FLCs: cohort-based and topic-based. Cohort-based communities provide opportunities for specific groups of individuals, such as junior or senior faculty, department heads, or adjunct faculty, to address those teaching and learning topics that are most relevant to their needs. On the other hand, as the name suggests, the work of topic-based FLCs focuses on specific interest areas related to teaching and learning that might include subjects such as integrating service learning into a class, redesigning courses, understanding student motivation, conducting undergraduate research, using active learning in history classes, or implementing electronic portfolios.

Certainly, FLCs can provide the "structures and occasions" for faculty discussion, collaboration and knowledge construction that are essential components of developing a teaching commons. A similar type of professional development group, the faculty inquiry group, provides another strategy by which instructors can discuss and investigate their questions about teaching and learning.

Faculty Inquiry Groups

While most members of FLCs take part in various forms of inquiry, the FIG model presented here is that used by the Carnegie Foundation for the Advancement of Teaching as part of its Strengthening Pre-collegiate Education in Community Colleges (SPECC) project. According to Huber (2008),

> The core work of faculty inquiry involves instructors asking questions about the teaching and learning that goes on in their own classrooms; seeking answers by consulting the literature, gathering and analyzing evidence, and engaging students in the process whenever possible; using what they find out to improve the experience of their students; and sharing this work with colleagues so that they and their students can benefit too. Usually, questioning begins with a problem the instructor has perceived— something that's not going right. (p. 8)

As is the case with FLCs, FIGs can be quite diverse in membership and focus. For example, FIGs can be formed by instructors who teach sections of the same course or by faculty across disciplines who wish to explore the use of a specific teaching strategy. Faculty and administrators within a program might form an inquiry group to develop and evaluate the use of an electronic portfolio system as a tool for assessing student learning. While there is considerable diversity in the composition and goals of FIGs, the groups implement at least four basic steps as they carry out their cyclical process of inquiry (Carnegie Foundation for the Advancement of Teaching, n.d.):

- Develop a question.
- Design a plan for research.

- Gather and evaluate evidence.
- Present and review findings.

In that this process is viewed as cyclical, the work of a FIG can become iterative. For example, additional research questions may arise as data are gathered, or supplementary data collection methods may be added as the data are analyzed. The final outcomes of the faculty inquiry process are as diverse as the groups themselves and can include transformed teaching or new courses, curricula, and pedagogies. These results may then serve as questions for a new cycle of faculty inquiry.

In the following discussion, we describe how the TSIG developed during its first year as an entity that possesses elements of both an FLC and an inquiry group as well as its own unique characteristics that have contributed to its success. And while we have continued to evolve, our primary focus remains that of providing a teaching commons in which teaching is valued as a scholarly activity worthy of reflection and inquiry.

Group Implementation and Functioning

The success of any faculty group is determined in large part by the abilities, skills, and personalities of its members. The FLC program at Miami University (n.d.) identifies several key factors for recruiting FLC participants.

The preliminary goals established for TSIG were more global than those typically found within traditional FLC programs. Moreover, the actual activities and functioning of the group were to be negotiated among its participants. As a result, the facilitator of the group offered membership to a small group of diverse faculty from four-year and two-year campuses based on their established interest in teaching. While any two-year college campus could benefit from a TSIG, this combination of faculty from our two-year campus and from our main university campus was especially enriching because it allowed us to build community on a larger scale. Doing this emphasized our common goals and built relationships and opportunities for collaborations where they might not normally exist. It could chip away at the perception that the two-year college instructor is less qualified. During the spring, 12 prospective members were sent e-mails describing the TSIG project and inviting them to take part in the group during the following academic year; 10 faculty members accepted the invitation. In May, an informal meeting of TSIG was held to discuss the project and research procedures and to provide an opportunity for members to meet each other.

The group has averaged eight meetings per year since its inception. The meetings include catered lunches, snacks provided by group members, or restaurant meals paid for by group members. While not specifically studied and evaluated, anecdotal evidence suggests that food and casual meeting space contribute to the trusting environment needed for honest, in-depth discussions about teaching and its role within a research institution.

Before each meeting, the group facilitator distributes an agenda, which typically includes the following items:

1. Selection of date, time, and location for the next one or two meetings. To the degree possible, all meetings for a given quarter are scheduled at one time.
2. Reading selection(s) for the next one or two meetings.
3. Discussion of the current reading selection.
4. Time for journaling (approximately 10 minutes). This is an opportunity for group members to reflect on the meeting. To facilitate this process, the following prompt is included on the agenda: "How could information from today's reading and/or discussion be applied directly to your own teaching?"

While the agenda is not followed strictly (these are not committee meetings, after all!), it does provide a general guideline. Meetings are scheduled for 90 minutes, and the group honors that time frame.

Funding for FLCs and FIGs can be extremely important to the long-term success of these groups because it demonstrates the institution's commitment to teaching and provides motivation for involvement in such an initiative. Small yearly grants from the university enabled us to provide reading materials and lunches for our group members.

For the first meeting, the group facilitator selected an article to serve as the focus for the group's discussion. From that point forward, group members contributed ideas for readings, which were then selected by an informal group vote. For the first three years, books were purchased through an internal organization's grant. Group members have expressed willingness to purchase their own readings should grant funding not be available in the future. A list of books purchased to date is provided in Appendix A.

Outcomes of the Teacher Scholar Inquiry Group

The most valuable aspects [of TSIG] for me were the absolute certainty that I could come away having learned something valuable, the collegiality

and supportive interaction of the group members, the inspiration to take
risks and assess the success of this risk-taking. (TSIG Member Survey
Response)

While the primary goal of the TSIG is to provide the opportunity for rich
conversation and deep thinking about teaching and learning, it has also provided an opportunity to investigate the value of the group as a model of
faculty development over time. As a result, an action research study was
planned, and data collection and analyses have continued for the three years
of TSIG's existence.

Action Research Study

To investigate the impact of TSIG experiences on its members, a collaborative action research methodology was adopted. Action research involves the
systematic inquiry of one's own practice over time and is typically portrayed
as iterative cycles of reflection and planning, implementing a plan or taking
action, collecting and analyzing data, and reflecting on the data and adjusting one's practice (Riel, 2010; Sagor, 2000). This method not only provides
us with data regarding individual members' development as teacher scholars
but also supports our problem solving and analysis of issues related to our
own group process and structure.

Data Collection

In preparation for deciding on data collection and analysis strategies, the
following research questions were generated:

- How do we claim the time to engage in meaningful conversation
  about our teaching in a research-intensive institution?
- How do we establish an effective forum that encourages self-reflection
  and discussion about our teaching, and what factors contribute to the
  development of such an environment?

To answer these questions, the following surveys were developed:

- Beginning-of-year survey: included two Likert-type and two open-
  ended questions
- Monthly surveys: three open-ended questions related to the value of
  the readings and monthly meeting

- End-of-year survey: five Likert-type questions and seven open-ended questions

Surveys were conducted through SurveyMonkey.com, and responses were anonymous.

Results

In this section we provide an overview of the results from our first year of data collection and analysis.

Beginning-of-Year Survey. The purpose of this survey was to encourage self-assessment of members' teaching and to determine what goals they had in mind for taking part in TSIG. Participants demonstrated significant interest in the teaching process yet considered their technical skill level and effectiveness as teachers to be just slightly above average. The results also showed that participants had high hopes for their upcoming experience as TSIG members. In general, participants identified the desire to improve their teaching and student learning and to form relationships with colleagues that would facilitate this process. The results also confirmed participants' desire to increase their teaching skills by participating in a collegial group. Primary goals mentioned for participation in TSIG included the following:

- Learn more about the SoTL.
- Explore ways to improve teaching and student learning.
- Become a member of a community of scholars with "like interests."
- Learn about ways to convert students from passive learners to active, engaged learners.
- Learn to assess and improve my teaching.
- Investigate ways to improve student perceptions of active learning strategies.

Monthly Meeting Surveys. Responses to the monthly surveys identified several important trends regarding the outcomes of the TSIG experience for participants, including the following:

- the critical importance of taking time to get to know one another and to develop a sense of trust and respect;
- the encouragement members felt as they listened to respected colleagues describe their own frustrations in the classroom and the significance of shared problem solving;

- the value of providing a premeeting lunch time that encouraged relationship formation and provided a gateway to the more formal discussion for the day;
- the importance of being able to discuss honestly those aspects of the group that are not working, such as assigning too much reading and changing readings when they do not meet the members' needs; and
- the tremendous value of the group as a whole to individual members' lives.

Participants felt professionally rejuvenated by the new information they were learning and spent considerably more time reflecting on their teaching as a result of TSIG.

End-of-Year Survey. This survey included both the self-assessment of teaching and numerous questions related to the impact and value of TSIG experiences during the previous academic year. By the end of the year, members felt their technical skill as well as their effectiveness as a teacher had increased.

The beginning-of-the-year survey identified numerous goals that members had in mind for taking part in the group, and end-of-year results indicated that individuals had achieved, or were achieving, many of these goals owing to TSIG participation. For example, results suggested that participants were already attempting to implement new teaching strategies, exploring ways to improve their teaching and student learning, and reflecting on their teaching in new and different ways because of their involvement in TSIG. All members strongly agreed that their participation had led to forming relationships with colleagues that supported their teaching or academic work. Members also said that the potential for collaboration, the monthly readings and associated discussion, and the group's multidisciplinarity and same-sex composition were all highly valuable factors contributing to the success of TSIG. Interestingly, however, it is the sharing and collegial nature of the group, rather than learning about teaching, that was identified as most valued.

The end-of-year survey also provided evidence that TSIG was influencing members' scholarly activity. More than half of the members indicated that they had made, or were planning to make, presentations related to TSIG participation at conferences. Additionally, one member said that she was planning to conduct an SoTL study about TSIGs as a result of her group experiences.

Discussion

As indicated previously, this study was undertaken to answer two basic questions related to our initial efforts in developing a teaching commons within our institution. In this section we discuss our interpretation of the results as they relate to these questions. However, it should be noted that these questions continue to be answered as data analysis of subsequent years continues.

How do we claim the time to engage in meaningful conversation about our teaching? Finding time for 10 busy individuals from two different campuses to meet was the most significant challenge TSIG members identified and is consistent with findings from other studies (e.g., Cummins, Adu-Poku, Bancroft, & Theall, 2008). While participants expressed tremendous enthusiasm for the experience and valued their developing relationships with colleagues, job- and family-related responsibilities occasionally hampered their participation. Nonetheless, the average attendance for the meetings throughout the year was 84%. TSIG members were highly motivated at the outset to be part of the voluntary group and were willing to make the time to take part in an activity that had the potential to contribute to their professional growth. As the year progressed, the motivation to continue attendance was reinforced as participants' initial goals to learn more about teaching and to establish relationships with like-minded peers were met. Ultimately, however, the facilitation of a highly motivated individual to coordinate the group's activities during the first year was critical.

An additional time-related theme arose from the data. TSIG members were interested in making sure that the limited amount of time they had was used effectively. For example, it became clear during the year that as members began to bond, time was needed for them to engage in informal conversation prior to our reading discussions. As a result, we added an additional 30 minutes to our meeting time to provide for socialization and eating.

How do we establish an effective forum that encourages self-reflection and discussion about our teaching and what factors contribute to the development of such an environment? The stage for success of TSIG was set from the very beginning. The invitation e-mail sent to prospective participants outlined how the idea for the group came into being, introduced the ideas of pedagogical solitude and the teaching commons, presented the goals for the group, described the research component, and provided potential dates for a preliminary meeting for TSIG members. Both the official invitation and initial gathering informed members about the general purpose and structure of the group. Moreover, it was shared that we would all be "owners" of the group, that it would be run democratically through collective decision making, and that the participants would determine what the group would ultimately become. In a study of a small faculty group, Hare and O'Neill (2000) found that lack of understanding among participants regarding a group's vision, mission, and goals can dramatically influence its impact:

> How can the group be effective, efficient, and productive if members do not fully understand the basic vision? Although group acceptance of these elements is important, it is a moot point if it is perceived that there is no vision, mission, or goals. The outcome, as we see, is that members can and do substitute their own vision, mission, and goals making the group eclectic and unfocused. (p. 37)

The democratic nature of the group enabled us to problem solve when issues arose. One of the wishes TSIG members expressed in their monthly surveys was the desire to "dig deeper" during our conversations. When this issue was raised at a meeting, there was unanimous support for the idea of paring down the number of readings to give us more opportunities for reflection and thoughtful discussion. Since that time, we have been mindful of not overloading ourselves with readings that become "assignments" rather than opportunities for achieving a deeper understanding of how our students learn and how best to facilitate that process.

Two group composition factors were identified in survey responses as being important to the success of discussions—sex and multidisciplinarity. Additionally, research team members noted in their journals that comments about the benefits of a single-sex, multidisciplinary, multi-experience, and multi-age group were made frequently during both formal discussions and informal conversations. The perception clearly exists among TSIG members that the single-sex makeup of the group is advantageous. When questioned about this observation, members suggested that differing communication styles between men and women may have influenced not only our relationship formation and willingness to share openly during discussions, but also how the group has evolved. The large body of literature on sex- and gender-related differences in communication supports this contention. Men tend to be more task-oriented in groups while women tend to focus on the interpersonal needs of the group members and demonstrate willingness to share feelings and emotions (Carli, 2006; Carli & Bukatko, 2000). Interestingly, however, these differences are found to be mitigated to some degree in mixed-sex groups.

While participants value the same-sex composition of TSIG, the tremendous diversity of disciplines, ages, campuses, and backgrounds represented is viewed as an important contributor to the group's success. This is consistent with previous research that links multidisciplinary group composition to richer discussion as well as participants' comfort in risk taking and sharing ideas outside one's own department (Harper, 1996; Wildman, Hable, Preston, & Magliaro, 2000).

A final point should be mentioned in considering best practices for developing an effective forum for discussion. As noted previously, the facilitator hand-selected the members of TSIG based on her previous experience with the individuals, and she did this to maximize the potential for success. In situations where membership is open to all faculty, the success of the group may differ from the TSIG experience. Nonetheless, one might assume that individuals who make the effort to be part of a learning community or inquiry group would possess a similar level of personal commitment to developing as a teacher scholar.

Conclusion

In this chapter we have chronicled the development of the TSIG during its first year. As discussed previously, FLC and FIG frameworks can be used to support the development of a teaching commons. Our model for TSIG blended elements of both FLCs and FIGs in that we designed collaborative activities that would facilitate a deeper understanding of teaching and learning while at the same time implementing a systematic process of inquiry to evaluate the impact of the group over time.

Several questions remain for future investigation. For example, how does the fact that TSIG was established as a group with the expressed potential to meet for more than a year influence how we have evolved? Would our experience have been less successful, or at least different, if there was no expectation for a multiyear experience?

The data provided here must be interpreted with some measure of caution. We report only on the first year of our experiences; the final story of the value and impact of TSIG can be told only when the data from subsequent years are analyzed and reported. Nonetheless, TSIG remains intact.

In her evaluation of a faculty group established to promote teaching-related reflection and conversation, Harper (1996) notes that "implicit in such a community is a quality of respect built on a sense of mutuality involved in true conversation. Such respect can sustain the relationship even in [the] face of sharp differences in knowledge, value or belief" (p. 264). We view our first year in TSIG as clear evidence of the validity of this statement. Moreover, it is the collegiality and admiration that exists among group members that has supported our individual growth as teacher scholars. In the words of one of our members:

> What the totality of this TSIG experience has meant for me in one word is . . . *change*. I have come away from this experience energized, determined, committed to do more and better, and, I think most importantly—to take more risks. There is much to do. I am looking forward to our next year of TSIG. I think the foundation has been set and I want to challenge myself more. I want to ask and explore the "harder" questions—mine and those of the rest of the group. I want to dig deeper and to understand more. I want to be able to evaluate what I am doing and implement changes with clarity and a well-formulated rationale. I am so very grateful that I have had this opportunity. Thank you!

References

Beach, A. L., & Cox, M. D. (2009). The impact of faculty learning communities on teaching and learning. *Learning Communities Journal, 1*(1), 7–27. Retrieved from http://celt.muohio.edu/lcj/

Boyer, E. L. (1990). *Scholarship reconsidered: Priorities of the professoriate.* Stanford, CA: Carnegie Foundation for the Advancement of Teaching.

Carli, L. L. (2006). Gender issues in workplace groups: Effects of gender and communication style on social influence. In M. Barrett & M. J. Davidson (Eds.), *Gender and communication at work* (pp. 69–83). Burlington, VT: Ashgate.

Carli, L. L., & Bukatko, D. (2000). Gender, communication, and social influence: A developmental perspective. In T. Eckes & H. M. Trautner (Eds.), *The developmental social psychology of gender* (pp. 295–331). Mahwah, NJ: Lawrence Erlbaum.

Carnegie Foundation for the Advancement of Teaching. (n.d.). *Faculty inquiry toolkit.* Retrieved from http://specctoolkit.carnegiefoundation.org/

Cox, M. D. (2001). Faculty learning communities: Change agents for transforming institutions into learning organizations. *To Improve the Academy, 19,* 69–93.

Cummins, L., Adu-Poku, S., Bancroft, K., & Theall, M. (2008). Promoting the scholarship of teaching and learning in a faculty-staff learning community. *Journal of Faculty Development, 22*(1), 40–51.

Hare, L. R., & O'Neill, K. (2000). Effectiveness and efficiency in small academic peer groups: A case study. *Small Group Research, 31*(1), 24–53. doi:10.1177/104649640003100102

Harper, V. (1996). Establishing a community of conversation: Creating a context for self-reflection among teacher scholars. *To Improve the Academy, 15,* 251–266.

Huber, M. T. (2008). *The promise of faculty inquiry for teaching and learning basic skills: Strengthening pre-collegiate education in community colleges (SPECC).* Stanford, CA: Carnegie Foundation for the Advancement of Teaching.

Huber, M. T., & Hutchings, P. (2005). *The advancement of learning: Building the teaching commons.* San Francisco: Jossey-Bass.

Huber, M. T., & Hutchings, P. (2006). Building the teaching commons. *Change, 38*(3), 25–31.

Miami University. (n.d.). *Faculty learning communities: Recommendations for initiating and implementing an FLC at your campus.* Retrieved from http://www.units .muohio.edu/flc/recommendations.php

Riel, M. (2010). *Understanding action research.* Retrieved from http://cadres.pepper dine.edu/ccar/define.html

Sagor, R. (2000). *Guiding school improvement with action research.* Alexandria, VA: Association for Supervision and Curriculum Development.

Shulman, L. S. (1989). Toward a pedagogy of substance. *AAHE Bulletin, 41*(10), 8–13.

Shulman, L. S. (2004). *Teaching as community property: Essays on higher education.* San Francisco: Jossey-Bass.

Shulman, L. S. (2005). Foreword. In M. T. Huber & P. Hutchings, *The advancement of learning: Building the teaching commons* (pp. v–viii). San Francisco: Jossey-Bass.

Wildman, T. M., Hable, M. P., Preston, M. M., & Magliaro, S. G. (2000). Faculty study groups: Solving "good problems" through study, reflection, and collaboration. *Innovative Higher Education, 24*(4), 247–263. doi:10.1023/B:IHIE.0000 047413.00693.8c

APPENDIX A
Group Readings

Angelo, T. A., & Cross, K. P. (1993). *Classroom assessment techniques: A handbook for college teachers* (2nd ed.). Jossey-Bass Higher and Adult Education. San Francisco: Jossey-Bass.

Arum, R., & Roksa, J. (2011). *Academically adrift: Limited learning on college campuses.* Chicago: University of Chicago Press.

Barkley, E. F. (2009). *Student engagement techniques: A handbook for college faculty.* Higher and Adult Education Series. San Francisco: Jossey-Bass.

Blumberg, P. (2008). *Developing learner-centered teaching: A practical guide for faculty.* San Francisco: Jossey-Bass.

Bok, D. (2007). *Our underachieving colleges: A candid look at how much students learn and why they should be learning more.* Princeton, NJ: Princeton University Press.

Davis, B. G. (2009). *Tools for teaching* (2nd ed.). San Francisco: Jossey-Bass.

Fink, L. D. (2003). *Creating significant learning experiences: An integrated approach to designing college courses.* Jossey-Bass Higher and Adult Education. San Francisco: Jossey-Bass.

Huber, M. T., & Hutchings, P. (2005). *The advancement of learning: Building the teaching commons.* Jossey-Bass/Carnegie Foundation for the Advancement of Teaching. San Francisco: Jossey-Bass.

Nathan, R. (2006). *My freshman year: What a professor learned by becoming a student.* Ithaca, NY: Cornell University Press.

O'Brien, J. G., Millis, B. J., & Cohen, M. W. (2008). *The course syllabus: A learning-centered approach* (2nd ed.). San Francisco: Jossey-Bass.

Pace, D., & Middendorf, J. (Eds.). (2004). Decoding the disciplines: Helping students learn disciplinary ways of thinking. *New Directions for Teaching and Learning, 98,* 109–110. doi:10.1002/tl.152

Palmer, P. J. (2007). *The courage to teach: Exploring the inner landscape of a teacher's life, 10th Anniversary Edition.* San Francisco: Jossey-Bass.

Walvoord, B. E., & Anderson, V. J. (2009). *Effective grading: A tool for learning and assessment in college.* San Francisco: Jossey-Bass.

Weimer, M. (2002). *Learner-centered teaching: Five key changes to practice.* San Francisco: Jossey-Bass.

Willingham, D. T. (2010). *Why don't students like school: A cognitive scientist answers questions about how the mind works and what it means for the classroom.* San Francisco: Jossey-Bass.

Zull, J. E. (2002). *The art of changing the brain: Enriching the practice of teaching by exploring the biology of learning.* Sterling, VA: Stylus.

189

11

WRITERS GROUPS

Composing a Balanced Faculty

Brenda Refaei, Susan Sipple, and Claudia Skutar

Consider this scenario: a college seminar room filled with faculty members from a variety of disciplines and career stages. Some sit at laptops; others write diligently with pen on paper. Over in the corner, two colleagues meet to talk about the assignment they're drafting for the class they're co-teaching. Occasionally, from the seminar table, someone breaks the silence to ask, "Did anybody see that article in the *Chronicle*," or "What's a better word for . . . ?" Over the past several years, colleges and universities across the country have been implementing writers groups to help busy faculty find time and space to work on writing related to all aspects of what they do: teaching, scholarship, or service. Faculty meet regularly to work together on individual or collaborative writing projects. While many faculty members work well on these projects alone, writers groups can allow for collaboration and provide the kind of schedule and structure that many faculty need to keep their work moving forward. These faculty learning communities (FLCs) can be particularly useful on two-year college campuses, providing faculty there with the kind of balance they need in their professional lives to complete a variety of writing tasks.

The "publish or perish" adage is familiar to all academics, though not every college professor is bound by it in the same way. Some two-year college faculty—particularly those at university branch campuses—must publish moderately to achieve promotion and tenure; other two-year college faculty have no administrative mandate to publish, yet they have a personal professional interest in doing so. Furthermore, even two-year college faculty who do not intend to present papers at conferences or publish their work in scholarly journals have a variety of writing tasks related to teaching and service that they cannot always fit into their busy schedules. An *interest* in writing does not always lead to a completed grant proposal, a new classroom assignment, or a peer-reviewed publication; in fact, it does not necessarily lead to the actual *act* of writing.

As so many two-year college faculty know, the demands of heavy teaching loads and committee service leave little time for sustained writing no matter how great the inclination or how forceful the mandate. However, they might also sense that without the creative pursuits writing can offer, they could burn out. The National Faculty Stress Research Project (Gmelch, Lovrich, & Wilke, 1984) found that among the three most common faculty responsibilities—teaching, service, and research—the most stressful role is teaching. In addition, Talbot (2000) and Quick (1987) have found that large universities and small colleges differ primarily in time spent on scholarship versus teaching, with university faculty being far more research-oriented and college faculty more teaching-oriented. Two-year college faculty, then, need to achieve some kind of balance in their roles, if only to ward off stress or burnout.

One way to encourage two-year college professors to find time to engage in writing is to form writing groups, as we did at our two-year branch of a major research university. Writers groups can bring faculty members together for dedicated individual writing time, team brainstorming sessions, reading and discussions of books designed to improve writing productivity, and peer review of works in progress. By creating a supportive interdisciplinary group for idea exchange, writers groups rely on internal expertise, inspire interdisciplinary discussions, and create community (Benson-Brown, 2006). In addition, scheduled writing time that leads to peer review of works in progress creates accountability that helps some faculty finish writing projects that otherwise might have languished.

Since the two-year college mission places an extraordinarily heavy emphasis on teaching and learning, many professors find reasons to dedicate time outside of the classroom to tasks that are linked more clearly to immediate teaching concerns: class preparations, grading, or student conferences. For that reason, writers groups on two-year college campuses will more easily garner the support of administration and attract and keep devoted teaching faculty by exposing clear links between writers group activities and teaching excellence. And these groups do encourage new insights about teaching and new potential for improved teaching practices. Writers groups raise awareness in participants by helping them to see challenges faced by student writers and by offering them an opportunity to reflect on teaching through their writing activities.

Literature Review

While little has been written about the need for or implementation of faculty writers groups on two-year college campuses, some work has been done on the use of these FLCs at four-year colleges and universities. In the face of increasing expectations for teaching, professional development, and service, faculty are often stressed about how to increase their writing productivity (Wilson, 2001). Wilson describes how requirements for tenure have been raised and are now more dependent upon publishing a number of scholarly articles or books. New faculty are under increasing pressure to meet the demands for publishing. Wilson asserts, "The bar for tenure is rising at major research universities and teaching institutions alike" (p. A12). The famous adage "publish or perish" is now reaching campuses with heavy teaching loads. This puts faculty developers in the position of designing programs to support this increased expectation for publishing.

Even institutions where faculty are not expected to publish may find writing groups helpful. Boice (1995) argues that helping early-career faculty develop good writing habits will help them to develop good teaching habits. He suggests that lessons learned from the scholarly writing process can inform reflection on teaching. For instance, the peer-review process in writing can be used to help mentor new faculty. Since new faculty are familiar with the process of seeking out feedback on their writing, they may be more willing to seek out similar support to improve their teaching. Faculty who participated first in his writing group and later in his teaching group reported increased motivation for both writing and teaching. The regular writing habits Boice recommends, then, help new faculty become more collaborative teachers.

These faculty-initiated writers groups can do more than help support writing or enhance teaching; they can also be places to foster collegial relationships that sustain new faculty, particularly women and minorities, who may feel isolated in academic departments (Friend & Gonzalez, 2009).

Most typical in the literature on faculty writing is the development of writing programs by faculty developers at four-year colleges or universities. Gillespie and colleagues (2005) describe how the University of Washington–Bothell developed research circles to support faculty writing. Elbow and Sorcinelli (2006) describe an idyllic writing program. The University of Massachusetts–Amherst created a writing center described as

"The Faculty Writing Place" in a lovely space. . . . It offers lots of windows and light, beautiful views of the campus, and a quiet carpeted space with comfortable writing tables and chairs. It will be open nearly 24/7. We are also going to have available an experienced editor for some one-to-one coaching for early career faculty. (Elbow & Sorcinelli, 2006, p. 18)

Although many institutions may not have such a space for faculty writing, Elbow and Sorcinelli do offer useful suggestions for beginning faculty writers groups. First, they suggest, "keep it simple" (p. 20). Writers groups do not need a lot of discussion; they need time to write. Second, writers groups should "focus on opportunity, rather than remediation" (p. 20), so that faculty feel welcome to participate. Third, they recommend "affirm[ing] the integration of scholarship and teaching" (p. 20). Fourth, the writing group should also "link the notions of academic work and community" (p. 20). Joining such a community can be especially helpful to new faculty who need to assimilate to the academic environment. Finally, they recommend using the "talent, perspectives, and expertise of your own faculty" (p. 22) to manage costs.

Although many faculty just need time to write, some may want more support for their writing. Gray and Birch (2000) take the work of Boice on scholarly productivity and develop a faculty writing program to improve time management, paragraph organization, and peer feedback. Benson-Brown (2006) developed an even more intensive program; the faculty developers she writes about provide one-on-one manuscript critiques to faculty. This helps them improve audience accessibility and voice, thereby teaching them how to revise manuscripts to reach a larger audience. In addition, they offer workshops on writing productivity, copyright issues, and converting dissertations into books. All of these examples describe groups at four-year research institutions; more research is needed to describe how such groups work at two-year institutions, with faculty's increased teaching loads and commitment to student learning.

Two-Year College Faculty Need Writers Groups

Expectations for publication vary at two-year colleges, just as those colleges themselves vary. At some community colleges, too many publications may even prevent a faculty member from being hired. In fact, Kozeracki (2002) says, "one of the perennial concerns expressed about hiring faculty with doctorates for community college teaching is that they are socialized toward research rather than teaching" (p. 53). Whether or not administrators express that fear as a caution to faculty against spending time on writing and scholarship, the fact remains that even if faculty choose to write, there is little time for it. In contrast, faculty at two-year branches of major universities may have real pressure to publish, although the expectations about how much are not necessarily the same as at those colleges' main campuses.

Regardless of how many classes two-year college faculty teach, or how much time they devote to other professional obligations, creative and scholarly writing remains a part of the professional lives of many faculty members. Palmer (2002) says that one-third of community college faculty regularly produce scholarly or creative writing. Furthermore, he notes that more than half of the writing completed by two-year college faculty is related to what is certainly the most important and time-consuming piece of their college mission: teaching. This writing allows instructors to devote time to reflection, analysis, and peer review of classroom practices and related research in a congenial and supportive environment. While some of these things could be (and are) done by instructors sitting alone in their offices, creating a space where others are taking the time to write and reflect could facilitate an increase in productivity and job satisfaction. One participant in our writers group likened her time in the FLC to "a spa day for your brain," suggesting a great deal about the way the professional time is divided at the two-year college. Time with students is frequently regarded as the most important aspect of a professor's job, with other aspects of the work feeling like a burden or a luxury; however, without time to reflect and create—without time to write—teaching and mentoring could suffer.

Furthermore, while the student-teacher relationship is quite often energizing to the individual professor, heavy teaching loads and long office hours can lead to isolation from colleagues, prohibiting intellectual exchange that is fundamental to good teaching. In addition, isolation is one of the factors contributing to faculty burnout (Baker-Fletcher, Car, Menn, & Ramsey, 2005; Maslach & Leiter, 1997). One antidote is professional development that brings colleagues together to reflect and create (Baker-Fletcher et al., 2005; Baldwin & Chang, 2006; Blaisdell & Cox, 2004; Karpiak, 2000; Sipple & Lightner, 2009). Writers groups may be effective in countering isolation in two-year colleges. While other professional obligations could help combat isolation—committee work, for instance—those duties do not always result in the fortifying interactions that FLCs devoted to writing can. One member of our writers group said,

> Unlike [committee] meetings, which are necessarily driven by the need for
> the group to come to a consensus, and other FLCs, which for better or for
> worse showcase our work juxtaposed with the work of colleagues . . . , the
> writers group is a more congenial and productive environment for personal
> interactions. . . . I have the opportunity to discuss what I'm doing with
> colleagues from different disciplines and with different degrees of experi-
> ence without the pressure of stacking my work up against theirs.

Not only do writers groups provide an environment where faculty can set
aside other obligations to focus on writing, they also provide important
opportunities for engagement that fortify the professional life.

Impact on Teaching and Learning

Writing completed in two-year college writers groups may be different from
the work completed in groups in four-year colleges or university FLCs
devoted to writing. While some members in our group work on creative or
scholarly writing intended for presentations or publication, many others use
the time to write assignments or exams, prepare grant or conference proposals, write documents related to college service, work on writing related to
ongoing education, or write professional correspondence. While some community college administrators are concerned that too much attention to
scholarship could detract from teaching (Grubb et al., 1999), the time spent
in the group—regardless of the task at hand—can be enormously beneficial
to a faculty member's teaching life. As previously mentioned, writing groups
can enhance teaching by making participants more aware of their own writing processes; this increased awareness can help instructors better model
good writing practices to students. When instructors know firsthand the
importance of outlining, prewriting, peer review, and revision, they can better explain their importance to students.

Furthermore, when group members share work for peer review with
participants from other fields, they encounter the kind of feedback they give
students on writing assignments. This can be particularly instructive, helping
group members see the most constructive ways to give and to receive feedback—information they can then transmit to students. Writing for a target
audience or reviewing work written for readers from unfamiliar fields allows
group members to better appreciate the differences in content, language, and
style they expect students to navigate across disciplines (Elbow & Sorcinelli,
2006). Something as simple as struggling to create or review a document

written in an unfamiliar documentation style can remind participants of the challenges their students face. More important, it can help them invent new ways to guide their students to conquer those challenges. One of our group members said,

> Making time to write, even if it's just once a month, helps me remember what difficult work writing and research are—that's a direct correlation with my students' experiences. I plan to take my own work into the classroom next quarter . . . and work on my project alongside my students, as they work on theirs. It will, I think, help them to see that even practiced scholars and writers struggle with new ideas and research. Writing is hard, tedious work, no matter who you are.

Instead of detracting from the work the faculty do in the classroom, then, participation in writers groups can directly contribute to that important work. In addition, writers groups may help faculty be more effective teachers in other ways as well. By providing professors with formal, regularly scheduled, institutionally supported writing time, writing and reflection are no longer treated like hobbies to be completed on a free weekend or during summer break. In this way two-year colleges can help faculty members organize their work. A member of our writers group said, "The group helped me focus on teaching by providing a scheduled time to work on other projects. Knowing I have that project space, I can keep focused on teaching without constantly worrying that I won't get to my own writing projects."

Finally, writers groups might be particularly useful for two-year college faculty who hope to move into positions at four-year colleges. "For many community college faculty, university teaching continues to be an appealing future occupation, supporting previous claims that for some, positions at the community college serve as a temporary step toward a faculty position in a four-year college or university" (Lee, 2002, p. 27). Anyone who hopes to attain a tenure-track job at a four-year college or university must maintain the kind of scholarly activity that comes from research and writing. Regular participation in a writers group could allow these faculty to pursue new employment opportunities without detracting from the important work they do in their two-year college classrooms.

Implementing a Writers Group on a Two-Year College Campus

Any administrator, faculty developer, or faculty member interested in implementing a writers group on his or her two-year college campus will likely find that these groups need little in terms of resources. However, as Miller, Finley, and Shedd Vancko (2000) warn, "good ideas do not implement themselves; people do. The best designed systems will flounder if implementation is left to chance" (p. 90). With that in mind, anyone initiating and attempting to maintain a writers group over time would be well-advised to consider a few fundamental ideas.

Finding faculty with the desire to join a writers group is probably the easiest part of starting one of these FLCs. Once faculty meet for the first time, however, a variety of individual needs and expectations for the group are likely to arise. Just as individual writing processes vary, so do individual needs from writing-intensive FLCs. Some members will want time to sit with others and write quietly; some will want the group to provide peer review of works in progress; others will look for the FLC to provide accountability to make them responsible to get writing done. Others might (somewhat problematically) view it as a social hour. Any institution considering implementing a writers group should consider that flexibility could attract members to the FLC and make the community long term. Since faculty development programs work best when they are individualized to meet the specific needs of their faculty, it makes good sense to craft a writers group with the faculty and even the college mission in mind (Miller et al., 2000; Murray, 2002).

To support the writing of faculty at our college, the Learning and Teaching Center director initiated a faculty writers group as an ongoing FLC. This group aids its self-selected faculty members through mutual support and accountability to write for teaching, service, research, publication, and presentation. Since its inception, the group has tested a number of ways to support this and has experienced both successes and failures. What has been key to the group's continuance and its growth (and it has grown steadily, both in number of participants and in meeting times and formats) is that it has paid close attention to its trial-and-error search for what works. Rather than set an unchanging structure, the group has remained organic and responsive to what members need by keeping things that work and throwing out things that do not.

One basic success has been use of a facilitator to set meeting schedules, obtain meeting space, and keep group members on task via their commitment to participate at regular times. This job is not overly taxing, but it is essential to the success of the FLC. While the group meetings function well with minimal intervention by a facilitator, someone must do the necessary work of promoting the group to faculty, requesting funding (if any) from administrators, scheduling meetings and retreats, e-mailing members, and providing evidence of participation in the form of letters or certificates to members who may need documentation for promotion or tenure. At colleges where a writers group is faculty driven, the leader is unlikely to be compensated by anything more than a line on his or her curriculum vitae, though perhaps this is not insignificant, given that leadership roles are frequently considered in tenure and promotion. At our college, the Learning and Teaching Center director took on this responsibility for the first years of the writing group, and other faculty members took over the leadership role as the group evolved. A good leader can help faculty members be more productive in the FLC. One member explained that participation in regularly scheduled writing sessions has been useful because it provides deadlines for completion of his work. Without facilitators, deadlines would exist as self-imposed requirements for individual faculty members working in isolation. In fact, the use of facilitators has worked so well that the group currently has two to manage growth in size, meeting times, and meeting format.

While there is no question that ongoing faculty development is a necessity at two-year colleges, administrators are frequently concerned about the cost of these opportunities (Miller et al., 2000). Like other FLCs, writers groups can be relatively low-cost endeavors, conducting their work with free or inexpensive resources; this has certainly been one of the successes of our group. Despite the fact that little funding is available, the facilitators have been able to maintain the essential flexibility that stands as a hallmark of our group. Facilitators use college meeting rooms as faculty gathering spaces, with a subgroup meeting at local coffee shops for peer review. Using what faculty development money is available, facilitators organize biannual off-campus retreats locally.

At our college, a continuity of meeting times has worked well, with an initial twice-a-quarter schedule as a faculty writers group starts up, moving to a bimonthly schedule as the group developed. Additionally, facilitators currently designate specific monthly meetings on the same days and times for the academic year. This setup technique, accompanied by monthly reminders, has helped busy faculty to build the dates into their calendars. Participants commit to attend only one of the two sessions but are welcome at both. Group participants sign in for their session and note the task on which they plan to work. When signing out, they note whether they were able to complete their task. Facilitators designed this sign-in as a simple technique for maintaining accountability, something that can help some writers maximize productivity. Originally, facilitators introduced the idea of accountability by asking members to keep a running record of writing conducted or completed during sessions. Members seemed to like the freedom to move among their many writing tasks without reporting specifics to colleagues, and for some, keeping the log was one more item on an already lengthy professional to-do list. Facilitators dropped the log in favor of the sign-in sheet, a simpler way to track participation and encourage attendance.

While some faculty in writers groups participate because doing so helps them to schedule time to work on projects, others need something different from the community: a group of peers who can review drafts and offer feedback for editing and revision. Even in interdisciplinary FLCs, the peer-review function can be very useful to members, providing them with commentary from a variety of perspectives. In our writers group, our first attempt at creating a regular peer-review process involved creating a buddy system that paired all participating faculty members for additional peer critique sessions. This system was based on the idea that, ultimately, all participants should be shaping and reviewing their writing products for use in the classroom, presentation, or publication. Yet participation was low, because only a few members wanted regular peer review; some who wanted peer review did not have the time, and some busy faculty wanted time simply to write.

Facilitators dropped this system and moved instead to a small self-selected subset of the entire faculty writers group that meets twice a quarter to peer-review work. Faculty who wanted the opportunity to talk about their writing projects were invited to join this small subgroup, playfully nicknamed Will Write for Coffee, which meets at a local coffee shop to review drafts in progress. One week before the group meets, members send short drafts—around five pages—of current manuscripts. Participants write comments, suggestions, and other feedback on each other's drafts. At the coffee shop, members first discuss their positive reactions to the piece and then move into supportive comments to help the writer revise the manuscript. The group works best when it has between three and seven participants. Fewer participants yield less useful advice, while a larger size does not allow enough time for the manuscripts to be discussed thoroughly. Although membership of this group varies, there are always enough participants from the larger writing group to give constructive feedback.

This shift in format succeeded and meets the needs of its participants and motivates them. Regardless of format, those who have taken part in peer review as part of the writers group have found it useful. One person valued the interdisciplinary feedback, observing that she benefited most from peer review from people both within and outside her discipline. A colleague agreed, stating, "It is good to hear comments from individuals other than those in my area of expertise so that I can better develop writing skills that can cross disciplines." Another appreciated both the accountability that attends the feedback process and the objectivity of his reviewers. Clearly, peer review of writing has been an important attribute of the faculty writers group.

Successful writers groups may function entirely as on-campus FLCs; however, some groups could find it useful to meet off-campus, at least periodically. Our faculty writers group does. Our off-campus retreats started with annual daylong sessions to provide space and longer time for writing; participants found them so productive that sessions evolved into biannual retreats that now garner about a dozen participants. Using a small college faculty development stipend, the group rents space and purchases lunch at a local retreat center, with no Internet accessibility. Faculty literally retreat to this setting to write for an entire day. One of our group members remarked, "the retreat in particular, reminds me that there's a variety of work going on around me, and that it's valuable work."

Conclusion

By providing a relatively easy-to-stick-to schedule for busy two-year college faculty, writers groups help to provide the kind of balance between the demands of teaching and scholarship or teaching and reflection that is so necessary to the successful academic. Furthermore, like other FLCs, writers groups bring participants together across disciplines and ranks and, in doing so, help to alleviate any faculty tendency toward isolation; these connections help those same faculty members make connections with each other that could lead to collaborative or mentoring relationships in other areas of their professional lives.

Writers groups—like other FLCs—may contribute to the institution as well. Faculty, students, and the institution as a whole benefit when faculty engage in writing with an eye toward publication or presentation. A more professional professoriate may be one outcome of active writers group participation. In addition, by reducing faculty propensity for isolation, writers groups could alleviate burnout, thereby reinvigorating members and, perhaps, inspiring them to greater productivity in other areas of their professional lives. Furthermore, students may benefit when faculty participate in writers groups. Instructors who are actively involved in writing and writers groups may develop a keener sense of their own writing processes and a deepened understanding of the writing problems their students face. When these instructors engage with student writers, it stands to reason that they will take to those conversations a better understanding of the challenges, struggles, and benefits that writing presents.

By fostering pursuits that are directly or indirectly related to teaching, then, writers groups help to enhance the mission of most two-year colleges without demanding much from already burdened faculty developers or their budgets. Quite simply, writers groups are a perfect choice for two-year colleges and their faculty.

References

Baker-Fletcher, K., Car, D., Menn, E., & Ramsey, N. J. (2005). Taking stock at mid-career: Challenges and opportunities for faculty. *Teaching Theology and Religion, 8*(1), 3–10. doi:10.1111/j.1467-9647.2005.00217.x

Baldwin, R. G., & Chang, D. A. (2006). Reinforcing our keystone faculty: Strategies to support faculty in the middle years of academic life. *Liberal Education, 92*(4), 28–35.

Benson-Brown, A. (2006, January). Where manuscript development meets faculty development. *Journal of Scholarly Publishing,* 131–135.

Blaisdell, M. L., & Cox, M. D. (2004). Midcareer and senior faculty learning communities: Learning throughout faculty careers. *New Directions for Teaching and Learning, 97,* 137–148. doi:10.1002/tl.140

Boice, R. (1995). Developing writing, then teaching, amongst new faculty. *Research in Higher Education, 36*(4), 415–456.

Elbow, P., & Sorcinelli, M. (2006, November/December). The faculty writing place: A room of our own. *Change,* 17–22.

Friend, J., & Gonzalez, J. (2009, January/February). Get together to write. *Academe,* 31–35.

Gillespie, D., Dolsak, N., Kochis, B., Krabill, R., & Lerum, K. (2005). Research circles: Supporting the scholarship of junior faculty. *Innovation in Higher Education, 30*(3), 149–162. doi:10.1007/s10755-005-6300-9

Gmelch, W. H., Lovrich, N. P., & Wilke, P. K. (1984). Sources of stress in academe: A national perspective. *Research in Higher Education, 20,* 477–479.

Gray, T., & Birch, J. (2000). Publish, don't perish: A program to help scholars flourish. In D. Lieberman & C. Wehlburg (Eds.), *To improve the academy: Resources for faculty, instructional, and organizational development* (pp. 268–284). Bolton, MA: Anker.

Grubb, W. N., Worthen, H., Byrd, B., Webb, E., Badway, N., Case, C., Goto, S., & Villeneuve, J. C. (1999). *Honored but invisible: An inside look at teaching in community colleges.* New York: Routledge.

Karpiak, I. (2000). The "second call": Faculty renewal and recommitment at mid-life. *Quality in Higher Education, 6*(2), 125–134.

Kozeracki, C. A. (2002). Faculty attitudes about students. In C. L. Outcalt (Ed.), *Community college faculty: Characteristics, practices, and challenges* (pp. 47–55). San Francisco: Jossey-Bass.

Lee, J. J. (2002). University reference group identification among community college faculty. In C. L. Outcalt (Ed.), *Community college faculty: Characteristics, practices, and challenges* (pp. 21–28). San Francisco: Jossey-Bass.

Maslach, C., & Leiter, M. P. (1997). *The truth about burnout: How organizations cause personal stress and what to do about it.* San Francisco: Jossey-Bass.

Miller, R., Finley, C., & Shedd Vancko, C. (2000). *Evaluating, improving, and judging faculty performance in two-year colleges.* Westport, CT: Bergin & Garvey.

Murray, J. P. (2002). The current state of faculty development in two-year colleges. In C. L. Outcalt (Ed.), *Community college faculty: Characteristics, practices, and challenges* (pp. 89–98). San Francisco: Jossey-Bass.

Palmer, J. C. (2002). Disciplinary variations in work of full-time faculty members. In C. L. Outcalt (Ed.), *Community college faculty: Characteristics, practices, and challenges* (pp. 9–19). San Francisco: Jossey-Bass.

Quick, J. C. (1987). Institutional preventive stress management. In P. Seldin (Ed.), *New Direction for Teaching and Learning* (pp. 75–84). San Francisco: Jossey-Bass.

Sipple, S., & Lightner, R. (2009, Fall). Two-year college faculty: Energy and entropy at mid-career. *Journal of the Ohio Association of Two-Year Colleges, 33,* 17–24.

Talbot, L. A. (2000). Burnout and humor usage among community college nursing faculty members. *Community College Journal of Research and Practice, 24,* 359–373. doi:10.1080/106689200263962

Wilson, R. (2001). A higher bar for earning tenure. *Chronicle of Higher Education, 47*(17), A12.

APPENDIX A

Writers Tips: An Annotated Bibliography

Allen, D. (2001). *Getting things done: The art of stress-free productivity.* New York: Penguin Group.

This is an excellent guide to setting up a simple time/project management system. To get some writing done, break down the associated tasks and get them on to-do lists. Allen shows how to do this using his proven time management strategies.

Becker, H. S. (2007). *Writing for social scientists: How to start and finish your thesis, book, or article.* (2nd ed.). Chicago: University of Chicago Press.

Becker acknowledges in his preface to this second edition that much "hangs on our ability to turn out acceptable prose on demand" (p. viii). Because of this daunting task, he says a writer may lose confidence, making the writing harder. His book offers a variety of suggestions to help writers move forward.

Belcher, W. L. (2009). *Writing your journal article in twelve weeks: A guide to academic publishing success.* Thousand Oaks, CA: SAGE Publications, Inc.

Belcher has created a detailed week-by-week plan to take the academic writer from article start to finish in 12 weeks through such steps as setup of a personal writing plan, starting the article, advancing an argument, selecting a journal, making use of peer feedback, submitting the piece, and responding to journal decisions.

Boice, R. (1990). *Professors as writers: A self-help guide to productive writing.* Stillwater, OK: New Forums.

This is a solid standard offering a four-step plan for writing productivity, advice on dealing with relapses, and an annotated bibliography on hindrances to writing.

Hart, J. (2006). *A writer's coach: The complete guide to writing strategies that work.* New York: Anchor Books, Random House.

Hart focuses on the basics because, he says, "All writers face similar problems, regardless of their medium" (p. ix). He talks about such things as process, structure, clarity, rhythm, voice, and mechanics to orient his readers to good writing style.

Huff, A. S. (1999). *Writing for scholarly publication.* Thousand Oaks, CA: SAGE Publications, Inc.

Huff argues that scholarly writing is a conversation between writer and audience "rooted in a lively exchange of ideas" (p. 3) and one that has the potential to shape ongoing conversations among colleagues (p. 3). She covers the entire process of writing for academic journals, from choosing a topic to submission, revision, and publication.

Silvia, P. J. (2007). *How to write a lot: A practical guide to productive academic writing.* Washington, DC: American Psychological Association.
For faculty struggling with writing, this is a good book; Silvia believes that "Writing is a skill, not a genetic gift, so you can learn how to do it" (p. xi). He takes a "practical, behavior-oriented approach to writing" (p. 3), laying out specific goal-setting steps for producing. The book also contains an excellent writing references section.

ABOUT THE CONTRIBUTORS

Editors

Robin Lightner is the codirector of the Learning and Teaching Center and professor of psychology at University of Cincinnati Blue Ash College. She teaches psychology courses, specifically introductory, personality, social, and research methods. She facilitates a number of FLCs, offers workshops for faculty, and consults with faculty about teaching and classroom-based research. Her own research topics include faculty development, transfer of learning, and self-regulated learning. She is a consultant-evaluator for the Higher Learning Commission, has been inducted into her university's Academy of Fellows for Teaching and Learning, and was awarded the Blue Ash College Distinguished Teaching Award.

Susan Sipple is an associate professor of English at University of Cincinnati Blue Ash College. She earned her PhD in twentieth-century American literature from Miami University. Sipple teaches literature, composition, and developmental writing and has won several awards for her teaching, including UC's A. B. "Dolly" Cohen Award for Excellence in Teaching and UC's Boyce Award for Outstanding Teaching. She is a member of UC's Academy of Fellows for Teaching and Learning. Her most recent scholarship includes research on study abroad, faculty learning communities, faculty burnout, and instructor feedback on student writing. In addition, she has won research awards from the National Association for Developmental Education and the Ohio Association for Developmental Education.

Contributors

Ruth Benander is codirector of the Learning and Teaching Center and professor of English at University of Cincinnati Blue Ash College. She teaches composition and multicultural literature both on campus and through study abroad. At UC she leads a number of FLCs, designs workshops for faculty both face-to-face and online, and participates in multidisciplinary SoTL research. Her own research topics include adult learning, transfer of learning, and acquisition of multicultural competence. She is a member of UC's Academy of Fellows for Teaching and Learning and received the Award for Innovative Excellence in Teaching, Learning and Technology at the International Conference on College Teaching and Learning.

Rhonda Berger is the technology training director of College Training & Development for Miami Dade College in Miami, Florida. She directs the technology training program at the college and supervises the technology trainers/instructional designers who provide workshops, manage the training labs, and work with faculty and staff on technology projects at seven campuses and outreach centers. She has been working with instructional technology and faculty and staff development for more than 20 years.

Margaret Cheatham is associate professor of information systems in the Business and Economics Department at University of Cincinnati Blue Ash College, where she teaches information systems and introduction to business courses. Her scholarly interests include concept mapping, problem-based learning, faculty inquiry groups, and technology tools for personal and professional productivity.

Lesta Cooper-Freytag is a professor emerita who taught in the Biological Sciences Department of University of Cincinnati Blue Ash College for 41 years. Her research interests during these years were human genetics and the scholarship of teaching and learning. During her tenure at the college, she also served as a department chairperson and as interim associate dean of academic affairs. She has won the University of Cincinnati's A. B. "Dolly" Cohen Award for Excellence in Teaching, Blue Ash College's Distinguished Teaching Award, and recognition at the state level for her work in SoTL.

Milton D. Cox is director emeritus of the Center for the Enhancement of Learning, Teaching, and University Assessment at Miami University, Ohio, where he founded and continues to direct the annual International Lilly Conference on College Teaching, now in its thirty-second year. He is also founder and editor-in-chief of the *Journal on Excellence in College Teaching* and the *Learning Communities Journal*. He facilitates the Hesburgh Award-winning Teaching Scholars Faculty Learning Community, now in its thirty-fourth year. Milt has been project director of state and federal grants establishing faculty learning community programs at other universities, is coeditor of *Building Faculty Learning Communities*, and has visited over 75 institutions in the U.S. and abroad to consult on various issues in higher education. He incorporates student learning portfolios and Howard Gardner's concept of multiple intelligences in his mathematics classes. He is recipient of the C. C. MacDuffee Award for distinguished service to Pi Mu Epsilon, the national mathematics honorary society, and a certificate of special achievement from the Professional and Organizational Development Network in Higher Education in recognition and appreciation of notable contributions to the profession of faculty, instructional, and organizational development.

Sarah Cummins-Sebree is an associate professor of psychology at University of Cincinnati Blue Ash College. She teaches introductory and developmental psychology courses as well as research methods and statistics. Her current research interests include multimodal perception and postural control development in children, and the relationship among motivation, student expectations, and academic performance of students at two-year colleges.

Janice Denton is professor and head of the Chemistry Department at University of Cincinnati Blue Ash College. She is a member of the university's Academy of Fellows for Teaching and Learning and was awarded the Blue Ash College Distinguished Teaching Award in 2001. She has presented workshops and papers at regional and national assessment and teaching conferences and has worked with faculty on student learning and classroom-based assessment at colleges and universities across the country. Since 2005, she has been mentoring institutions that participate in the Assessment Academy and workshops offered by the Higher Learning Commission.

Ronald A. Elizaga is a full-time psychology instructor at Columbus State Community College in Ohio. He regularly teaches introduction to psychology, personality psychology, and social psychology. He is the cofounder of Generation One Trailblazers, a faculty-driven resource group for first-generation college students at CSCC. Among his research interests are construal-level theory, goal persistence, and other social cognitive applications toward learning and academic achievement.

Traci Haynes is an associate professor and interim chair of the Psychology Department at Columbus State Community College in Ohio. She regularly teaches introduction to psychology, life span development, and child development. She began teaching at CSCC as an adjunct instructor and has remained a strong advocate for adjuncts in her roles as both faculty and administrator. She chairs the department's Adjunct Faculty Appreciation Committee and is a representative on the college's Advanced Adjunct Workshop Committee. She was a co-facilitator for the original Psychology Faculty Learning Community and is a cofounder of the Generation One Trailblazers. In addition to her focus on the concerns of adjuncts and first-generation students at Columbus State, Haynes is very involved in service learning and autism advocacy on campus.

Gene Kramer is a professor of mathematics at University of Cincinnati Blue Ash College. He teaches developmental and undergraduate-level mathematics courses. At Blue Ash College, he has been a member of several faculty learning communities focusing on transfer of learning, first-year experience, and self-regulated learning. His present research interests are in developing and researching interventions to promote transfer of learning and self-regulated learning for developmental mathematics students.

Ellen Lynch is associate professor of early childhood education in the College of Education, Criminal Justice and Human Services at the University of Cincinnati. She is a member of the Academy of Fellows for Teaching and Learning at UC. She has facilitated and conducted research on an FLC for the past four years that has focused on scholarly teaching and SoTL, and she is on the editorial boards of both the *Problem-Based Learning Clearinghouse* and the *International Society for the Scholarship of Teaching and Learning Journal*. She has presented both nationally and internationally on SoTL research and the use of problem-based learning in the college classroom.

Joanne Munroe is an instructional designer and faculty developer/trainer at Tacoma Community College. She is part of an eLearning team that helps faculty to create and sustain learning environments enhanced through technology. A catalyst for Munroe's research into informal learning, Web 2.0 participatory learning, and open educational resources was her preparation for a plenary for the Ohio Online Learning Network and her opportunity for interactions as a "critical colleague" during the 2007 Ohio Learning Network Conference. Munroe's experience includes designing and implementing FLCs for administrators, executive leaders, faculty, and staff at community colleges. She is also a master reviewer and independent trainer for Quality Matters.

Patrick Nellis is the district director of College Training and Development for Miami Dade College in Miami, Florida. He coordinates faculty and staff development for the college across a wide spectrum of job requirements, from custodians to faculty to administrators, which affords him an opportunity to design learning experiences for adults in many different contexts, including faculty learning communities. He has worked in faculty and staff development in community colleges for 18 years.

Brenda Refaei is the composition coordinator and assistant professor of English at University of Cincinnati Blue Ash College. She teaches preparatory, first-year, and intermediate composition; facilitates FLCs on course redesign and qualitative research; and offers workshops for faculty on problem-based learning, Lesson Study, and student engagement. Her own research topics include second-language acquisition, literacy acquisition, and service-learning and problem-based learning pedagogies. She has been inducted into the University of Cincinnati's Academy of Fellows for Teaching and Learning.

Charlotte Skinner is an associate professor of mathematics at University of Cincinnati Blue Ash College, where she teaches a variety of math courses, from the developmental level through calculus for science and engineering majors. She is the department's adjunct coordinator, assisting with the hiring, mentoring, and evaluation of adjunct math faculty. Her research interests include assessment, retention, and self-regulated learning (SRL). She participated in a three-year, federally funded research project on SRL, and she has given several presentations on the subject at the regional and national levels.

Claudia Skutar is an assistant professor of English at University of Cincinnati Blue Ash College, where she teaches composition and literature. Her writing spans creative work in poetry and nonfiction, literary analysis, and research on her classes. Participation in the college Faculty Writers Group since its inception has provided her time for writing, which has led to publication of creative work, presentation of a literary paper, and presentations and published articles on classroom research.

Frank Wray is a professor of biology at University of Cincinnati Blue Ash College, where he teaches biology courses with an emphasis on ecology. His present research interest involves faculty attitudes toward teaching online and face-to-face courses, and he has published articles concerning the use of technology in the classroom. He has been inducted into his university's Academy of Fellows for Teaching and Learning.

I anticipate that this book will lead many more faculty members to see their teaching as an opportunity to engage in SOTL. And, even though it is clearly an effective guide for individual thinking, it will be even more effective when used as the focus of a Faculty Learning Community or by a less formal group of faculty working together. Indeed, the core structure and especially the worksheets will help groups to stay focused and productive. However used, it will help teachers use SOTL as a way to improve their students' learning and to foster more advanced learning outcomes while simultaneously enhancing the faculty members' own professional development and careers. I hope you find it as interesting and helpful as I did."—*Craig E. Nelson, Emeritus Professor of Biology, Indiana University, and Founding President, International Society for the Scholarship of Teaching and Learning*

Linked Courses for General Education and Integrative Learning
A Guide for Faculty and Administrators
Edited by Margot Soven, Dolores Lehr, Siskanna Naynaha, and Wendy Olson
Foreword by Betsy Barefoot, EdD

"This book provides a unique contribution to the learning community literature by focusing exclusively on linked courses—a learning-community format that has the most realistic potential for promoting *bona fide* integrative learning—in contrast to creating merely a cohort of students via 'block scheduling.' Among the book's other distinctive features are discussion of linked courses that span diverse disciplines and diverse campus settings (2-year, 4-year, residential and commuter), as well as its comprehensive coverage of key issues that underlie or undermine creation of successful learning communities, such as faculty motivation, faculty development, program administration, and program assessment. This book is a must read for anyone interested in creating learning communities that fulfill their promise of promoting meaningful, integrated learning, and a coherent general education experience."—*Joseph B. Cuseo, professor emeritus of psychology at Marymount College and member of the editorial board to the National Resource Center for The First-Year Experience and Students in Transition*

22883 Quicksilver Drive
Sterling, VA 20166-2102

Subscribe to our e-mail alerts: www.Styluspub.com

Also available from Stylus

Powerful Learning Communities
A Guide to Developing Student, Faculty, and Professional Learning Communities to Improve Student Success and Organizational Effectiveness
Oscar T. Lenning, Denise M. Hill, Kevin P. Saunders, Alisha Solan, and Andria Stokes
Foreword by Vincent Tinto

"Oscar Lenning and his colleagues have produced a landmark scholarly and policy statement on effective learning communities. It should be read by every faculty member and administrator in postsecondary education who is concerned with maximizing the developmental potential of this powerful educational intervention for students."—**Ernest T. Pascarella**, *Professor and Mary Louise Petersen Chair in Higher Education, The University of Iowa*

Learning communities have been demonstrated to dramatically improve student outcomes by engaging students in their learning.

This book constitutes a comprehensive guide for readers who want a broad strategic view of learning communities, enabling them to identify which type of LC best meets the learning needs of their students, and the context and mission of their institution. It also provides the tools for planning, designing and implementing what the authors define as "powerful" LCs, and for understanding the assessment implications of their decisions.

The potential power of LCs is realized through effective facilitation, appropriate team-building activities, linkages, planning, and active collaboration that promotes learning of the group and the individual group members—all of which topics are covered in this volume.

This book is organized around the three themes of setting the stage, designing an LC, and building or enhancing a powerful LC, and covers three types of learning communities—student, professional (faculty, staff), and institutional LCs concerned with student learning—providing a range of tools and forms to facilitate planning. The authors also address designing and maintaining hybrid and virtual LCs.

This book is intended as a practical resource for anyone at any level in higher education who wants to champion, develop, or redesign student or professional LCs, or even explore broader initiatives to develop their institution into a "learning organization." Administrators in academic and student affairs administrators will find guidance for setting appropriate policies and allocating resources.

Engaging in the Scholarship of Teaching and Learning
A Guide to the Process, and How to Develop a Project From Start to Finish
Cathy Bishop-Clark and Beth Dietz-Uhler
Foreword by Craig E. Nelson

"Bishop-Clark and Dietz-Uhler have made a unique contribution in the present volume. It is an exceptionally fine, straight-forward and brief guide for faculty looking at their first SOTL project. For most such readers, it will probably seem to be the most helpful of the [available] guides. And, although it is written with the novice in mind, many of us with more experience also will benefit from reading through it.